The Translators and Editor

BENJAMIN R. FOSTER is Laffan Professor of Assyriology at Yale University. He is the author and translator of *Before the Muses: An Anthology of Akkadian Literature* and *From Distant Days: Myths, Tales, and Poetry of Ancient Mesopotamia*, as well as numerous other works in the field of Assyriology and Babylonian literature.

DOUGLAS FRAYNE was Lecturer in the Department of Near Eastern Studies at the University of Toronto. The author of *The Early Dynastic List of Geographical Names*, he was an editor at the Royal Inscriptions of Mesopotamia Project (RIME) and translated and edited three books in the RIME series: *Sargonic and Gutian Periods (2334–2113 BC), Ur III Period (2112–2004 BC),* and *Old Babylonian Period (2003–1595 BC).*

GARY BECKMAN is Professor of Near Eastern Studies at the University of Michigan. He is the author of *Hittite Birth Rituals* and *Hittite Diplomatic Texts*. With Jack Sasson and others, he edited the encyclopedic *Civilizations of the Ancient Near East*. He is also an editor of the *Journal of Cuneiform Studies* and the *Journal of the American Oriental Society.*

NORTON CRITICAL EDITIONS
Ancient, Classical, and Medieval Eras

For a complete list of Norton Critical Editions, visit
wwnorton.com/nortoncriticals

A NORTON CRITICAL EDITION

THE EPIC OF GILGAMESH

A NEW TRANSLATION
ANALOGUES
CRITICISM AND RESPONSE

SECOND EDITION

Translated and Edited by

BENJAMIN R. FOSTER
YALE UNIVERSITY

W · W · NORTON & COMPANY · *New York* · *London*

W. W. Norton & Company has been independent since its founding in 1923, when William Warder Norton and Mary D. Herter Norton first published lectures delivered at the People's Institute, the adult education division of New York City's Cooper Union. The firm soon expanded its program beyond the Institute, publishing books by celebrated academics from America and abroad. By midcentury, the two major pillars of Norton's publishing program—trade books and college texts—were firmly established. In the 1950s, the Norton family transferred control of the company to its employees, and today—with a staff of four hundred and a comparable number of trade, college, and professional titles published each year—W. W. Norton & Company stands as the largest and oldest publishing house owned wholly by its employees.

Manufacturing by: Maple Press
Production manager: Stephen Sajdak

Library of Congress Cataloging-in-Publication Data

Names: Foster, Benjamin R. (Benjamin Read), translator, editor.
Title: The epic of Gilgamesh / a new translation, analogues, criticism and
    response ; translated and edited by Benjamin R. Foster.
Other titles: Gilgamesh. English. | Norton critical edition.
Description: Second edition. | New York ; London : W.W. Norton & Company,
    2018. | "A Norton critical edition." | Includes bibliographical references.
Identifiers: LCCN 2018044162 | ISBN 9780393643985 (pbk.)
Subjects: LCSH: Epic poetry, Assyro-Babylonian—Translations into English.
Classification: LCC PJ3771.G5 E5 2018 | DDC 892/.1—dc23 LC record
    available at https://lccn.loc.gov/2018044162

ISBN: 978-0-393-64398-5 (pbk.)

W. W. Norton & Company, Inc., 500 Fifth Avenue, New York, NY 10110
                    wwnorton.com
W. W. Norton & Company, Ltd., 15 Carlisle Street, London W1D 3BS

1 2 3 4 5 6 7 8 9 0

Contents

Illustrations

Figures 1, 3, and 5 drawn by Karen Polinger Foster and reproduced with permission.

Figures 2, 4, 6, 8–10 reproduced with the permission of the Trustees of the British Museum. © The Trustees of the British Museum. All rights reserved.

Figure 4 also reproduced with the permission of Benjamin R. Foster, Curator of the Yale Babylonian Collection.

Figure 7 reproduced with the permission of the Penn Museum, image #B17167 and #B16695.

Figure 11 reproduced with the permission of Dr. Gaëlle Coqueugniot, editor of *Syria*.

Acknowledgments

The revised and expanded translation of *The Epic of Gilgamesh* in this Norton Critical Edition owes many readings, interpretations, and felicitous turns of phrase to the monumental work of Andrew George, *The Babylonian Gilgamesh Epic: Introduction, Critical Edition and Cuneiform Texts* (2003; see Selected Bibliography for full citations). George's work on *Gilgamesh* is a turning point in the history of this complicated text, and I have benefited immensely from both his text edition and commentary. His treatments of important sources that have appeared since 2003, such as the Suleimaniyah, Schöyen, and Ugarit manuscripts, are likewise invaluable and exemplary. In the words of the epic, "he has revealed what was hidden" and brought understanding of this masterpiece to a far higher level than was possible forty-five years ago, when I first delved into its mysteries.

The 2005 German translation by Stefan Maul, *Das Gilgamesch-Epos, Neu Übersetzt und Kommentiert*, offers both new sources and many original proposals. I am also grateful for Martin Worthington's acute and thought-provoking studies of various difficult passages. I thank Mary Frazer for allowing me to benefit from her new edition of the Gilgamesh Letter.

There is no comprehensive edition of the Sumerian Gilgamesh material. These translations are based first of all on the text editions of W. H. P. Römer, Aaron Shaffer and Alhena Gadotti, Dietz O. Edzard, Antoine Cavigneaux and Farouk N. H. Al-Rawi, and the editions and translations of the Electronic Text Corpus of Sumerian Literature, prepared by Jeremy Black and collaborators. Translations, collations, and commentary by many other scholars, including Pascal Attinger, Miguel Civil, Jerrold Cooper, Andrew George, Thorkild Jacobsen, Dina Katz, Piotr Michalowski, Jeremiah Peterson, Herman Vanstiphout, and Niek Veldhuis, have offered me good guidance over rough terrain, where Samuel Noah Kramer led the way for us all.

My particular thanks go to Karen Polinger Foster for her assistance with cover design and illustrations, for her repeated readings of this work in conjunction with the original Akkadian and with the best modern translations, and for discussing it with me line by line. She greatly improved the English expression, readability, and accuracy of the translation.

For errors or shortcomings that remain, I alone am responsible.

Benjamin R. Foster

Introduction

This four-thousand-year-old tale of love, death, and adventure is the world's earliest epic masterpiece. Over a millennium before the *Iliad* and the *Odyssey*, Mesopotamian poets wrote of Gilgamesh, hero-king of the Sumerian city of Uruk. The story has five main sections: first, Gilgamesh's abuse of his subjects occasions the creation of the wild man Enkidu—as his rival—who becomes his boon companion; second, Gilgamesh persuades Enkidu to accompany him on a heroic quest to the forest of cedars, where they slay Humbaba, its monstrous guardian, and bring back a gigantic tree, thus winning immortal fame for Gilgamesh; third, the two heroes slay the Bull of Heaven, sent by the goddess Ishtar to kill Gilgamesh because he rejected her sexual advances; fourth, Enkidu dies, leaving Gilgamesh terrified at the prospect of his own death; and finally, Gilgamesh sets out on an arduous search for Utanapishtim, the survivor of the Flood granted immortality by the gods, to learn how he too can live forever.

Who Was Gilgamesh?

According to Mesopotamian tradition, Gilgamesh was a long-ago king of the city of Uruk and builder of its legendary city walls, traces of which are still visible today. Archaeologists date one phase of these massive ramparts, nearly ten kilometers long, with over nine hundred towers, to about 2700 B.C.E., so if Gilgamesh was a historical person, he may have ruled Uruk at that time. Anam, a king of Uruk during the nineteenth century B.C.E., mentions Gilgamesh as builder of the walls of his city in an inscription commemorating his own work on them, thereby comparing himself to his royal predecessor. Significantly, the walls of Uruk are the setting for the beginning and end of *The Epic of Gilgamesh*.

A list of ancient Mesopotamian kings, compiled in the late third millennium B.C.E., names Gilgamesh in the following passage, in which he, like other kings of his era, is given a fabulously long reign: "The divine Lugalbanda, a shepherd, reigned for 1200 years. The divine Dumuzi, a fisherman, whose city was Ku'ara, reigned for 100 years. The divine Gilgamesh, whose father was a phantom, lord of the city of Kullab, reigned for 126 years."[1] In *The Epic of Gilgamesh* and the Sumerian poems about Gilgamesh, on the other hand, his father is Lugalbanda, king of Uruk. They also identify his mother as the goddess Ninsun, a deified wild cow. The riddle of Gilgamesh's parentage is reflected in the epic, where he is described as two-thirds divine and one-third human (see also below, "Use of Fantastic Numbers"). As for the name *Gilgamesh*, it may mean "Ancestor-Was-a-Hero," though this is disputed. It was spelled and pronounced in different ways over the millennia.

Stories about the exploits of Gilgamesh were first written in Sumerian around 2100 B.C.E. They appear in this Norton Critical Edition in "The Sumerian Gilgamesh Poems," translated by Douglas Frayne and Benjamin R. Foster. The kings ruling in Sumer during that period, the Third Dynasty of the city of Ur, claimed that they were descended from the ancient royal house of Gilgamesh of Uruk. One king of Ur even called Gilgamesh his "brother." The kings may well have come from Uruk, but their vaunted kinship with such a remote figure of the past was perhaps little more than a bid for prestige and antiquity for their royal family. They may also have wanted to avoid referring to the more recent past, when Sumer, especially Uruk and Ur, resented being ruled by a non-Sumerian dynasty. Whatever the reasons, poets of the Third Dynasty of Ur composed narratives extolling the life and deeds of Gilgamesh, as well as those of his father, Lugalbanda, which were enjoyed at the royal court.

A document studied in Sumerian schools of the early second millennium B.C.E., supposedly a copy of a lost ancient inscription, names Gilgamesh and his son Ur-lugal (who appears in "The Death of Gilgamesh") as having rebuilt a cult structure at Nippur called the Tummal. This fanciful piece states that the Tummal was originally built by King Enmebaragesi of Kish and his son Akka, the aggressor in "Gilgamesh and Akka."

In later times, Gilgamesh was honored as a netherworld deity, in accordance with the destiny pronounced for him in "The Death of Gilgamesh," and was invoked in funerary rites. A prayer to him found on tablets from Assyria dating to the first millennium B.C.E. reads, in part, as follows:

> O Gilgamesh, perfect king, judge among the netherworld gods,
> Deliberative prince, neckstock of the peoples,[2]
> Who examines all corners of the earth,
> Administrator of the netherworld,
> You are the judge and you examine as only a god can!

1. Kullab was originally a separate place around the sanctuary of Anu that became part of Uruk when that city expanded.
2. A neckstock was a device of wood used to restrain prisoners, here signifying Gilgamesh's control of the human race.

When you are in session in the netherworld,
You give the final verdict,
Your verdict cannot be altered nor can your sentence
    be commuted.
Shamash, the Sun, has entrusted to you his powers
    of judgment and verdict.
Kings, governors, and princes kneel before you,
You examine the omens that pertain to them,
You render their verdicts.

Memory of Gilgamesh outlasted Mesopotamian civilization. Gilgamesh—and perhaps Utanapishtim—are mentioned in a fragmentary version of the *Book of Giants* found among the Dead Sea Scrolls, perhaps dating to the first century C.E. Aelian, a Roman author of the third century C.E., tells a story of the birth of Gilgamesh (translated below, p. 171). Since this does not correspond to anything in the extant sources, it may not represent an authentic Mesopotamian tradition.

What Is The Epic of Gilgamesh?

The Sumerian poems of the late third millennium B.C.E. provided material for those written in the Babylonian language around 1700 B.C.E., called here the "old versions" of *The Epic of Gilgamesh*. The most original of these took episodes from the Sumerian poems and recast them into a new, cohesive plot showing how an arrogant and overbearing king was chastened by the realization that he had to die, like everybody else. The surviving pieces of various old versions show that they gave rise to the Babylonian epic tradition about Gilgamesh, which was to last more than fifteen hundred years.

Fragments of many different versions of the epic have been recovered on clay tablets from Iraq, Syria, Israel, and Turkey, attesting to its wide distribution in ancient times. The manuscripts of *The Epic of Gilgamesh* dating to the period 1500–1000 B.C.E., the "middle versions," preserve only scattered episodes. The longest and most complete text, known from a group of manuscripts of the seventh century B.C.E., has been termed the "standard version." "Late versions" are manuscripts postdating the seventh-century ones.

Portions of *The Epic of Gilgamesh* were translated into such non-Mesopotamian languages as Hittite and Hurrian. "The Hittite Gilgamesh" is translated here by Gary Beckman (below, pp. 159–67). The Hurrian versions are too broken and poorly understood to translate. The so-called Elamite version found in some translations is actually a misunderstanding of two tablets that have nothing to do with Gilgamesh. "The Gilgamesh Letter" (translated below, pp. 169–70) is an ancient parody of the epic.

When Babylonian and Sumerian tablets were rediscovered and deciphered in modern times, the story of Gilgamesh and Enkidu was gradually pieced together from numerous fragmentary manuscripts. Though episodes and passages are still missing, enough of the text has been found to enable modern reading of a coherent extended narrative.

Form, Authorship, and Audience of The Epic of Gilgamesh

The Mesopotamians had no word corresponding to "epic" or "myth" in their languages. Ancient scholars of Mesopotamian literature referred to the epic as the "Gilgamesh Series," that is, a lengthy work on more than one tablet, each corresponding to a "book" or "canto" in modern terms, twelve in the case of *The Epic of Gilgamesh*. Eleven of these tablets form the continuous narrative poem of the standard version. The twelfth is a partial Babylonian translation of the Sumerian poem "Gilgamesh, Enkidu, and the Netherworld," which was appended to the narrative, perhaps during the later second millennium B.C.E., because it seemed germane. This has been omitted here in preference to the more complete Sumerian original (below, pp. 109–25). It is impossible to say how many tablets comprised the old versions, but there were probably far fewer than eleven.

The Mesopotamians preserved no memory of the original Babylonian author of *The Epic of Gilgamesh* but associated the eleven-tablet version with Sin-leqi-unninni, a scholar who lived in the second half of the second millennium B.C.E., centuries after the old versions were written. Nothing further is known about this man except that long after his death he was claimed as an ancestor by certain distinguished families in Babylonia.

One common assumption about ancient epics, such as the *Iliad* or the *Odyssey*, is that their written form was based on oral tradition. This does not seem to be true of *The Epic of Gilgamesh*. There is no evidence that *The Epic of Gilgamesh* began as an oral narrative performed by bards or reciters and only later coalesced as a written text. In fact, the poem as we now have it shows many signs of having been a formal written literary work composed and perhaps performed for well-educated people. Rather than being popular or folkloristic literature, the story of Gilgamesh may have been mostly of interest to the small circle of men and women who belonged to the social, economic, and intellectual elite of their day. Alleged classic features of oral poetry, such as extensive repetition and fixed epithets, are more characteristic of the late than the early versions of the epic, the reverse of what one might expect. A short excerpt from Tablet II, found on a student's exercise tablet from Babylon and dating from the late first millennium B.C.E., shows that the epic was studied in schools of that time. It was also quoted or alluded to in various commemorative and literary works, whose authors no doubt expected that their audience would recognize the source of the passage.

Reading The Epic of Gilgamesh

DIRECT SPEECH AND NARRATIVE

The Epic of Gilgamesh contains considerable direct speech by the characters, normally introduced by the formula, "X made ready to speak, saying to Y." But in situations in which the narrator wishes to convey a sense of urgency, abruptness, anger, or excitement, this formula is often omitted (I, 188; III, 47, 95; VI, 7, contrast 22–23; VI, 84, contrast 87–88; VI, 156; VII, 139, 167; IX, 3; XI, 190, 199, contrast 201–02).[3] The story opens and closes using the same words, addressed by an omniscient narrator to the audience in the beginning and addressed by Gilgamesh to the exiled boatman at the end. The poem also contains first-person discourse by individual characters relating their past (XI, 9–230) or present (IX, 5–12) deeds. In general, there is more direct speech by the characters than narration of their actions.

The pace of the narrative is sometimes rapid, sometimes slow. Suspense is built up by repetition (I, 121–95) or by lengthy speeches at climactic moments (V, 145–217). Passage of time may be conveyed by serial repetition of lines (VII, 176–82; IX, 90–122). Particularly dramatic moments or speeches of great emotion may be repeated in full, as if pausing for effect (II, 62–65, 96–100). Action is presented in short episodes, often with direct speech, such as instructions, assertions, or statements of will, setting the stage for events to follow (X, 193–202). The second half of the poem makes extensive use of retrospective speech concerning incidents already narrated or that took place before the time of the poem, climaxing in the long soliloquy of Utanapishtim narrating the story of the Flood (XI, 9–230). While these speeches are progressively more important for Gilgamesh's broadening understanding, their effect is to slow the action in the second half of the poem. The denouement, however, is surprisingly rapid.

PARALLELISM

In Babylonian poetry, each line usually consists of a complete sentence or thought. Lines tend to be divided into two, three, or more parts, with roughly the same number of words, two to four, in each part. There are many variations on this pattern even within the same poem. There is no strict meter, but the symmetry of poetic lines can give passages a kind of rhythm or beat that may be modified

---

3. References are to tablet and line of the translation in this Norton Critical Edition.

for artistic purposes. For example, in *The Epic of Gilgamesh*, rapid rhythms are used for a fight scene (II, 96–102), slow ones for an anxious mother's prayers (III, 47–100).

Lines of poetry often come in pairs or quatrains, related to each other in sound, rhythm, and meaning. Meaning is developed in part of a line or a whole line, in pairs or groups of lines through parallelism, that is, repeated formulations of a message such that subsequent statements may restate, expand, complete, contrast, render more specific, or carry further the original message.

The following two-line description of Enkidu illustrates this:

> He anointed himself with oil, turned into a man,
> He put on clothing, became like a warrior.
>   (II, 41–42)

In this case, the first half of each line gives complementary, sequential actions that describe Enkidu's progress in grooming himself into a civilized state. The second half of each line proclaims his progress from becoming a human being to becoming a leader among men.

In this five-line example, Enkidu enters Uruk to challenge Gilgamesh:

> The whole of Uruk was standing beside him,
> The people formed a crowd around him,
> A throng was jostling toward him,
> Young men were mobbed around him,
> Babyish, they were fawning before him.
>   (II, 81–85)

Activity increases the more closely the scene focuses on Enkidu: the outermost people stand in a crowd, some within jostling each other for position; the nearer ones have formed a tighter crowd; and the youths next to him are falling at his feet. This quickening of action is paralleled by ever greater specification of those involved, from all the citizens of Uruk to the groveling young men of the city. One senses, too, increasing derogation by the narrator, as the onlookers become progressively more unruly and idolizing.

Contrastive parallelism is exemplified by a description of Gilgamesh as both defender and aggressor:

> Mighty flood-wall, protector of his troops,
> Furious flood-surge, smashing walls of stone.
>   (I, 34–35)

NARRATIVE CONTRASTS

The reader will observe that another favored literary device of the standard version of the epic is the use of contrasts or symbols that are redefined or even reversed in meaning over the course of the poem. For instance, in the beginning, Gilgamesh stays up all night roistering and abusing his subjects; at the end, he cannot stay awake more than a few minutes. Gilgamesh the king, at the apex of society, is supposed to act as shepherd of his subjects but instead mistreats them; Enkidu, the wild man grown up outside human society, watches all night over the shepherds' flocks. Before coming to Uruk, Enkidu roams the steppe, saving wild beasts from hunters; grief-stricken after Enkidu's death, Gilgamesh takes to the steppe, killing wild beasts.

FIGURES OF SPEECH

Babylonian literature makes extensive use of similes and other figures of speech familiar to the modern reader. In the epic, similes are more typical of direct speech, often with high emotional content, than of the narrative voice. Noteworthy examples include Shamhat's encouragement of Enkidu (II, 6), Gilgamesh's ridicule of Enkidu's fears (VII, 38), Enkidu's dream narrative (VII, 135–36), and Utanapishtim's depiction of the onset of the Flood (XI, 132–35). Their context suggests that similes were deemed features of elevated speech in dramatic moments.

Simile comparisons include human beings, deities, animals, products of civilization, and nature. Men are compared to men in terms of positive and negative status, the former being to men of skill (slaughterer, VI, 138) or men in respected positions (warrior, II, 42), the latter being to men without authority (weakling, II, 210; wayfarer, I, 129; X, 9; bandit, X, 73). When men are compared to women and children, the more a man acts like them, the greater depth and range of feeling, and the more open expression of that feeling, are attributed to him (I, 264–66; III, 185; VIII, 13, 45). Comparisons to deities imply exceptional characteristics of a person's activities (I, 133; II, 89). Comparisons to animals are well known in Mesopotamian literature; most striking in the epic are those that compare the gods to dogs and flies (XI, 140, 187), which are highly negative. Humbaba's comparison of Enkidu to a turtle is presumably humorous, as the epic has previously stressed his hairiness and fleetness (V, 97). Comparisons to material culture are generally positive (battlement, II, 24; arrow, X, 121), whereas comparisons to nature are mostly negative (rain, cloud, vapor, reed, V, 136; X, 295; XI, 235), suggesting that poets were inclined to glorify civilization over natural phenomena.

Metaphors, or implied comparisons, include such examples as "Whatever they attempt is a puff of air" (II, 194); "Humbaba's cry is the roar of a deluge. His maw is fire, his breath is death" (II, 164–65); Enkidu is Gilgamesh's axe, sword, shield, and favorite garment (VIII, 46–48). Both similes and metaphors are used to build chains

of associations. In Tablet I, line 31, for instance, Gilgamesh is com-
pared to a charging wild bull, an image common enough in praise
of Mesopotamian royalty, but the figure gains richness a few lines
later by reference to his mother, Ninsun, as a wild cow: Gilgamesh
behaves like a wild bull, as a brave king should, but that is also his
birthright (I, 79; II, 68–69). Figures of speech sometimes come in
clusters, as in the lament of the mother goddess over the drowned
human race, in which two similes relating to childbirth occur
within fifteen lines (XI, 141, 156).

WORDPLAY

The Epic of Gilgamesh abounds in wordplay, that is, suggestion of
one word through use of another with the same or similar sound. In
modern Western literature, this technique is normally a game or
joke, but in Mesopotamian literature wordplays were used in solemn
literary and scholarly contexts as well as for humor. Several word-
plays in the narration of Gilgamesh's dream (I, 254–94), for exam-
ple, provide clear reference to homosexual love: "force" (I, 256) can
suggest "male wearing his hair in a distinctive manner to suggest pros-
titution," and "axe" (I, 287) suggests "female impersonator." Espe-
cially complicated wordplays occur in Ea's advice to Utanapishtim as
to how to deceive the human race about the true nature of the events
presaged by construction of the ark (XI, 43–47). According to one
interpretation, these depend on "cakes" suggesting "darkness" or a
specific ominous sign in divination, "grains" suggesting something
like "grievous", and "rains" suggesting "provide for." In Enkidu's curse
of the hunter (VII, 58–63), the words for "friend" (*ibru*) and "subsis-
tence" (*epru*) sound very similar. When the gardener rejects Ishtar's
advances (VI, 70–73), he chooses the word "reed" (*elpetu*) to echo
harshly Ishtar's use of "touch" (*luput*).

USE OF FANTASTIC NUMBERS

Of all ancient Mesopotamian literary works, *The Epic of Gilgamesh*
makes the most frequent use of fantastic numbers for quantity, size,
weight, time, and distance. Sometimes the unit counted is not
expressed but left to the reader's imagination, as in Tablet XI, line 67,
"thrice thirty-six hundred measures of tar I poured into the oven."
The precise numbers may vary among different versions of the poem.
In some instances, they do not seem to add up (II, 214–18) or simply
defy calculation (I, 58–62; X, 214). Some of these figures may have
been jokes intended for people with a Mesopotamian mathematical
education, while others may be exaggerations for literary ends.
Among the epic's most celebrated riddles is Gilgamesh's genealogy
as two-thirds divine and one-third human, for which various expla-

nations have been offered. The fraction two-thirds appears again in the name of the boatman, Ur-Shanabi, "Servant of Two-Thirds," and in connection with completing the ark (XI, 97).

PECULIARITIES OF SPEECH

Tone and usage in such an ancient text are hazardous topics for discussion, but *The Epic of Gilgamesh* differentiates the speech of some characters, including their style, diction, grammar, and even pronunciation. Utanapishtim, for example, expresses himself in an elevated, opaque style suitable for an antediluvian sage. He also has a curious mannerism of rolling or doubling consonants, which may have suggested to an ancient audience some social or personal distinction now no longer apparent. Shamhat, the harlot, is eloquent and persuasive (I, 232–52), whereas Ishtar, the goddess, speaks like a person of little education, as a streetwalker might (VI, 83–99, 152). The elders of Uruk are pompous and long-winded, causing Gilgamesh to laugh in derision (II, 282). Ishullanu, the gardener, uses a nonstandard form in VI, 71, which could be seen either as archaic and proverbial ("Hath my mother not baked?") or as a colloquialism ("Hain't my mother baked?"). Deliberate distortion of normal poetic language to reflect individual speech habits occurs elsewhere in Mesopotamian literature, but no other work develops the device to the same extent.

COMPOUND EXPRESSIONS

Another distinctive usage in *The Epic of Gilgamesh* is the formation of compounds with the word "man," such as "trapping-man" or "entrapping-man" (I, 121; VII, 58), "mightiness-man" (I, 147), "happiness-man" (I, 242), "yokel-man" (V, 94), and "human-man" (I, 186). The most elaborate of these is the name of the old man who is supposed to test the plant of rejuvenation: "Old Man Has Become Young-Again-Man" (XI, 323). This type of formation is very rare outside of this poem, so may be considered a special feature of its style, though the tone and intent are no longer discernible.

QUOTATIONS AND ALLUSIONS

An educated Mesopotamian audience would have recognized passages in the epic that occur in other literary works. The poem called "Ishtar's Descent to the Netherworld"[4] is one such example. Enkidu echoes some of its lines when describing his descent to the land of no return (VII, 144–52). Ishtar's threats to release the dead (VI, 98–99) are likewise found in her "Descent." Mesopotamian readers

---

4. Translated in *Muses*, pp. 402–09. (See list of abbreviations below, p. xxiii.)

might have relished the contrast between how this passage was used in the epic and how it was used in the other poem. In the epic, Ishtar speaks these lines when she goes up to heaven, whereas in the "Descent" she speaks them at the gates to the netherworld. They would have appreciated too that in threatening to break down the tavern keeper's door (X, 22), Gilgamesh uses the same words as Ishtar uses in the other poem when threatening to break down the doors of the netherworld. Perhaps they thought this a humorous touch. Furthermore, Enkidu curses Shamhat the harlot (VII, 82, 84) just as the queen of the netherworld curses the male imperson-ator of women in "Ishtar's Descent."

Other literary works quote the epic, such as a lament written by a Babylonian prince of the sixth century B.C.E., which borrows the phrase otherwise unique to the epic, "At the first glimmer of dawn" (VIII, 81).[5] These intertextual allusions to Mesopotamian intellec-tual tradition suggest that the anticipated audience was primarily an educated elite responsive to literary cross-references and the adroit reuse of stock phraseology.

THEMES

Certain themes of the epic would likewise have been familiar from other widely studied literary works. The idea that human mortality was a consequence of divine selfishness, for example, was well known, as was a concept of the hero as a man striving toward greater accomplishments than those of ordinary people, regardless of the limitations imposed by chance and destiny.

The Mesopotamians preferred literary works to be set in ancient times, involving kings and gods, narrating events largely outside of everyday experience. Yet both divine and human characters often display imperfections and personal failings, as if remoteness of time and empirical background were no obstacles to projecting inglori-ous weakness onto long-ago figures. The theme of the partiality and unpredictability of divine justice was familiar to Babylonian readers as well. They would not have been surprised at the unfair condemnation of Enkidu, nor at the intervention of the sun god, Shamash, to the crucial advantage of the heroes.

Mesopotamians expected their serious literature to stress the importance of knowledge. In the standard version of the epic, the significance of Gilgamesh's story lies not so much in the deeds themselves as in the lessons his experiences offered to future gen-erations. The standard version of the epic highlights progressive acquisition of knowledge as a fundamental attribute of a civilized

5. Translated in *Muses*, pp. 852–56.

human being. Enkidu becomes sexually aware, learns how to consume cooked foods and fermented beverages, is taught to wear manufactured garments, and defends the interests of his community. Both Gilgamesh and Enkidu move to a higher stage of knowledge by learning to love another human being, but Enkidu's untimely death turns this joy into the pain of loss. Gilgamesh gains from his bereavement a new form of knowledge, an enhanced awareness of himself. He must finally accept that he too will die and that his immortality must be memory of what he has accomplished in his lifetime. The epic teaches that his experience has a broader meaning only because it was written down for the benefit of those who come after. It privileges literate culture, the preserve of a small but influential segment of the population. To the Mesopotamians, written tradition thus offered both a gateway to the past and a key to the closed door of the future.

The modern reader may well find other themes of special interest, such as its explicit male–female eroticism and its depiction of the same-sex love of Gilgamesh and Enkidu. Women, moreover, are more active in this narrative than in many Mesopotamian literary works, to the extent that Gilgamesh's success in his quests for fame and immortality is largely owed to their intervention. His mother's prayers to the sun god lead to his defeat of Humbaba. The wife of the scorpion monster evidently persuades her husband to let Gilgamesh into the sun's tunnel under the earth. Siduri, the tavern keeper, tells him how to get across the sea. The wife of Utanapishtim persuades her dour spouse to give Gilgamesh a parting gift, which turns out to be how to find the plant of rejuvenation. While Mesopotamian literary convention held that women were more susceptible to emotion than men, *The Epic of Gilgamesh* develops this into a major theme with no clear ancient parallel. Its feminization of Gilgamesh was perhaps intended to show that not only was the king bigger, stronger, more handsome and courageous than ordinary men, he also felt more deeply. This was a major factor in his achieving immortal fame, and it set him apart from other heroes of the past.

Today, the satirical and humorous elements of the poem may seem surprising, as a canon of Western culture is that epic should be solemn and high-minded. Such passages include the pedantic correction of the scorpion monster's wife, Enkidu's abrupt substitution of a magnanimous blessing for his irreversible curse of the harlot, his denunciation of an insensate door, and the sun god's hollow promise of a fine funeral as consolation for his unjust death. There are also fleeting but memorable images, such as the worm dropping out of Enkidu's nose or the fearsome monster Humbaba bursting into tears, for which ancient parallels will not readily be found. Taken with the quantitative exaggerations of the story, among them

Gilgamesh's extraordinary journeys in time and space, his race against the sunset, and the topographical consequences of his struggle with Humbaba, such passages may betoken a complex intent that blended humor and a sophisticated pleasure in the implausible with meditation about knowledge, love, death, and the human condition. No one can say for sure.

New in This Second Edition

The revised edition of *The Epic of Gilgamesh* incorporates over 150 previously unknown lines from recently discovered manuscripts. The entire poem has been retranslated on the basis of the text established by the 2003 edition of Andrew George, which includes new copies of all the manuscripts of the Babylonian epic then known, plus a translation and extensive commentary that substantially advance understanding of many key passages. All modern studies of the epic must begin with George's work, which had not appeared when the first edition of this translation was published. Important additional manuscripts that have been discovered since 2003 have also been incorporated.

Although there is no comprehensive edition of the Sumerian Gilgamesh poems, they have been retranslated by the editor for this edition taking into account new manuscript discoveries, improved readings of manuscripts previously known, and advances in understanding of this difficult material made by many philologists over the past fifteen years. The two versions of "Gilgamesh and Huwawa" have been combined into one and "The Gudam Epic" has been omitted, since it does not mention Gilgamesh. "The Hittite Gilgamesh," translated by Gary Beckman, incorporates additional fragments as well.

Two critical essays by Susan Ackerman and Andrew George have been added that take more recent scholarship and research agendas into account, revised with the authors' permission and keyed to this translation for ease of reference.

This is therefore the most complete and up-to-date treatment of the ancient Mesopotamian epic tradition about Gilgamesh available today.

Abbreviations and Symbols

Babylonian Gilgamesh Epic: George, Andrew. *The Babylonian Gilgamesh Epic: Introduction, Critical Edition and Cuneiform Texts.* Oxford: Oxford UP, 2003.

Epics: Vanstiphout, Herman. *Epics of Sumerian Kings: The Matter of Aratta.* Writings from the Ancient World 20. Atlanta: Society of Biblical Literature, 2003.

Harps: Jacobsen, Thorkild, ed. *The Harps That Once . . . : Sumerian Poetry in Translation.* New Haven, CT: Yale UP, 1987.

Muses: Foster, Benjamin R. *Before the Muses: An Anthology of Akkadian Literature,* 3rd ed. Bethesda, MD: CDL Press, 2005.

[ ] indicates translator's restoration of missing text.
( ) indicates explanatory insertion by the translator.
< > indicates material erroneously omitted by the scribe.

The Text of
THE EPIC OF GILGAMESH

Tablet I

[The prologue introduces Gilgamesh as a man who gained knowledge through exceptional experiences and preserved it for the future. The narrator invites us to admire Gilgamesh's architectural legacy in Uruk, then to read the story of his hardships.]

He who saw the wellspring, the foundations of the land,
Who knew the world's ways, was wise in all things,
Gilgamesh, who saw the wellspring, the foundations of
   the land,
Who knew the world's ways, was wise in all things,
He it was who studied seats of power everywhere,   5
Full knowledge of it all he gained.
He saw what was secret and revealed what was hidden,
He brought back tidings from before the Flood,
From a distant journey came home, weary, but at peace,
Set out all his hardships on a monument of stone,   10
He built the walls of ramparted Uruk,
The lustrous treasury of hallowed Eanna!   *Temple Tower*
See its upper wall, which girds it like a cord,
Gaze at the lower course, which no one can equal,
Mount the wooden staircase, there from days of old,   15
Approach Eanna, the dwelling of Ishtar,
Which no future king, no human being can equal.
Go up, pace out the walls of Uruk,
Study the foundation terrace and examine the brickwork.
Is not its masonry of kiln-fired brick?   20
And did not seven masters lay its foundations?
One square mile of city, one square mile of gardens,
One square mile of clay pits, a half square mile of Ishtar's
   dwelling,
Three and a half square miles is the measure of Uruk!
Open the foundation box of cedar,   25
Release its lock of bronze,
[Raise] the lid upon its hidden contents,
Take up and read from the lapis tablet
Of all the miseries that he, Gilgamesh, came through.

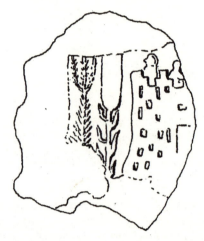

1. *Go up, pace out the walls of Uruk.* Seal impression from the end of
the fourth millennium B.C.E. depicting people atop the walls of Uruk.

[*The narrator extols the extraordinary characteristics of Gilgamesh. An
old version of the epic began here.*]

Surpassing all kings, for his stature renowned,   30
Heroic offspring of Uruk, a charging wild bull,
He leads the way in the vanguard,
He marches at the rear, defender of his comrades.
Mighty flood-wall, protector of his troops,
Furious flood-surge, smashing walls of stone,   35
Wild calf of divine Lugalbanda, Gilgamesh is perfect in strength,
Suckling of the sublime wild cow, divine Ninsun,
Towering Gilgamesh is uncannily perfect.
Opening passes in the mountains,
Digging wells at the highlands' verge,   40
Traversing the ocean, the vast sea, to the sun's rising,
Exploring the furthest reaches of the earth,
Seeking everywhere for eternal life,
Reaching in his valor Utanapishtim the Distant One,
Restorer of holy places that the deluge had destroyed,   45
Founder of rites for the teeming peoples,
Who could be his like for kingly virtue?[1]

---

1. Mesopotamian rulers sometimes boasted of restoring ancient temples that had been
   destroyed and forgotten long ago. In line 45, the poet suggests that Gilgamesh became a
   dutiful king of this kind. Mesopotamian rulers also sometimes boasted of endowing
   temples with new offerings. This pair of lines (45–46) sums up religious duties expected
   of a good king by citing two extremes of benefactions: those from the remote past and
   those beginning in his own reign.

And who, like Gilgamesh, can proclaim, "I am king!"?
Gilgamesh was singled out from the day of his birth,
Two-thirds of him was divine, one-third of him was human! 50
The Lady of Birth drew his body's image,
The God of Wisdom brought his stature to perfection.[2]

[gap, partially filled by a middle version]

Gilgamesh could wrestle with fifty companions, wearing out
   young men every day,
He kept the young men of Uruk fearful of mistreatment.
The locks of his hair grew thick as a grain field,
His teeth gleamed like the rising sun, 55
His hair was dark as deep blue strands of wool.
Eleven cubits was his height,
His chest four cubits wide,
A triple cubit his feet, his leg six times twelve, 60
His stride was six times twelve cubits,
A triple cubit the beard of his cheek.
He was perfection in height,
Ideally handsome [. . .]

[Gilgamesh, in his arrogance and superior strength, abuses his male sub-
jects, apparently through some strenuous athletic competition at which
he excelled, as well as his female subjects, ravishing them at will. Heed-
ing the complaints of the women, the gods create a wild man, Enkidu, as
a fitting rival for Gilgamesh.]

In ramparted Uruk he strode back and forth,
Lording it like a wild bull, his head thrust high. 65
The onslaught of his weapons had no equal.
His companions stood forth by his game stick,
He was harrying the young men of Uruk beyond reason.
Gilgamesh would leave no son to his father,
Day and night he would rampage fiercely. 70
Gilgamesh, king of this numberless people,
He, the shepherd of ramparted Uruk,
Gilgamesh would leave no girl to her mother!
Soon [. . .] 75
[Their plaints] . . . before them.

2. According to one Mesopotamian tradition, the first human being was created by Mami,
goddess of birth, whom the gods thereupon rewarded with the title "Mistress of All the
Gods," and Enki, god of wisdom, working together. Subsequent human beings were
born naturally. This passage means that Gilgamesh was physically a perfect human
being, so much so that he resembled the first human created by the gods more than the
product of a normal birth.

Bold, superb, accomplished, . . .
Gilgamesh would leave no young woman to her husband!
He was their bull, they were the kine!
Their bitter clamor rose up to the sky,   80
The warrior's daughter, the young man's chosen,
Ishtar kept hearing their plaints,[3]
Their bitter complaint reached the heaven of Anu.
The gods of heaven, the lords who command,
[Said to Anu]:   85

> Have you created a headstrong wild bull in ramparted Uruk?
> The onslaught of his weapons has no equal.
> His companions stand forth by his game stick,
> He is harrying the young men of Uruk beyond reason.
> Gilgamesh leaves no son to his father!   90
> Day and night he rampages fiercely.
> This is the shepherd of ramparted Uruk,
> This is the people's shepherd,
> Bold, superb, accomplished, [. . .]!
> Gilgamesh leaves no young woman to her [husband]!   95

The warrior's daughter, the young man's chosen,
Anu(?)[4] kept hearing their plaints.

[*Anu speaks.*]

> Let them summon Aruru, the great one,
> She created the human race.
> Let her create a match for Gilgamesh, mighty in strength,   100
> Let them contend with each other, that Uruk may
>   have peace.

They summoned Aruru, the great one:

> You, Aruru, created [the human race],
> Now, create what Anu commanded,
> To his stormy heart, let that one be equal,   105
> Let them contend with each other, that Uruk may
>   have peace.

---

3. The goddess Ishtar was believed to pay particular attention to the prayers of women.
4. This restoration is uncertain; the next four lines are not present in the manuscripts but have been supplied by the translator because the text seems to be in disorder here.

When Aruru heard this,
She conceived within her what Anu commanded.
Aruru wet her hands,
She pinched off clay, she cast it down upon the steppe,   110
She created valiant Enkidu in the steppe,
Offspring of silence,[5] with the force of the valiant Ninurta.
Shaggy with hair was his whole body,
He was made lush with head hair, like a woman,
The locks of his hair grew thick as a grain field.   115
He knew neither people nor inhabited land,
He dressed as animals do.
He ate grass with gazelles,
With beasts he jostled at the water hole,
With wildlife he drank his fill of water.   120

[*A distraught hunter seeks his father's advice as to how to stop Enkidu's interference with his trapping. The father counsels him to go to Gilgamesh, who will give him a woman to seduce Enkidu from his feral way of life.*]

A hunter, a trapping-man,
Encountered him at the water hole,
One day, a second, and a third he encountered him at the
    water hole.
When he saw him, the hunter stood stock-still with terror,
As for (Enkidu), he went home with his beasts.   125
(The hunter) was aghast, struck dumb,
His feelings were in turmoil, his face drawn,
There was sorrow in his heart,
His face was like a traveler's from afar.
The hunter made ready to speak, saying to his father: 130

   My father, there is a certain fellow who comes [to the
       water hole],
   He is the mightiest in the land, strength is his.
   Like the force of heaven, so mighty is his strength![6]
   He constantly ranges over the uplands,
   Constantly eating grass with beasts,   135

---

5. This unique expression may mean that he was brought into the world without the tumult that normally accompanies childbirth (*Babylonian Gilgamesh Epic*, p. 789).
6. Many scholars understand the obscure expression "force of heaven" to mean a meteorite, but this is difficult to harmonize with "force of the valiant Ninurta," a terrestrial deity, in line 112.

Constantly making his way to the water hole.
I am too frightened to approach him.
He has filled in the pits I dug,
He has torn out my traps I set,
He has helped the beasts, wildlife of the steppe, slip from
    my hands,   140
He will not let me work the steppe.

His father made ready to speak, saying to the hunter:

[My son], in Uruk [. . .] Gilgamesh,
[There is no one mightier] than he.
Like the force of heaven, so mighty is his strength.   145
Take the road, set off [toward Uruk],
[Tell Gilgamesh of] the mightiness-man.
[He will give you Shamhat the harlot], take her with you,
[Let her prevail over him], instead of a mighty man.
[When the wild beasts] draw near the water hole,   150
[Let her strip off her clothing], laying bare her charms.
[When he sees her], he will approach her.
His beasts [that grew up with him] on the steppe will
    deny him.

[Giving heed] to the advice of his father,
The hunter went forth [. . .],   155
He took the road, set off toward Uruk,
To [the king], Gilgamesh, [he said these words]:

There is a certain fellow who comes [to the water hole],
He is the mightiest in the land, strength is his.
Like the force of heaven, so mighty is his strength.   160
He constantly ranges over the uplands,
Constantly feeding on grass with beasts,
Constantly making his way to the water hole.
I am too frightened to approach him.
He has filled in the pits I dug,   165
He has torn out my traps I set,
He has helped the beasts, wildlife of the steppe, slip from
    my hands,
He will not let me work the steppe.

Gilgamesh said to him, to the hunter:

Go, hunter, take with you Shamhat the harlot,   170
When the wild beasts draw near the water hole,

Let her strip off her clothing, laying bare her charms.
When he sees her, he will approach her.
His beasts that grew up with him on the steppe will deny
    him.

Forth went the hunter, taking with him Shamhat the harlot,   175
They took the road, going straight on their way.
On the third day they arrived at the appointed place.
Hunter and harlot sat down to wait.
One day, a second day, they sat by the water hole,
The beasts came to the water hole to drink,   180
The wildlife came to drink their fill of water.
But as for him, Enkidu, born in the uplands,
Who ate grass with gazelles,
Who drank at the water hole with beasts,
Who, with wildlife, drank his fill of water,   185
Shamhat looked upon him, a human-man,
A barbarous fellow from the depths of the steppe—

There he is, Shamhat, open your embrace,
Open your loins, let him take your charms!
Be not bashful, take his vitality!   190
When he sees you, he will approach you,
Toss aside your clothing, let him lie upon you,
Treat him, a human, to woman's work!
His beasts will deny him, though he grew up with them,
As in his ardor he caresses you!   195

Shamhat loosened her garments,
She opened her loins, he took her charms.
She was not bashful, she took his vitality.
She tossed aside her clothing and he lay upon her,
She treated him, a human, to woman's work,   200
As in his ardor he caressed her.
Six days, seven nights was Enkidu aroused, flowing into
    Shamhat.
After he had his fill of her delights,
He set off toward his beasts.
When they saw him, Enkidu, the gazelles shied off,   205
The wild beasts of the steppe shunned his person,
Enkidu had polluted his virginal body.
His knees stood still, while his beasts were going away,
Enkidu was too slow, he could not run as before,
But he had gained [reason], broadened his understanding.   210

[*Shamhat urges Enkidu to return with her to Uruk, artfully piquing his interest with tales of pleasures awaiting him there, then feigning second thoughts as she describes Gilgamesh.*]

He returned, he sat at the harlot's feet,
The harlot was looking into his face,
While he listened to what the harlot was saying.
The harlot said to him, to Enkidu:

> You are handsome, Enkidu, you are become like a god,   215
> Why roam the steppe with wild beasts?
> Come, let me lead you to ramparted Uruk,
> To the hallowed temple, abode of Anu and Ishtar,
> The place of Gilgamesh, who is perfect in strength,
> And so, like a wild bull, he lords it over the young men.   220

As she was speaking to him, her words found favor,
He was yearning for one to know his heart, a friend.
Enkidu said to her, to the harlot:

> Come, Shamhat, escort me
> To the lustrous hallowed temple, abode of Anu and Ishtar,   225
> The place of Gilgamesh, who is perfect in strength,
> And so, like a wild bull, he lords it over the young men.
> I myself will challenge him, [I will speak out] boldly,
> [I will] raise a cry in Uruk: I am the mighty one!
> [I am the one who will] change destinies!   230
> He who was born in the steppe [is mighty], strength
>   is his!

[*Shamhat speaks.*]

> [Come then], let him see your face,
> [I will show you Gilgamesh], where he is I know full well.
> Come then, Enkidu, to ramparted Uruk,
> Where young men are resplendent in holiday clothing,   235
> Where every day is set for a celebration,
> Where drums never stop beating.
> And the harlots too, they are fairest of form,
> Rich in beauty, full of delights.
> Even the great (gods) are kept from sleeping at night![7]   240
> Enkidu, you who [have not] learned how to live,

7. The Mesopotamians considered a small group of the gods "great" or "superior," above all the others. The stillness of night was sometimes expressed as the time when even the great gods had retired for their rest.

Oh, let me show you Gilgamesh, the happiness-man.
Look at him, gaze upon his face,
He is radiant with virility, manly vigor is his,
The whole of his body is seductively gorgeous.   245
Mightier strength has he than you,
Never resting by day or night.
O Enkidu, renounce your audacity!
Gilgamesh is beloved of Shamash,
Anu, Enlil, and Ea broadened his wisdom.   250
Ere you come down from the uplands,
Gilgamesh will dream of you in Uruk.

[*The scene shifts to Uruk, where Gilgamesh is telling his mother, Ninsun,
his dreams. She explains them to him.*]

Gilgamesh went to relate the dream, saying to his mother:

Mother, such a dream I had last night:
There were stars of heaven around me,   255
As the force of heaven kept falling toward me,
I tried to carry it but it was too strong for me,
I tried to move it but I could not budge it.
The whole of Uruk was standing beside it,
[The people formed a crowd] around it,   260
A throng [was jostling] toward it,
[Young men] were mobbed around it,
[Babyish], they were fawning before it!
[I fell in love with it] like a woman, I caressed it,
I carried it off and laid it down before you,   265
Then you were making it my partner.

The mother of Gilgamesh, knowing and wise,
Who understands everything, said to her son,
[The wild cow] Ninsun, knowing and wise,
Who understands everything, said to Gilgamesh: 270

The stars of heaven around you,
[As] the force of heaven fell upon you,
Your trying to move it but being unable to budge it,
Your laying it down before me,
Then my making it your partner,   275
Your falling in love with it like a woman, your caressing it,
(Means) there will come to you a strong one,
A companion who rescues a friend.
He will be mighty in the land, strength will be his,

Like the force of heaven, so mighty will be his strength.   280
You will fall in love with him like a woman, you will
    caress him.
He will be mighty and rescue you, time and again.

He had a second dream,
He arose and went before the goddess, his mother,
Gilgamesh said to her, to his mother: 285

Mother, I had a second dream.
An axe was cast down in a street of broad-marted Uruk,
They were crowding around it,
The whole of Uruk was standing beside it,
[The people] formed a crowd around it,   290
A throng was jostling toward it,
Young men were mobbed around it.
I carried it off and laid it down before you,
I fell in love with it like a woman, I caressed it,
Then you were making it my partner.   295

The mother of Gilgamesh, knowing and wise,
Who understands everything, said to her son,
The wild cow Nin[sun], knowing and wise,
Who understands everything, said to Gilgamesh:

My son, the axe you saw is a man.   300
Your loving it like a woman and caressing it,
And my making it your partner
(Means) there will come to you a strong one,
A companion who rescues a friend.
He will be mighty in the land, strength will be his,   305
Like the strength of heaven, so mighty will be
    his strength.

Gilgamesh said to her, to his mother:

Let this befall me according to the command of the great
    counselor Enlil,
I want a friend for my very own confidant,
For my own confidant do I want a friend!   310

Even while he was having his dreams,
Shamhat was telling the dreams of Gilgamesh to Enkidu,
As the pair of them were making love together.

Tablet II

[Shamhat begins the process of educating Enkidu. She takes him to an encampment of shepherds, where he learns how to eat, drink, dress, and groom himself, as well as to defend his community. Whereas Gilgamesh keeps his subjects awake at night with his roistering, Enkidu stays up all night to protect the flocks. Much of this tablet is known from older versions, freely combined here with later ones.]

While Enkidu was seated before the harlot,
The pair of them were making love together,
Enkidu forgot the steppe where he was born.
Six days, seven nights was Enkidu aroused, flowing
    into Shamhat.[1]
The harlot said to him, to Enkidu: 5

    As I look at you, Enkidu, you are become like a god,
    Why roam the steppe with wild beasts?
    Come, let me lead you to broad-marted Uruk,
    To the hallowed temple, abode of Anu,
    Up then, Enkidu, let me lead you to broad-marted Uruk,   10
    To Eanna, abode of Anu,
    Where they do things that long abide,
    And you too, like a man, can make something of yourself,
    You already know where the shepherd ranges.

He heard what she said, accepted her words,   15
The counsel of Shamhat touched his heart.
She took off her clothing, with one piece she dressed him,
The second she herself put on.
Clasping his hand, she led him as if he were a god,[2]
To the shepherds' huts, where a sheepfold was.   20
The shepherds crowded around him,
(They said) to themselves, of their own accord:

---

1. A newly discovered fragment shows that this line refers to a second week of heroic intercourse, this time in the shepherds' camp, A. George, "Another Fragment of Old Babylonian Gilgamesh," *Zeitschrift für Assyriologie* 108 (2018): 10–21.
2. Statues of Mesopotamian gods were sometimes led in procession by worshipers. Enkidu, escorted by Shamhat, now resembles one of these (this tablet, line 6).

This fellow, how like Gilgamesh in stature,
In stature tall, proud as a battlement.
I am sure, being born in the steppe,   25
He was nursed on the milk of wild beasts!

They set bread before him,
They set beer before him.
Enkidu did not eat the bread.
He eyed it uncertainly, then stared,   30
Enkidu did not know to eat bread,
Nor had he ever learned to drink beer!
The harlot made ready to speak, saying to Enkidu:

Eat the bread, Enkidu, the staff of life,
Drink the beer, the custom of the land.   35

Enkidu ate the bread until he was sated,
He drank seven juglets of the beer.
His mood became relaxed, he was singing joyously,
He felt lighthearted and his features glowed.
A barber treated his hairy body,   40
He anointed himself with oil, turned into a man,
He put on clothing, became like a warrior.
He took his weapon, did battle with lions,
As the [shepherds] rested at night,
He slew many wolves, defeated many lions!   45
The head herdsmen lay down to sleep,
Enkidu was their watchman, a wakeful man

[gap]

[A passerby on his way to a wedding feast tells Enkidu of Gilgamesh's tyran-
nical prerogative: he is the first to have the bride. Enkidu, aghast, strides off
to Uruk. Whereas before Shamhat had led him, now he walks in front like
a challenger.]

He was having fun with Shamhat.
He lifted his eyes, he saw a man.
He said to the harlot: 50

Shamhat, bring that man here!
Why has he come? I will ask him to account for himself.

The harlot summoned the man,
He came over, Enkidu said to him:

Fellow, where are you rushing?   55
What is this, your wearisome errand?

The man made ready to speak, said to Enkidu:

They have invited me to a wedding.
Is it (not) people's custom to get married?
I have heaped high on the festival tray   60
The fancy dishes for the wedding.
For the king of ramparted Uruk,
The people's veils are open for his choosing,
For Gilgamesh, king of broad-marted Uruk,
The people's veils are open for his choosing!   65
He mates with the lawful wife,
He first, the groom after.
By divine decree pronounced,
From the cutting of his umbilical cord, she is his due.[3]

At the man's account, his face went pale.   70

[*gap*]

Enkidu was walking in front, with Shamhat behind him.

[*As foretold in Gilgamesh's dream, a crowd gathers around Enkidu as he
enters Uruk. He has arrived in time for the wedding ceremony.*]

When he entered the street of broad-marted Uruk,
A multitude crowded around him.
He stood there in the street of broad-marted Uruk,
With the people crowding around him.   75
They said about him:

He is equal to Gilgamesh in build,
Though shorter in stature, he is stronger of frame.
I am sure, being born in the steppe,
He was nursed on the milk of wild beasts!   80

The whole of Uruk was standing beside him,
The people formed a crowd around him,
A throng was jostling toward him,
Young men were mobbed around him,
Babyish, they were fawning before him.   85
In Uruk the sacrifices were as usual,

---

3. This means that by his birthright Gilgamesh can take brides first on their wedding
nights then leave them to their wedded husbands.

2. *It was Gilgamesh who knelt for the win, his foot on the ground.* This seal image shows a triumphant hero immobilizing a lion with what may have been the same gesture described here.

The young men were jubilant,
Against the young man headed straight on his way,
    a champion stood ready,
Against the godlike Gilgamesh, a rival stood ready!
For the goddess of lovemaking, the bed was made,   90
Gilgamesh was to join with the girl that night.

[*gap*]

[*Enkidu blocks the king's way to the wedding ceremony. They wrestle in the doorway. Gilgamesh wins by lifting Enkidu over his shoulders while keeping one foot and the other knee on the ground. The match over, Enkidu praises Gilgamesh's superiority.*]

Enkidu approached him,
They met in the public street.
Enkidu blocked the door to the wedding with his foot,
Not allowing Gilgamesh to enter.   95
They grappled with each other, crouching like bulls,
They shattered the doorpost, the wall shook.
Gilgamesh and Enkidu grappled with each other,
Crouching like bulls,
They shattered the doorpost, the wall shook!   100
They grappled with each other at the door to the wedding,

They fought in the street, the public square.
It was Gilgamesh who knelt for the win, his foot on the ground.
His fury abated, he turned away.
After he turned away,   105
Enkidu said to him, to Gilgamesh:

> As one unique did your mother bear you,
> The wild cow of the ramparts, Ninsun,
> Exalted you above the most valorous of men!
> Enlil has granted you kingship over the people.   110

[*gap*]

They kissed each other and made friends.
They discussed [. . .] together . . .

[*gap*]

[*Gilgamesh is speaking.*]

> I have found the friend, the confidant whom I saw
>   [in my dreams],
> Enkidu, the confidant whom I saw [in my dreams]!

Enkidu said to her, to the harlot: 115

> Come, harlot, let me do something good for you,
> Because you brought me to ramparted Uruk,
> Because you showed me a fine companion, a friend

[*gap*]

[*As foretold in the dream, Gilgamesh goes to his mother, Ninsun, to tell her
of his new friend. She responds that Enkidu has no family, perhaps mean-
ing that he is not suitable for her son. She may also predict that Gilgamesh
will live to regret this friendship (line 127). Enkidu bursts into tears. When
Gilgamesh asks him why, Enkidu says that he is afraid of something, pos-
sibly the loss of the happiness he has just found.*]

> He is mighty in the land, strength is his,
> Like the force of heaven, so mighty is his strength,   120
> In stature tall, proud as a battlement.

The mother of Gilgamesh made ready to speak,
Said to Gilgamesh,
Ninsun, the wild cow, made ready to speak,
Said to Gilgamesh: 125

My son, [. . .]
Bitterly [. . .]
Enkidu has neither [father nor mother],
He was overgrown with hair [. . .]
He was born in the steppe, no one [. . .]   130

[*In the old version used here, Enkidu becomes angry when he overhears
Ninsun's speech. But in the standard version, which resumes in line 151
below, he is apprehensive.*]

Enkidu froze, he heard [what she said],
He thought about it and collapsed [. . .]
His eyes filled with tears,
His heart felt resentment,
He sighed bitterly.   135
Enkidu's eyes filled with tears,
His heart felt resentment,
He sighed bitterly!
He was listless, his strength turned to weakness.
They clasped each other [. . .]   140
They joined hands like [. . .]
Gilgamesh felt sorry for him,
Saying to Enkidu:

> Why did your eyes fill with tears
> Your heart feel resentment,   145
> You sigh bitterly?
> Why are you listless, your strength turned to weakness?

Enkidu said to him, to Gilgamesh:

> Cries of sorrow, my friend, have cramped my muscles,
> I am listless, my strength turned to weakness.   150
> Fear has made its way into my heart.

[*Perhaps to legitimate their friendship, Gilgamesh proposes a joint quest to
kill a divine monster named Humbaba, in order to cut a giant cedar tree in
the forest Humbaba guards. Felling evergreens on distant mountains was a
well-known demonstration of kingly power in early Mesopotamia. Enkidu,
horrified, tries vainly to dissuade him.*]

Gilgamesh made ready to speak,
Saying to Enkidu:

[*gap*]

[There dwells in the forest] a fierce monster, Humbaba,
[You and I shall] kill [him]   155
[And] wipe out [something evil from the land].
[Let us] surprise him in his dwelling.

Enkidu made ready to speak,
Saying to Gilgamesh:

My friend, I knew of him in the steppe   160
When I roamed with the wild beasts.
The forest is a wilderness, sixty double leagues in every
     direction,
Who can go into it?
Humbaba's cry is the roar of a deluge,
His maw is fire, his breath is death.   165
The dwelling of Humbaba is a hopeless quest.

Gilgamesh made ready to speak,
Saying to Enkidu:

My friend, I must go up the mountain [. . .]

[*gap*]

Enkidu made ready to speak,   170
Saying to Gilgamesh:

How shall the likes of us go to the forest of cedars, my friend?
In order to safeguard the forest of cedars,
Enlil appointed him to frighten off the people,
Enlil ordained him seven direful radiances.[4]   175
That journey is not to be undertaken,
That creature is not to be looked upon.
The guardian of [. . .], the forest of cedars,
Humbaba's cry is the roar of a deluge,
His maw is fire, his breath is death.   180
He can hear rustling in the forest for sixty double
     leagues.
Who can go into his forest?
Adad is first and Humbaba is second:[5]
Who, even among the gods, could attack him?

---

4. The Mesopotamians believed that divine beings were surrounded by blinding, awe-inspiring radiances. In the old versions of *The Epic of Gilgamesh*, these are considered removable, like garments or jewelry, whereas in "Gilgamesh and Huwawa" (below, pp. 125–38) they resemble tree branches.
5. In the mountain lands northwest of Mesopotamia, where the cedars grew, Adad, god of storm and thunder, reigned supreme; Humbaba was second only to him.

In order to safeguard the forest of cedars,   185
Enlil appointed him to frighten off the people,
Enlil ordained him seven direful radiances.
Besides, whoever goes into his forest, numbness over
    powers him.

Gilgamesh made ready to speak,
Saying to Enkidu: 190

Who, my friend, can go up to heaven?
The gods took up their dwellings in the light of the sun,
But people's days are numbered,
Whatever they attempt is a puff of air.
Here you are, even you, afraid of death.   195
What good is your bravery's might?
I will go before you,
You can call out to me, "Go on, be not afraid!"
If I fall, I'll have established my name:
"Gilgamesh, who joined battle with fierce Humbaba,"
    (they'll say).   200
You who were born and grew up on the steppe,
When lions sprang at you, you knew what to do.
Young men fled before you,
The evening [star came out] for you.
But now you talk like a weakling,   205
How you pule! You make me ill.
I must set [my hand] to cutting a cedar tree,
I must establish eternal fame.
Come, my friend, let's be off to the foundry,
Let them cast axes such as we'll need.   210

[*After supervising the casting of enormous axes and weapons, Gilgamesh
informs the citizenry of Uruk of his planned quest. First he addresses the
elders, speaking of his desire for eternal fame, next the young men, appeal-
ing to their sense of adventure. He promises to return in time to celebrate
the springtime festival of the new year. Enkidu and the elders attempt
unsuccessfully to dissuade him.*]

Off they went, hand in hand, to the workshop.
The craftsmen, seated around, conferred.
They cast great axes,
Axe blades weighing 180 pounds each they cast.
They cast great daggers,   215
Their blades were 120 pounds each,
The fittings of the daggers each thirty pounds of gold.
Gilgamesh and Enkidu bore ten times sixty pounds each!

He bolted the seven gates of Uruk,
He summoned [the assembly], the multitude convened,   220
[All the land] turned out in a street of broad-marted Uruk.
Gilgamesh [took his place] upon his throne,
[. . . in a street] of broad-marted Uruk,
[Enkidu] sat before him.
[Gilgamesh spoke to the elders of broad-marted Uruk]:   225

    [Hear me, O elders of broad-marted Uruk],
    The god of whom they speak
    I, Gilgamesh, would see!
    The one whose name resounds across the whole world,
    I will hunt him down in the forest of cedars.   230
    I will make the land hear
    How mighty is the scion of Uruk.
    I will set my hand to cutting a cedar,
    An eternal name I will make for myself!

[*In an old version of this episode, Gilgamesh addresses the elders, lines 226–234, and they respond, lines 265–79. In the standard version, he addresses the young men, lines 235–46, and the elders respond, lines 265–79. Both speeches are incorporated here.*]

    Hear me, O young men [of ramparted Uruk],   235
    Young men of Uruk who understand [this cause]!
    I have taken up a noble quest,
    I travel a distant road, to where Humbaba is,
    I face a battle I do not know,
    I mount a campaign I do not know.   240
    Give me your blessing that I may go,
    [That I may indeed] see your faces [safely again],
    That I may indeed re-enter joyfully the gate of ramparted
      Uruk,
    That I may indeed return to hold the New Year festival
      twice in a year![6]
    May that festival be held, the fanfare sound!   245
    May the drums resound [before the wild cow, Ninsun]!

Enkidu pressed advice upon the elders,
Upon the young men of Uruk who understood this cause:

    Tell him he must not go to the forest of cedars,
    That journey is not to be undertaken,   250

6. The Babylonian New Year festival centered on the triumphal return of the city god from a place of rustication in the steppe. Gilgamesh's return will be a second such triumph.

That being is not to be looked upon.
The guardian of the forest [. . .]
Humbaba's cry is the roar of a deluge,
His maw is fire, his breath is death,
He can hear rustling in the forest for sixty double leagues.   255
Whoever goes into his forest, numbness overpowers him,
Who can go into his forest?
Adad is first and Humbaba is second:
Who, even among the gods, could attack him?
In order to safeguard the forest of cedars,   260
Enlil appointed him to frighten off the people,
Enlil ordained him seven direful radiances.

The elders of ramparted Uruk arose,
They responded to Gilgamesh with their advice:

You are young, Gilgamesh, your courage carries you away,   265
You are ignorant of what you speak,
You do not know what you are attempting.
We hear of Humbaba that his features are eerie,
Who is there who could face his weaponry?
He can hear rustling in the forest for sixty double leagues.   270
Whoever goes into his forest, numbness overpowers him,
Who can go into it?
Humbaba's cry is the roar of a deluge,
His maw is fire, his breath is death!
Adad is first and Humbaba is second: 275
Who, even among the gods, could attack him?
In order to safeguard the forest of cedars,
Enlil appointed him to frighten off the people,
Enlil ordained him seven direful radiances.

When Gilgamesh heard the speech of his counselors,   280
He looked toward his friend and laughed:

Now then, my friend, [do you say the same?]
Am I too afraid to approach him?
I must go [. . .]
I will [slay] Humbaba like a lion,   285
I will lash together logs of cedar, cypress, [and evergreen]
     trees,
I will gather [the boughs] upon it,
I will cut off Humbaba's head and I will navigate down-
     stream [. . .]

[gap]

Tablet III

[Resigned to Gilgamesh's departure, the elders entrust his safety to Enkidu. Line 11 may contain a pun on the Babylonian word meaning both "brides" and "excavations," portending Enkidu's fate.]

The elders spoke to him, saying to Gilgamesh:

> [Come back safely to] Uruk's haven,
> Trust not, Gilgamesh, in your strength alone,
> Let your eyes see all, make your blow strike home.
> He who goes in front saves his companion,   5
> He who knows the path protects his friend.
> Let Enkidu walk before you,
> He knows the way to the forest of cedars,
> He has seen battle, been exposed to combat.
> Let Enkidu protect his friend, safeguard his companion,   10
> Let him return, to be a grave husband.
> We in our assembly entrust the king to you,
> On your return, entrust the king to us.

[Gilgamesh and Enkidu go off to the temple of Ninsun, to ask her blessing.]

Gilgamesh made ready to speak,
Saying to Enkidu: 15

> Come, my friend, let us go to the sublime temple,
> To go before Ninsun, the great queen.
> Ninsun the wise, who is versed in all knowledge,
> Will send us on our way with good advice.

Clasping each other, hand in hand,   20
Gilgamesh and Enkidu went to the sublime temple,
To go before Ninsun, the great queen.
Gilgamesh came forward and entered before her,
Gilgamesh said to her, to [Ninsun]:

> O Ninsun, I have taken up a noble quest,   25
> [I travel] a distant road, to where Humbaba is,

23

To face a battle I do not know,
To mount a campaign I do not know.
Give me your blessing, that I may go,
That I may indeed see your face safely again,   30
That I may indeed re-enter joyfully the gate of
    ramparted Uruk,
That I may indeed return to hold the New Year festival twice
    in a year,
That I may indeed celebrate the New Year festival twice
    in a year!
May that festival be held, the fanfare sound!
May the drums resound before you!   35

*[Ninsun, after ritual preparations, prays to Shamash to help her son on his
quest.]*

[The wild cow] Ninsun heard them out with sadness,
The speeches of Gilgamesh, her son, and Enkidu.
Ninsun entered the bathhouse seven times,
She bathed herself in water with tamarisk and soapwort.[1]
[She put on] a garment as beseemed her body,   40
[She put on] an ornament as beseemed her breast.
[Her . . .] was in place, she was wearing her tiara.
[. . .] harlots [. . .] the ground,
She climbed the staircase, mounted to the roof terrace,
She went up onto the roof, set up an incense offering to
    Shamash.   45
She made the offering, to Shamash she raised her hands
    in prayer:

    Why did you endow my son Gilgamesh with a restless
        heart?
    Now you have moved him to travel
    A distant road, to where Humbaba is,
    To fight a battle he does not know,   50
    To mount a campaign he does not know.
    Until he goes and returns,
    Until he reaches the forest of cedars,
    Until he has slain fierce Humbaba,
    And wipes out from the land the evil thing you hate,   55
    In the day, [when you traverse the boundaries of the sky],
    May Aya, your bride, not hesitate to remind you:
    "Entrust him to the watchmen of the night."
    At nightfall [. . .]

1. A medicinal plant used in cleansing and magic.

[*gap*]

O [Shamash], you opened [the mountains] for the beasts
    of the steppe,   60
You came out for the land to [. . .],
The mountains [glow], the heavens [brighten],
The beasts of the steppe [behold] your fierce radiance.
They wait [for you to . . .] them,
The wild creatures [. . .] you.   65
The dying man [finds] life [through you],
You [incline] your head to judges.
At your light's rising, the [multitudes] assemble,
The great gods stand in attendance [upon your glow].
May Aya your bride not hesitate to remind you: 70
"Entrust him to the watchmen of the night."
The campaign that [. . .]
Touch [. . .]

[*gap*]

While Gilgamesh journeys to the forest of cedars,
May the days be long, may the nights be short,   75
May his loins be girded, his [stride be strong].
At night, let him make a camp for sleeping,
Let them lie down for the night [. . .].
May Aya, your bride, not hesitate to remind you:
["Entrust him to the watchmen of the night."]   80
When Gilgamesh, Enkidu, and Humbaba meet,
Raise up for his sake, O Shamash, great winds against
    Humbaba,
South wind, north wind, east wind, west wind,
    moaning wind,
Blasting wind, lashing wind, contrary wind, dust storm,
Demon wind, freezing wind, storm wind, whirlwind: 85
Let thirteen winds rise, that Humbaba's face
    be darkened,[2]
Then let Gilgamesh's weapons defeat Humbaba.
As soon as your own [radiance] flares forth,
At that very moment, O Shamash, look to the man who
    reveres you.
May your swift mules [convey] you,   90
A comfortable seat, a [fragrant] bed is laid for you,
May the gods, your brethren, serve you your [favorite] foods,

---

2. This may mean that the buffeting winds will temporarily deprive Humbaba's face of its
   radiant magic powers of destruction.

May Aya, the great bride, dab your face with the fringe
  of her spotless garment.

The wild cow Ninsun made a second plea to Shamash:

O Shamash, will not Gilgamesh [become a judge among]
  the gods?   95
Will he not share heaven with you?
Will he not share a scepter with the moon?
Will he not be a sage with Ea in the depths?
Will he not rule the human race with Irnina?
Will he not dwell with Ningishzida in the Land of No
  Return?   100

[gap]

[Ninsun adopts Enkidu and says his female descendants will henceforth
serve a temple dedicated to Gilgamesh.]

After the wild cow Ninsun had made her plea,
The wild cow Ninsun the wise, who is versed in all knowledge,
[. . .] Gilgamesh [. . .].
She snuffed the incense, [she came down from the roof
  terrace],
She summoned Enkidu to impart her message: 105

Mighty Enkidu, though you are no issue of my womb,
Your offspring shall be among the devotees of Gilgamesh,
The priestesses, votaries, cult women of the temple.

She placed a token around Enkidu's neck:

The priestesses have hereby taken in this foundling,   110
And the daughters of the gods will bring up this foster child.
I herewith take Enkidu, who [was born in the steppe], for
  my adopted son,
May Gilgamesh treat Enkidu well [as a brother should].

[gap]

While you journey [with him] to the forest of cedars,
May the days be long, may the nights be short,   115
May your loins be girded, your stride be strong.
At night make a camp for sleeping,
Let [. . .] watch over [. . .]

[gap]

[*The following two episodes are taken from an old version, which arranged the material differently from the standard version. Gilgamesh goes to a temple, presumably that of Shamash, god of oracles, to ask for an omen portending the successful outcome of their quest. Divination, often by slaughtering a sheep or goat and looking for certain marks or formations on the liver or entrails, was normal practice in Mesopotamia to predict the success or failure of an undertaking. The result is evidently unfavorable, so Gilgamesh, in desperation, tries to change the prognosis by offering various blandishments to Shamash.*]

Gilgamesh was kneeling before [Shamash],
The words he spoke [. . .]:   120

    I am going, O Shamash, to the place of [Humbaba],
    Let me be safe there, [keep me] alive.
    Bring me back to the haven of [broad-marted Uruk],
    Place your protection [upon me].

Gilgamesh summoned [. . . the diviners],   125
His oracle [. . .]
The palace [. . .]

[gap]

Tears were pouring down Gilgamesh's [face]:

    [I will take], my god, a road I have never traveled,
    Its [. . .], my god, I do not know.   130
    [Let me return] here safely,
    [Let me gaze on] you as long as I like.
    [I will build] a house for your delight,
    [I will seat you on thrones]

[gap]

[*In the large gap in the old and standard versions that occurs here, Gilgamesh and Enkidu are still in Uruk, perhaps carrying out various rites and drawing up plans for a great door to be made from the giant cedar tree they plan to bring back. When the text resumes, Gilgamesh is giving instructions for governing the city in his absence. The city elders wish him well.*]

    The young men should not form a crowd in the
        street [. . .],   135
    Judge the lawsuit of the weak, call the powerful to
        account,[3]

---

3. Mesopotamian rulers were supposed to ensure that poor and defenseless people received the same legal process as the rich and powerful.

While we have it our way, as children do,
And set up our [battle standard] at Humbaba's gate.

His dignitaries stood by, wishing him well,
In a crowd, the young men of Uruk ran along behind him,   140
While his dignitaries made obeisance to him:

Come back safely to Uruk's haven!
Trust not, Gilgamesh, in your strength alone,
Let your eyes see all, make your blow strike home.
He who goes in front saves his companion,   145
He who knows the path protects his friend.
Let Enkidu walk before you,
He knows the way to the forest of cedars,
He has seen battle, been exposed to combat.
[. . .] in the mountain passes,   150
Let Enkidu protect his friend, safeguard his companion,
Let him return, to be a grave husband.
We in our assembly entrust the king to you,
On your return, entrust the king to us.

Enkidu made ready to speak, saying to Gilgamesh: 155

Turn back, my friend, [. . .]
You must not [. . .] this journey!

[*In an old version, the two heroes take up their weapons. The elders bless Gilgamesh, and Enkidu at last gives up his objections.*]

[. . .] his equipment,
[. . .] the great daggers,
[The bow] and the quiver   160
[. . .] in their hands.
He took up the axes,
[. . .] his quiver, the Anshanite bow,[4]
[He set] his dagger in his belt.
[Equi]pped, they set forth on the journey.   165
[The young men] hailed Gilgamesh:

You will bring back [. . .] into the city!

The elders [hailed him],
Counseled Gilgamesh for the journey:

---

4. Anshan was a place in southwestern Iran famous for the quality of its bows.

Trust not, Gilgamesh, in your own strength,   170
Let your vision be clear, take care of yourself.
Let Enkidu go before you,
He has seen the road, has traveled the way.
He knows the ways into the forest
And all the tricks of Humbaba.   175
He who goes first safeguards his companion,
His vision is clear, [he protects himself].
May Shamash help you to your goal,
May your eyes show you the things you have spoken of,
May he open for you the barred road,   180
Make straight the pathway to your tread,
Make straight the upland to your feet.
May nightfall bring you good tidings,
May Lugalbanda stand by you in your cause.
Have it your way, as children do,   185
Wash your feet in the river of Humbaba whom you seek.
When you stop for the night, dig a well,
May there always be pure water in your waterskin.[5]
You should libate cool water to Shamash
And be mindful of Lugalbanda.   190

Enkidu made ready to speak, saying to Gilgamesh:

[As] you insist, make the journey.
Do not be afraid, watch me.
I know his dwelling in the forest,
[And the pathways] where Humbaba goes.   195

[gap]

[. . .] who goes with me,
[I will bring him safely back] to you,
[. . .] in joy!

[. . .] upon hearing this speech,
The young men [hailed him]:   200

Go, Gilgamesh, may [. . .]
May your god go [by your side],
May [Shamash] help you [to your goal]!

Gilgamesh and Enkidu [. . .]

[gap]

5. Mesopotamian travelers carried drinking water in leather bags.

Tablet IV

[Gilgamesh and Enkidu go on their journey, covering a vast distance at a fantastic speed. As they camp each night, Enkidu makes Gilgamesh a shelter and lays out a magic circle for him to sleep in. This may be a circle of flour, as known from Mesopotamian sorcery and oath-taking. Gilgamesh prays for a dream to portend the outcome of the expedition. He dreams three times of mountains. The first falls upon him, the second holds him fast, and the third erupts. Enkidu explains each time that the mountain is Humbaba, who will make a terrifying attack but will collapse and die. Next he dreams of a lion-headed monster-bird and then a bull attacking him. Since the text is very damaged here and various versions exist, the number, sequence, and contents of the dreams, as well as the narrative connecting them, vary considerably. The rendering here sews together a choice of the best-preserved episodes from various periods.]

At twenty double leagues they took a bite to eat,
At thirty double leagues they made their camp,
Fifty double leagues they went in a single day,
A journey of a month and a half in three days.
They approached Mount Lebanon.   5
Toward sunset they dug a well,
Filled [their waterskin with water].
Gilgamesh went up onto the mountain,
He poured out flour for an [offering, saying]:

  O Mountain, bring me a dream, let me see [a good omen]!   10

Enkidu made Gilgamesh a shelter for receiving dreams,
He fastened the door against the blast.
He had him lie down in a circle [of flour],
And spreading out like a net, Enkidu [. . . and] lay down in
  the doorway.
Gilgamesh rested his chin on his knees.   15
Sleep, which usually steals over people, fell upon him.
In the middle of the night he awoke,
Got up, and said to his friend:

30

My friend, did you not call me? Why am I awake?
Did you not touch me? Why am I disturbed?   20
Did a god not pass by? Why does my flesh tingle?
My friend, I had a dream,
And the dream I had was very disturbing.
[We . . .] on the flanks of a mountain,
The mountain fell [upon us],   25
We [. . .] like flies!

The one born in the steppe could advise,
Enkidu explained the dream to his friend:

      My friend, your dream is favorable [. . .],
      The dream is very precious [as an omen].   30
      My friend, the mountain you saw is [Humbaba],
      We will catch Humbaba, we will [kill him],
      We will throw down his corpse on the field of battle.
      Then at dawn we will see good tidings from Shamash.

At twenty double leagues they took a bite to eat,   35
At thirty double leagues they made their camp,
Fifty double leagues they went in a single day,
A journey of a month and a half in three days.
They approached Mount Lebanon.
Toward sunset they dug a well,   40
Filled [their waterskin with water].
Gilgamesh went up onto the mountain,
He poured out flour for an [offering, saying]:

      O Mountain, bring me a dream, let me see [a good omen]!

Enkidu made Gilgamesh a shelter for receiving dreams,   45
He fastened the door against the blast.
He had him lie down in a circle [of flour],
And spreading out like a net, Enkidu [. . . and] lay down in
      the doorway.
Gilgamesh rested his chin on his knees.
Sleep, which usually steals over people, fell upon him.   50
In the middle of the night he awoke,
Got up, and said to his friend:

      My friend, did you not call me? Why am I awake?
      Did you not touch me? Why am I disturbed?
      Did a god not pass by? Why does my flesh tingle?   55
      My friend, I had a dream,

And the dream I had was very disturbing.
I was heaving my shoulder against a mountain,
The mountain fell over on me and pushed me over,
Numbness had enfolded my knees,   60
Something awful had pinned my arms!
Then there was a man, he approached me like a lion,
Radiant he was, throughout the land, handsome as can be.
He grasped my upper arm,
He pulled me out from under that very mountain,   65
He gave me water to drink and my heart grew calm,
He set my feet on the ground again.

The one born in the steppe could advise,
Enkidu explained the dream to his friend:

My friend, your dream is favorable,   70
The dream is very precious [as an omen].
Now, my friend, the one toward whom we go,
Is he not that mountain? He is something passing strange,
Now, Humbaba, the one toward whom we go,
Is he not that mountain? He is something passing strange!   75
You and he will strain against each other and you will do a
    matchless deed,
The duty of a warrior, the mission of a man.
His rage will mount to a frenzy against you,
Terror of him will enfold your knees.
Then the one you saw was Shamash the king,   80
In time of trial he will grasp your hand.

It was favorable, Gilgamesh was happy with his dream,
His heart rejoiced, his features beamed.
At twenty double leagues they took a bite to eat,
At thirty double leagues they made their camp,   85
Fifty double leagues they went in a single day,
A journey of a month and a half in three days.
They approached Mount Lebanon.
Toward sunset they dug a well,
Filled [their waterskin with water].   90
Gilgamesh went up onto the mountain,
He poured out flour for an [offering, saying]:

O Mountain, bring me a dream, let me see [a good omen]!

Enkidu made Gilgamesh a shelter for receiving dreams,
He fastened the door against the blast.   95

He had him lie down in a circle [of flour],
And spreading out like a net, Enkidu [. . . and] lay down in
   the doorway.
Gilgamesh rested his chin on his knees.
Sleep, which usually steals over people, fell upon him.
In the middle of the night he awoke,   100
Got up, and said to his friend:

> My friend, did you not call me? Why am I awake?
> Did you not touch me? Why am I disturbed?
> Did a god not pass by? Why does my flesh tingle?
> My friend, I had a dream,   105
> And the dream I had was very disturbing.
> The heavens cried out, the earth began to rumble,
> Daylight faded, darkness fell,
> Lightning flashed, fire broke out,
> The flames spread, death was raining down.   110
> I turned faint from the din of thunder.
> Daylight darkened, where I was going I could not tell.
> On it went this way, then the raging fire died down,
> The flames went to naught, they turned to embers.
> The darkness brightened, the sun came out.   115
> [. . .] led me thence and [. . .]

Enkidu [explained], helped him understand his dream,
Saying to Gilgamesh:

[*Enkidu's explanation is mostly lost, but perhaps it was that the volcano-
like explosion was Humbaba, who flared up, then died.*]

> Humbaba, like a god [. . .]
> [. . .] the light flaring, we will [. . .]   120
> We will be [victorious] over him, we [will bind] his arms,
> [. . .]
> [. . .] we will prevail over him.
> Then at dawn we will see good tidings from Shamash.

At twenty double leagues they took a bite to eat,   125
At thirty double leagues they made their camp,
Fifty double leagues they went in a single day,
A journey of a month and a half in three days.
They approached Mount Lebanon.
Toward sunset they dug a well,   130
Filled [their waterskin with water].
Gilgamesh went up onto the mountain,
He poured out flour for an [offering, saying]:

O Mountain, bring me a dream, let me see
  [a good omen]!

Enkidu made Gilgamesh a shelter for receiving dreams,   135
He fastened the door against the blast.
He had him lie down in a circle [of flour],
And spreading out like a net, Enkidu [. . . and] lay down
  in the doorway.
Gilgamesh rested his chin on his knees.
Sleep, which usually steals over people, fell upon him.   140
In the middle of the night he awoke,
Got up, and said to his friend:

  My friend, did you not call me? Why am I awake?
  Did you not touch me? Why am I disturbed?
  Did a god not pass by? Why does my flesh tingle?   145
  My friend, I had a dream,
  And the dream I had was very disturbing.
  My friend, I had a fourth dream,
  More terrible than the other three.
  I saw the lion-headed monster-bird Anzu in the sky,   150
  It rose up and soared above us, like a cloud,
  It was something ghastly and its face was eerie,
  Its maw was fire, its breath death.
  Then there was a young man, wonderful in form,
  He [. . .] and stood there in my dream.   155
  He [cut off] its feathers, he grasped my arm,
  He [. . .] and threw it down [before] me.

[gap]

[Enkidu explains the fourth dream.]

  [The lion-headed monster-bird Anzu you saw in the sky],
  [That rose up] and soared above us, like a cloud,
  That was something ghastly, whose face was eerie,   160
  Whose maw was fire, whose breath was death—
  While you, for your part, will be afraid of its frightfulness,
  I will . . . its foot, I will help you up.
  The young man you saw was mighty Shamash

[gap]

At twenty double leagues they took a bite to eat,   165
At thirty double leagues they made their camp,
Fifty double leagues they went in a single day,

A journey of a month and a half in three days.
They approached Mount Lebanon.
Toward sunset they dug a well,   170
Filled [their waterskin with water].
Gilgamesh went up onto the mountain,
He poured out flour for an [offering, saying]:

   O Mountain, bring me a dream, let me see [a good omen]!

Enkidu made Gilgamesh a shelter for receiving dreams,   175
He fastened the door against the blast.
He had him lie down in a circle [of flour],
And spreading out like a net, Enkidu [. . . and] lay down in
   the doorway.
Gilgamesh rested his chin on his knees.
Sleep, which usually steals over people, fell upon him.   180
In the middle of the night he awoke,
Got up, and said to his friend:

   My friend, did you not call me? Why am I awake?
   Did you not touch me? Why am I disturbed?
   Did a god not pass by? Why does my flesh tingle?   185
   My friend, I had a dream,
   And the dream I had was very disturbing.

[*It is not clear how many dreams there were in all, though one version
refers to five. A poorly preserved manuscript of an old version includes the
following dream that could be inserted here, as portions of it are fulfilled in
Tablet VI.*]

   I was grasping a wild bull of the steppe!
   As it bellowed, it split the earth,
   It raised clouds of dust, hurtling toward the sky.   190
   I crouched down before it,
   It seized [. . .], wrapped around my arms.
   [. . .] pulled me out, [his face was . . .]
   [. . .] stroked my cheek, he gave me to drink from his
      waterskin.

                           [*gap*]

[*Enkidu explains the dream.*]

   The god, my friend, to whom we go,   195
   Is he not that wild bull? He is something passing strange!
   The face you saw was radiant Shamash,

In time of trial he will grasp our hands.
The one who gave you water to drink from his waterskin
Was Lugalbanda, your protective god who esteems you.   200
We will join together and do a matchless deed, unheard of
    in the land.

[*In an old version, the two friends hear from afar the voice of Humbaba
roaring in the forest. Enkidu loses courage.*]

Onward they rushed, day and night,
They approached Hamran, they sat on its ridge,
The mountain where the Amorite dwells.
Every day they could hear the voice of Humbaba,   205
He was watching them, the guardian of the cedars,
The one who turns back everyone who confronts him,
Humbaba, the guardian of the cedars,
The one who turns back everyone who confronts him!
[Enkidu looked] up and saw the cedars,   210
Their splendor veiling the ranges.
His face turned pale, like something severed,
Fear entered his heart.
Gilgamesh felt sorry for him, saying to Enkidu:

> Why, my friend, did your face turn pale,   215
> And fear enter your heart?

Enkidu made ready to speak, saying to Gilgamesh:

> I looked, my friend, and I saw the cedars,
> Their splendor veiling the ranges.
> Who can attack that god,   220
> Whose weapon is mightiest among his fellow gods?
> Shall we attack Humbaba,
> Whose weapon is mightiest in the four quarters of the
>   earth?
> So, my friend, my face turned pale,
> Fear entered my heart.   225

Gilgamesh made ready to speak, saying to Enkidu:

> Did not my courage carry me beyond what I thought I could
>   do?
> Shamash said to me, "I will go with you."
> Do not be afraid, Enkidu, watch me,
> I will wage such a battle as you have never known!   230

[*gap*]

Tablet V

[*The friends are found admiring the wondrous forest and the paths of Humbaba, its guardian.*]

They stood there, marveling at the forest,
They gazed at the height of the cedars,
They gazed at the way into the forest.
Where Humbaba would walk, a path was made,
Straight were the ways and easy the going.   5
They beheld the cedar mountain, dwelling of the gods, sacred
    to the goddess Irnina.
On the slopes of that mountain, the cedar bore its abundance,
Agreeable was its shade, full of pleasures.
The undergrowth was tangled, the forest dense,
Cedars and balsam [grew] so close together, there was no way
    in among them.   10
The cedars sent out shoots for a league,
The cypress [branches] for two-thirds of a league.
The cedar was dappled sixty cubits high with exudation,
The resin [oozed] out, dribbling down like raindrops,
It flowed out so that ditches had to carry it away.   15
Throughout the forest birdlife was chirping,
[. . .] answering each other in rhythmic din,
The cicada raised a shrill chorus,
[. . .] was singing, [. . .] was piping,
A pigeon was cooing, a turtledove answering,   20
The forest was joyous with the [cry] of the stork,
The forest was lavishly joyous with the francolin's [lilt].
Mother monkeys kept up their calls, baby monkeys chirruped.
Like a band of musicians and drummers,
They resounded all day long in the presence of Humbaba.   25
As the cedar [cast] its shadow,
Gilgamesh was beset by [fear].
Stiffness seized his arms,
Then numbness befell his legs.
Enkidu made ready to speak, saying to Gilgamesh: 30

37

3. *They gazed at the height of the cedars.* This wall relief suggests how the poet may have visualized the cedar mountain.

Let's go into the forest,
On with it, let's raise our challenge!

[*In the speech that follows, Gilgamesh offers brave words of encouragement to Enkidu, whereas it is he who is terrified, not his friend.*]

Gilgamesh made ready to speak, saying to Enkidu:

Why, my friend, are we trembling like weaklings,
We, who crossed all the mountains?   35
[Signs will appear] before us,
[Further along] we will see some light.
[My friend is a veteran] of combat,
One who has experienced [battle] is not afraid of death,
[You have spattered yourself with gore], you are not afraid
     of death!   40
[Get your blood up, like] an oracle, work yourself into a trance,
[Your battle cry should boom like a drum]!
[Get the stiffness out of your arms, drive the numbness
     from] your legs,
[Take hold of me, my friend, let us . . .],
[Your thoughts should focus on battle]!   45

[*gap*]

[*Weapons at the ready, the two friends advance.*]

Thereupon, swords [. . .]
And from the scabbards [. . .]
Axes touched with [the whetstone],

Hatchets and swords [. . .]
One [after the other . . .]   50
They crept forward [. . .]

[*The scene shifts to Humbaba, who evidently is uncertain about the heroes'
intent.*]

Humbaba de[bated with himself, saying]:

  No see[ker of cedar] has come,
  No [seeker of cypress] has come,
  Why are the [birds] perturbed?   55
  Why are my very own [birds alarmed]?

                    [*gap*]

  How could [. . .]
  [. . .] in my very bed?
  Surely En[lil . . .]
  In goodwill [. . .]   60
  If I shall be the one to die [. . .]
  May Enlil curse [the one who kills me]!

                    [*gap*]

[*Meanwhile, Enkidu is encouraging Gilgamesh.*]

Enkidu made ready to speak, [saying to Gilgamesh]:

  My friend, Humbaba [. . .]
  My friend, one is one [but two are double],   65
  Though one be weak, two [together are strong].
  If one cannot scale a slippery slope, two [can do it together].
  A three-strand rope [is stronger when doubled],
  Two cubs are [stronger] than a mighty lion.

                    [*gap*]

  My friend, aside from the winds of Shamash, [what have we]? 70
  Behind him is a whirlwind, [in front of him a blast].
  Speak to Shamash, that he give [you his thirteen winds]!

Gilgamesh looked up, [weeping before Shamash],
Facing the sun's radiance, [his tears flowed down].

  [Forget not] that day, O Shamash, I put my trust in you,   75
  Stand by me now [. . .]
  [Protect] Gilgamesh, scion of Uruk!

Shamash heard what he said,
Straightaway a warning cry [called out to him from heaven]:

> Hurry, confront him, do not let him go off [into
>   the forest],   80
> Do not let him enter the thicket nor [. . .]!
> He has not donned [all] of his seven [fearsome] cloaks,[1]
> One he has on, six he has left off.

They [. . .]
They charged forward like wild bulls [. . .]   85
He let out a bloodcurdling cry [. . .],
The guardian of the forest was shrieking aloud,
[. . .]
Humbaba was roaring like thunder

[*gap*]

[*At this point, in a damaged passage, Gilgamesh unexpectedly mentions
that Humbaba has children. Some versions give Humbaba seven sons, as
in this tablet, line 248, although in the Sumerian poem "Gilgamesh and
Huwawa," line 275, the monster says he lives alone.*]

Gilgamesh made ready to speak, saying to Enkidu: 90

> My friend, have not [Humbaba and his wife(?) . . .]
> Have they not produced [seven] children?

[*gap*]

[*When the heroes finally meet Humbaba, he proves to be something of a
snob, disdaining the steppe-born Enkidu, whom he ridicules as a midget
and a reptile. Gilgamesh then has second thoughts.*]

Humbaba made ready to speak, saying to Gilgamesh:

> Let fools, Gilgamesh, take advice from a yokel-man!
> Why have you made your way here?   95
> Come now, Enkidu, small-fry, who does not know his
>   father,
> Spawn of a turtle or tortoise, who sucked no mother's milk!
> I used to see you when you were younger but would not go
>   near you.
> [Had I killed the likes of] you, would I have filled my belly?

---

1. In one old version, Humbaba has seven magic garments, in other versions seven direful
   radiances, and in others seven glories. See p. 19, n. 4.

4. *My friend Humbaba's features grow ever more eerie.* These demonic faces show how Mesopotamians imagined Humbaba.

[Why] have you brought Gilgamesh to me with evil intent,   100
And taken a stand there, like some foreign foe?
I should slash the throat and neck of Gilgamesh,
I should let flying insects, screaming eagles, and vultures
     feed on his flesh!

Gilgamesh made ready to speak, saying to Enkidu:

My friend, Humbaba's features have grown ever more eerie,   105
We strode up to him like heroes to vanquish him,
Yet my fearful heart does not calm itself quickly.

[*Enkidu urges him on, quoting his brave words at Uruk and seeking to stiffen his resolve.*]

Enkidu made ready to speak, saying to Gilgamesh:

> Why, my friend, do you talk like a weakling?
> How you pule! You make me ill.   110
> Now, my friend, this has dragged [on long enough].
> The time has come to lift the copper from the mold.
> Will you take another hour to blow the bellows,
> An hour more to let it cool?
> To launch a flood weapon, to wield a lash?   115
> Retreat not a foot, you must not turn back,
> [Let your eyes see all], let your blow strike home!

>   [*gap*]

> He took a prisoner whenever he could.[2]
> Be mindful of your god, Lugalbanda,
> Those dreams you had, one after the other, are now
>   clear to you.   120

[*Humbaba evidently throws huge rocks at the heroes.*]

Gilgamesh advanced, heeding his friend's advice.
The ninth boulder hurtled down, the mountain exploded, fell
    into dust.
He sprang like a lion,
While Enkidu rushed forward, like a bodyguard.
Then they seized Humbaba in the forest,   125
His cry filled the forest,
They took hold of his direful radiances.
Humbaba roared, for his part, a challenge:

> I will lift them up so high, I will go up to heaven!
> I will smite the earth so hard, they will go down to the
>   watery deep!   130

He lifted them up toward heaven, but heaven was too
    far away.
He smote the earth, but a boulder stood in his way.

[*In the combat with Humbaba, the valley of Lebanon is formed by their circling feet.*]

At their heels the earth split apart,
As they circled, the ranges of Lebanon were sundered!

---

2. Lines 118–32 come from a fragment known only in German translation; the original
   words are mostly unpublished.

The white clouds turned black,   135
Death rained down like a vapor upon them.
Shamash raised the great winds against Humbaba,
South wind, north wind, east wind, west wind, moaning wind,
Blasting wind, lashing wind, contrary wind, dust storm,
Demon wind, freezing wind, storm wind, whirlwind: 140
The thirteen winds rose up and Humbaba's face was darkened,
He could not charge forward, he could not retreat.
Then Gilgamesh's weapons defeated Humbaba.

[*Humbaba begs for his life, appealing to Gilgamesh's superior sensibilities
and noble birth. Gilgamesh is willing to spare Humbaba, with no further
mention of the alleged evil that Shamash hates, but Enkidu urges him to
the deed.*]

Humbaba begged for life, saying to Gilgamesh:

> You were once a child, Gilgamesh, you had a mother who
>   bore you,   145
> You are the offspring [of the wild cow Ninsun].
> [You grew up to fulfill] the oracle of Shamash, lord of the
>   mountain:
> "Gilgamesh, scion of Uruk, is to be king."
> O Gilgamesh, a dead man cannot [serve a master],
> A living [slave] is [profitable] for his master.   150
> O Gilgamesh, spare my life! You will be master, wherever
>   I am.
> Let me dwell here to serve you in the cedar forest,
> Say however many trees, I will keep them for you,
> I will keep evergreen, cedar, and cypress,
> Tall, full-grown trees, the pride of your palace.   155

Enkidu made ready to speak, saying to Gilgamesh:

> My friend! Do not listen to what Humbaba [says],
> [Do not heed] his entreaties!

[gap]

[*Humbaba is speaking to Enkidu.*]

> You know the lore of my forest, the lore of everything,
> And you understand all I have to say.   160
> I might have lifted you up, dangled you from a twig at the
>   entrance to my forest,
> I might have let flying insects, screaming eagles, and
>   vultures feed on your flesh.

Now then, Enkidu, [mercy] is up to you,
Tell Gilgamesh to spare my life!

[*Enkidu urges Gilgamesh to carry out their mission as soon as possible,
before Enlil and the other gods learn of it.*]

Enkidu made ready to speak, saying to Gilgamesh: 165

My friend! Humbaba is guardian of the forest [of cedars],
Finish him off for the kill, put him out of existence.
Humbaba is guardian of the forest [of cedars],
Finish him off for the kill, put him out of existence,
Before Enlil the foremost one hears of this!   170
The [great] gods will become angry with us,
Enlil in Nippur, Shamash [in Larsa . . .],
Establish [your reputation] for all time:
"Gilgamesh, who slew Humbaba."

[*Humbaba prays to Shamash, saying that he never felt hostile to the young
Enkidu and had guarded the forest well. He seeks to have Enkidu identify
with him, both of them parentless and raised in the wild.*]

When Humbaba heard [what Enkidu said],   175
Humbaba [looked up, weeping before Shamash],
[Facing the sun's radiance, his tears flowed down]:

                         [*gap*]

While Enkidu lay sleeping with his animals, I made no cry
   against him,
The ranges of Lebanon, which produce the cedars, had not
   been [despoiled].
You, O Shamash, are my king and my judge!   180
I knew no mother who bore me, I knew no father who
   brought me up.
The mountain bore me and you brought me up!
Now, Enkidu, mercy is up to you.
Tell Gilgamesh to spare my life!

Enkidu made ready to speak, saying to Gilgamesh: 185

My friend! Humbaba is guardian of the forest
   [of cedars],
Finish him off for the kill, put him out of existence.
Humbaba is guardian of the forest [of cedars],
Finish him off for the kill, put him out of existence,

Before Enlil the foremost one hears of this!   190
The [great] gods will become angry with us,
Enlil in Nippur, Shamash [in Larsa . . .].
Establish [your reputation] for all time:
"Gilgamesh, who slew Humbaba."

When Humbaba heard [what Enkidu said],   195

[*gap*]

[*Realizing he is doomed, Humbaba curses them.*]

May they never [. . .],
May the pair of them never reach old age!
May Enkidu have none to bury him but Gilgamesh!

Enkidu made ready to speak, saying to Gilgamesh:

My friend, I speak to you, but you do not heed me [. . .]   200
So long as the curse [. . .]
[. . .] from his mouth!

[*An old version contains the following exchange between Gilgamesh and Enkidu concerning the seven direful radiances of Humbaba, in that version called "glories," whereas the standard version proceeds directly to line 219 below. Another late version inserts lines 211–18. In that version, Humbaba has seven sons whom the heroes kill, below, line 248, perhaps a different formulation of this episode.*]

Gilgamesh said to Enkidu:

Now my friend, let us go on to victory!
The glories are escaping into the forest,   205
The glories are escaping and their brightness is fading into
    the gloom.

Enkidu said to Gilgamesh:

My friend, catch the bird and where will its chicks go?
Let us search out the glories later,
They will run around in the woods like chicks.   210

[*Humbaba disdains Enkidu as a menial rather than a warrior.*]

[Humbaba] heard [what Enkidu said],
Humbaba looked up, [weeping before Shamash],
Facing the sun's radiance, [his tears flowed down]:

> Even if you did come into [the forest], Enkidu,
> In the moment of combat [you just advise Gilgamesh],   215
> For fighting is [not] what household servants [do].
> Will you sit there like a shepherd in front of him,
> And, like an underling, [wait for his command]?

[*Gilgamesh kills Humbaba.*]

[Gilgamesh] heeded his friend's words,
He drew out the sword at his side.   220
Gilgamesh [smote him] in the neck,
Enkidu [. . .] until he drew out his lungs.
Springing [the length of his] body,
He plucked teeth from his head as a trophy.
Masses of [. . .] fell on the mountain,   225
Masses of [. . .] fell on the mountain,
[. . .]
He struck him, Humbaba the guardian, down to the ground.
His blood [. . .]
For two leagues the cedars [were spattered with his blood],   230
He killed the [glories] with him.

5. *He struck him, Humbaba the guardian, down to the ground.* This scene from a bronze bowl shows this episode.

He slew the monster, guardian of the forest,
At whose cry the mountains of Lebanon [trembled],
At whose cry all the mountains [quaked].
He slew the monster, guardian of the forest,   235
[He trampled on] the broken [. . .],
He struck down the seven [glories].
The battle net [of two times sixty pounds], the sword weighing
   eight times sixty pounds,
He took the weight of ten times sixty pounds upon him,
He forced his way into the forest,   240
He opened the forbidden dwelling of the supreme gods.

[gap]

[They cut heroic numbers of cedars, then make a gigantic door that they float down the Euphrates as a gift to Enlil, to placate him for their killing the guardian of the forest. Enkidu, not anticipating the fatal consequences for himself, hopes that Enlil will be grateful to Gilgamesh for the door.]

[. . .] aromatics from that cedar were they bringing [for
   the . . .] of Enlil.
[Enkidu] made ready to speak, saying to Gilgamesh:

  [My friend], we have made a wasteland of the forest,
  [How] shall we answer for it to Enil in Nippur (when he
    says):   245
  "You slew the guardian as a deed of valor,
  "But what was this, your fury, that you decimated the
    forest?"

After they had slain his seven sons,
Cricket, Screamer, Blaster, Howler, Cunning, [. . .], Stormy,
Their axes weighing two times sixty pounds each,   250
They cut down [. . . cedars],
The woodchips made by the blows were three and a half
   cubits long.
Gilgamesh was cutting the trees,
While Enkidu kept looking for the tallest one.

[Enkidu speaks.]

  My friend, we have felled the lofty cedar,   255
  Whose crown once pierced the sky.
  Now make a door six times twelve cubits high, two times
    twelve cubits wide,

One cubit shall be its thickness.
Its hinge pole, ferrule, and pivot box shall be unique.
Let no stranger approach it, may the god love it!   260
Let the Euphrates bring it to Nippur,
Nippur, the sanctuary of Enlil.
May Enlil be delighted with you,
May Enlil rejoice over it!

[They gathered] cypress [. . .] boughs along with [. . .],   265
They lashed a raft together, they laid the [boughs upon it].
Enkidu rode [at the front],
And Gilgamesh rode [at the rear, bearing] the head of
    Humbaba.

Tablet VI

[Gilgamesh strips to put on fresh garments after the expedition. Ishtar, goddess of love and sex, is attracted to him and proposes marriage, offering him power and riches.]

He washed his matted locks, cleaned his head strap,[1]
He shook his hair down over his shoulders,
He threw off his filthy clothes, he put on clean ones.
Wrapping himself in a cloak, he tied on his sash,
Gilgamesh put on his kingly diadem.   5
The princess Ishtar coveted Gilgamesh's beauty:

Come, Gilgamesh, you shall be my bridegroom!
Give, oh give me of your lusciousness!
You shall be my husband and I shall be your wife.
I will ready for you a chariot of lapis and gold,   10
With golden wheels and fittings of gemstones,
You shall harness storm demons as if they were giant mules.
Enter our house amidst fragrance of cedar!
When you enter our house,
The magnificent doorframe shall do you homage,   15
Kings, nobles, and princes shall kneel before you,
They shall bring you gifts of mountain and lowland
    as tribute.
Your goats shall bear triplets, your ewes twins,
Your pack-laden donkey shall overtake the mule,
Your horses shall run proud before the wagon,   20
Your ox in the yoke shall have none to compare!

[Gilgamesh spurns Ishtar's proposal, heaping scorn upon her. He enumerates her past lovers, each of whom she doomed to a cruel destiny.]

Gilgamesh made ready to speak,
Saying to the princess Ishtar:

1. This may refer to a band of cloth that held up Gilgamesh's long hair. When it was released, the hair fell free over the shoulders, a sign of undress in Mesopotamia. Such a band is visible behind the ear of Gilgamesh in figure 5 (above, p. 46).

49

[If I were to] take you to wife,
[. . .] body and clothing?   25
[. . .] nourishment and drink?
[Shall I give you] food, worthy of a god?
[Shall I give you] drink, worthy of a king?
Shall I bind [you sheaves . . .]?
Shall I pile up [heaps of grain . . .]?   30
[Shall I wrap . . .] in a cloak?
[What will I get if] I marry you?
[You are a brazier that goes out] when it freezes,
A flimsy door that keeps out neither wind nor draught,
A palace [that crushes a] warrior,   35
An elephant that [knocks down] its housing,
Tar that [smears] its bearer,
Waterskin that [soaks] its bearer,
Weak stone that [undermines] a wall,
Battering ram that destroys the wall for an enemy,   40
Shoe that pinches its wearer!
Which of your lovers [lasted] forever?
Come, I call you to account for your lovers:
He who had [jugs of cream] on his shoulders and [. . .] on
    his arm,
For Dumuzi, your girlhood lover,   45
You ordained year after year of weeping.
You fell in love with the brightly colored hoopoe bird,
Then you struck him and broke his wing.
In the woods he sits crying "My-wing!"
You fell in love with the lion, perfect in strength,   50
Then you dug for him ambush pits, seven times seven.
You fell in love with the wild stallion, eager for the fray,
Whip, goad, and lash you ordained for him,
Seven double leagues of galloping you ordained for him,
You ordained that he muddy his water when he drinks,   55
You ordained perpetual weeping for his mother, divine Silili.
You fell in love with the shepherd, keeper of herds,
Who always set out cakes baked in embers for you,
Slaughtered kids for you every day.
You struck him and turned him into a wolf.   60
His own shepherd boys harry him off,
And his own hounds snap at his thighs!
You fell in love with Ishullanu, your father's gardener,
Who always brought you baskets of dates,
Who made your table splendid every day.   65
You wanted him, so you sidled up to him:
"My Ishullanu, let's have a taste of your vigor!

"Bring out your member, touch our sweet spot!"
Ishullanu said to you,
"Me? What do you want of me?   70
"Hath my mother not baked? Have I not eaten?
"Shall what I taste for food be insults and curses?
"In the cold, is my cover to be the touch of a reed?"
When you heard what he said,
You struck him and turned him into a midget,[2]   75
You left him stuck in his own garden patch,
His well sweep goes up no longer, his bucket does not
    descend [. . .],
As for me, now that you've fallen in love with me, you will
    [treat me] like them!

[Ishtar rushes off to her parents in a passion and sobs out her indigna-
tion. Her speech is noteworthy for its jarring colloquialisms. Her father,
Anu, the sky god, attempts mildly to pacify her, but Ishtar will have pun-
ishment at any price. She demands that her father's Bull of Heaven kill
Gilgamesh. She gets her way after threatening to release the dead from
the netherworld. She also promises to garner food against the seven years
of famine that will follow the attack of the bull.]

When Ishtar heard this,
Ishtar was furious and [went] up to heaven,   80
Ishtar went [sobbing] before Anu, her father,
Before Antum, her mother, her tears flowed down:

    Father, Gilgamesh has said outrageous things about me,
    Gilgamesh's been spouting insults about me,
    Insults and abuse against me!   85

Anu made ready to speak,
Saying to the princess Ishtar:

    Well now, did you not provoke the king, Gilgamesh,
    And so Gilgamesh spouted insults about you,
    Insults and abuse against you?   90

Ishtar made ready to speak,
Saying to Anu, her father:

    Well then, Father, pretty please, the Bull of Heaven,
    So I can kill Gilgamesh on his home ground.

2. Ishullanu's name suggests the Babylonian word *shullānu*, possibly "dwarf" or a person
with pockmarks.

If you don't give me the Bull of Heaven,   95
I'll strike the [nether fastness], as well as where its
     (inmates) dwell,
I'll turn the nether regions upside down,
I'll raise the dead to devour the living,
The dead shall greatly outnumber the living!

Anu made ready to speak,   100
Saying to the princess Ishtar:

   If you insist on the Bull of Heaven from me,
   Let the widow of Uruk gather seven years of chaff,
   [Let the farmer of Uruk] raise [seven years of hay].

Ishtar made ready to speak,   105
Saying to Anu, her father:

   [. . .] I stored up,
   [. . .] I provided,
   [The widow of Uruk has] gathered seven years of chaff,
   The farmer [of Uruk] has raised [seven years] of hay.   110
   At the Bull of Heaven's [fury I will kill him]!

When Anu heard what Ishtar said,
He placed the lead rope of the Bull of Heaven in her hand,
Ishtar led the Bull of Heaven away.

[*The bull rampages around Uruk, lowering the Euphrates' water level
with great gulps and opening up enormous pits in the ground with its
snorts. Hundreds of men fall into them. Enkidu pinions the animal from
the rear, and Gilgamesh stabs it to death.*]

When it reached Uruk,   115
It dried up groves, reedbeds, and marshes,
It went down to the river, it lowered the river by seven cubits.
At the bull's snort, a pit opened up,
One hundred men of Uruk fell into it, one after another.
At its second snort, a pit opened up,   120
Two hundred men of Uruk fell into it, one after another.
At its third snort, a pit opened up,
Enkidu fell into it, up to his middle.
Enkidu sprang out and seized the bull by its horns,
The bull spewed its foam in his face,   125
[Swished dung] at him with the tuft of its tail.
Enkidu made ready to speak,
Saying to Gilgamesh:

My friend, we boasted of ourselves in the city,
How shall we answer for the piles of (dead) people?   130
I have seen, my friend, the strength of the Bull
    of Heaven,
So knowing its strength, [I know] how to deal with it.
I will get around [and . . .] the strength of the Bull of
    Heaven,
I will [circle around] behind the Bull of Heaven,
I will grab it [by the tuft of its tail].   135
I will set [my foot on its hock],
[I will . . .] by its [. . .]
Then [you], like a strong, skillful slaughterer,
Thrust your dagger between nape, horn, and kill-point!

Enkidu circled around behind the Bull of Heaven,   140
He grabbed it by the tuft of its tail,
He set his foot on its hock,
[He . . .] by its [. . .],
Then Gilgamesh, like a strong, skillful slaughterer,
Thrust his dagger between nape, horn, and kill-point!   145

[*Gilgamesh and Enkidu offer the creature's heart to Shamash. Ishtar is dis-
traught, again using colloquial language. Enkidu rips off the bull's haunch
and throws it at her. He insults her, saying he would butcher her too if he
could. Ishtar summons her cult women to mourn over the bull's haunch.*]

After they had killed the Bull of Heaven,
They ripped out its heart and set it before Shamash.
They stepped back and prostrated themselves before
    Shamash,
Then the two sat down together, one beside the other.
Ishtar went up on the walls of ramparted Uruk,   150
She writhed in grief, she let out a wail:

    That bully Gilgamesh who belittled me, he's killed the Bull
        of Heaven!

When Enkidu heard what Ishtar said,
He tore off the bull's haunch and flung it at her:

    You too, if I could vanquish you, I'd treat you like this,   155
    I'd drape the guts over your arms!

Ishtar convened the cult women, prostitutes, harlots,
She set up a lament over the haunch of the bull.

6. *Then Gilgamesh, like a strong, skillful slaughterer, / Thrust his dagger between nape, horn, and kill-point!* This seal image shows this episode, with Ishtar standing by in anguish.

[*The bull's immense horns are marvels of craftsmanship. Gilgamesh hangs them up in his bedroom as a trophy.*]

Gilgamesh summoned all the expert craftsmen,
The craftsmen marveled at the massiveness of its horns.   160
They were molded from thirty pounds each of lapis blue,
Their outer shell was two thumbs thick!
Six times three hundred quarts of oil, the capacity of both,
He donated to anoint the statue of his protective god,
   Lugalbanda.
He brought them inside and hung them up in his lordly
   bedroom.   165

[*Gilgamesh and Enkidu parade in triumph. Gilgamesh makes a short speech to his servants. The victorious heroes celebrate then fall asleep.*]

They washed their hands in the Euphrates,
Clasping each other, they came away.
As they paraded through a street of Uruk,
The people of Uruk crowded to look [upon them].
Gilgamesh made a speech   170
To the servant-women of [his palace]:

Who is the handsomest of young men?
Who is the most glorious of males?
Gilgamesh is the handsomest of young men!
[Gilgamesh] is the most glorious of males!   175
[For what . . .] we knew [. . .] in our passion,
I will have no belittler in the street!
[. . .]

Gilgamesh held a celebration in his palace.
The young men stretched out, asleep on the couch of night.   180
While Enkidu slept, he had a dream.
Enkidu went to relate his dream,
Saying to his friend:

Tablet VII

My friend, why were the great gods in council?

[*gap*]

[*According to a Hittite version (see below, pp. 164–65), Enkidu dreams that the gods Anu, Enlil, Ea, and Shamash were in council. Anu decrees that because Gilgamesh and Enkidu killed the bull and cut cedars, one of them must die. Enlil, perhaps grateful for the cedar door, decrees that it should be Enkidu. Shamash considers this unfair, but Enlil overrules him. When the standard version resumes, the two heroes are evidently in Nippur, perhaps with the intent of persuading Enlil to change his judgment. Enkidu curses the cedar door, saying he now wishes he had given it to Shamash. The concluding words of his curse parody traditional Mesopotamian inscriptions on monuments, which called down the wrath of the gods upon anyone who damaged, removed, or usurped them.*]

Enkidu lifted [his head toward the door],
He spoke to the door [as if it were human]:

> O bosky Door, insensate,
> Which lends an ear that is not there, 5
> I sought your wood for twenty double leagues,
> Till I beheld a lofty cedar [whose crown had pierced the sky]
> No rival had your tree [in the forest . . .].
> Six times twelve cubits is your height, two times twelve
>   cubits is your width,
> One cubit is your thickness, 10
> Your hinge pole, ferrule, and pivot box are unique.
> I made you, I set you up in Nippur, . . .
> Had I known, O Door, how you would [requite me],
> And that this would be your favor toward me,
> I would have raised my axe, I would have chopped you down, 15
> I would have floated you as a raft to the temple of
>   Shamash,
> I would have [brought you] into the temple of Shamash,
> I would have set up the cedar [. . . in the . . .] of the
>   temple of Shamash,

I would have set up the lion-headed monster-bird Anzu at
   its gate (to protect it),
[. . .] access to you [. . .]   20
I would have [. . .] the city [. . .] of Shamash,
Then in Uruk [. . .] you,
Because Shamash heard my plea [. . .]
He gave me the weapon to [kill Humbaba].
Now then, O Door, it was I who made you, it was I who set
   you up,   25
Shall I [cast you down], shall I tear you out?
May a king who shall arise after me despise you,
May a god [allow . . .] to conceal you,
May he alter my inscription and put on his own!

He tore out [his hair], threw away [his clothing].   30
When he heard this speech, swiftly, quickly his tears flowed
   down,
When Gilgamesh heard out Enkidu's speech, swiftly, quickly,
   his tears flowed down.

[*Gilgamesh comforts Enkidu by suggesting that death may be a greater
burden for those left behind than for the deceased. Gilgamesh promises
that he will make a gold statue of Enkidu, presumably to offer to Enlil to
induce him to change his judgment.*]

Gilgamesh made ready to speak, saying to Enkidu:

[. . .] superb,
My friend, you are rational but [you said] strange things,   35
Why, my friend, did your heart speak strange things?
The dream is a most precious omen, though very frightening,
Your [lips] are buzzing like flies.
[Though frightening], the dream is a precious omen.
They left mourning for the living,   40
[The dead] left woe for the living.
Now I shall go pray to the great gods,
I will be assiduous to [my own god], I will pray to yours,
I will seek the blessing of [Anu], father of the gods,
May Enlil, counselor of the gods, hear my prayer about you,   45
May [Ea . . .].
I will make your image of gold beyond measure—

[*Enkidu interrupts him.*]

[My friend], pay out no silver, [squander] no gold!
What Enlil has commanded is not like the [. . .] of the
    gods,
What he has commanded, he will not [erase],   50
The verdict he has announced, he will not reverse or erase,
My friend, [my destiny] is scrivened.
People often die before their time.

[*At sunrise, Enkidu prays to Shamash, god of justice and right-dealing.
He calls his curse upon the two human agents whom he blames for his
destiny, the hunter and the harlot. For the hunter he wishes a poor catch,
for the harlot the worst of a whore's life. Lines 59–60 depend on a word-
play on the Babylonian words for "friend" and "food ration."*]

At the first glimmer of dawn,
Enkidu lifted his head, weeping before Shamash,   55
Before the sun's fiery glare, his tears flowed down:

I have turned to you, O Shamash, for the sake of my
    precious life!
As for that hunter, the entrapping-man,
Who did not let me get as much (life) as my friend,
May that hunter not get enough to make him a living.   60
Make his profit loss, cut down his take,
May his income, his portion evaporate before you,
[Any wildlife] wherever it enters [his traps], may it go out as
    if through a window!

When he had cursed the hunter to his heart's content,
He resolved to curse the harlot Shamhat: 65

Come, Shamhat, I will ordain you a destiny,
A destiny that will never end, forever and ever!
I will lay on you the greatest of all curses,
Swiftly, inexorably, may my curse come upon you.
May you never make a home that you can enjoy,   70
May you never caress [a child] of your own,
May you never be received among decent women,
May the ground besmirch your best garment,
May the drunkard bespatter your best clothes in the dust.
May you never [have a house with] fine things,   75
May your house be [the pit] where potters get their clay.
May you never have a bedroom, family chapel, or reception
    room,

May no bed, chair, or table to be proud of be set up in your
    home,
May the nook you enjoy be a doorstep,
May the dusty crossroads be your dwelling,   80
May vacant lots be your sleeping place,
May the shade of a wall be your counting house.
May brambles and thorns flay your feet,
May toper and sober slap your cheek,[1]
May the lawful wife scream at you when you meet.   85
May no builder keep your roof in repair,
May the screech owl roost in (your ruin of a) home,
May no feast ever be held in your dwelling.

[*gap*]

May your purple finery [be stolen],
May filthy underwear [be all you can buy],   90
[May one] whose loins are putrid [be your lover],
Because you [diminished] me, an innocent,
Yes me, an innocent, you [diminished] me in my steppe.

[*Shamash remonstrates, asserting that friendship with Gilgamesh was
worth an untimely death and promising Enkidu a fine funeral. He also tells
him that Gilgamesh will take his place as "wild man" of the steppe, no
doubt the fullest possible observance of the loss of his friend, short of taking
his place in the netherworld.*]

When Shamash heard what he said,
From afar a warning voice called out to him from the sky: 95

O Enkidu, why curse Shamhat the harlot,
Who gave you bread to eat, fit for a god,
Who poured you beer, fit for a king,
Who dressed you in a noble garment,
And gave you handsome Gilgamesh for a comrade?   100
Now Gilgamesh, your friend and brother,
Will lay you out in a noble resting place,
In a perfect resting place he will lay you out!
He will settle you in peaceful rest in that dwelling sinister,
[Potentates] of the netherworld will do you homage.   105
He will have the people of Uruk shed bitter tears for you,
He will burden the [pleasure-loving] people of Uruk with a
    task for you,[2]

1. This means that all her clients will beat her; see below, note 4.
2. This refers to the construction of an elaborate tomb, as in the Sumerian poem "The
Death of Gilgamesh" (below, pp. 155–56).

And, as for him, after your death, he will let his hair grow
    matted,
He will put on a lion skin and roam the steppe.

[*At this cold comfort, Enkidu, with bitter humor, immediately reverses the
"destiny that will never end" for the harlot. He now wishes her the best of
a whore's life: an eager, generous clientele from all levels of society.*]

When Enkidu heard the speech of the valiant Shamash,   110
His raging heart was calmed,
[. . .] his furious [heart] was calmed:

Come, [Shamhat, I will ordain you a destiny],
My mouth that cursed you, let it bless [you] instead.
May [governors] and dignitaries fall in love with you,   115
May the man one double league away slap his thighs in
    excitement,
May the man two double leagues away be letting down
    his hair.
May the soldier [not hold back] from you, but open his
    trousers,
May he [pay] you with obsidian,[3] lapis, and gold,
May fancy granulated ear bangles be your compensation.   120
To the man whose wealth is [secure], whose granaries
    are full,
May Ishtar, [enabler] of the gods, introduce you,
[For your sake] may the wife and mother of seven be
    abandoned.

Enkidu was sick at heart,
He lay there, lonely, [brooding],   125
[He told] his friend what was weighing on his mind.

[*Enkidu tells Gilgamesh his dream of dying and the afterlife. Mesopota-
mian tradition was unanimous on this grim view of the netherworld,
characterized by darkness, hunger, thirst, dust, and no rewards beyond
those provided by the solicitude of one's surviving kin.*]

My friend, what a dream I had last night!
Heaven cried out, earth made reply,
I was standing between them.
There was a certain man, his face was somber,   130
His face was like that of the lion-headed monster-bird Anzu,

3. A dark, glassy volcanic stone, prized in Mesopotamia for implements because it could
hold a sharp edge.

His hands were the paws of a lion,
His fingernails were the talons of an eagle.
He seized me by the hair, he was too strong for me,
I hit him but he bounced back like a swing rope,   135
He hit me and capsized me like a raft.
Like a mighty wild bull he trampled me down,
He [. . .] my body with his slaver,
"Save me, my friend!"—[but you did not save me],
You were afraid and did not [save me].   140
You [. . .]

[gap]

[. . .] and turned me into a dove,
[He trussed] my arms like a bird's.
Holding me fast, he took me down to the house of shadows,
    the dwelling of the infernal regions,
To the house that none leaves who enters,   145
On the road from which there is no way back,
To the house whose dwellers are bereft of light,
Where dust is their fare and their food is clay.
They are dressed like birds in feather garments,
Yea, they shall see no daylight, for they abide in darkness.   150
[Dust lies thick] on the door [and bolt],
[A ghastly stillness reigns] over that house of dust.
When I entered that house of dust,
I saw crowns in a heap,
There dwelt [the kings], crowned heads who once ruled
    the land,   155
Who always set out roast meat on the altars of Anu and Enlil,
Who always set out baked offerings, libated cool water
    from waterskins.
In that house of dust I entered,
Dwelt high priests and acolytes,
Dwelt reciters of spells and ecstatics,[4]   160
Dwelt the anointers of the great gods,
Dwelt old king Etana and the god of the beasts,
Dwelt the queen of the netherworld, Ereshkigal.
Belet-seri, scribe of the netherworld, was kneeling
    before her,

---

4. Mesopotamian poets often used extremes to convey totality or inclusiveness: high
priests were at the top of the hierarchy, assistants, or "acolytes," at the bottom, so line
159 means that all ranks of the educated priesthood were in the netherworld despite
their service to the gods in their lifetimes. Since reciters of spells had memorized
magic words, while prophets, or "ecstatics," were people who spoke in a trance without
having learned their words, line 160 therefore refers to all who communicated or made
use of the words of the gods.

She was holding a [tablet] and reading to her.   165
[She lifted her head], she looked at me:
"Who brought this man?
"[Who] brought [. . .]?
"[Who] has made ready [his burial goods]?
"[Who . . .] the grave?   170
"[Who . . .] the interment?"

[gap]

[*Whereas the two friends have interpreted or, one might say, explained away the grim symbolism of all the dreams they have had since the beginning of their friendship, this dream is so obvious and compelling in its portent that no interpretation is called for. When the text resumes, Enkidu is still speaking.*]

It was I who [went with you] through all hardships,
Remember me, my friend, [do not forget] what I have
    undergone!
"My friend had a dream needing no [interpretation]."

[*Enkidu's final illness is conveyed by somber repetition of the twelve days of its course. Little of his bitter final speech is now preserved, so the restorations proposed here are merely guesses.*]

The day he had the dream, his strength ran out.   175
Enkidu lay there one day, [a second day] he was ill,
Enkidu lay in his bed, [his illness grew worse].
A third day, a fourth day, [Enkidu's illness grew worse].
A fifth day, a sixth, a seventh,
An eighth, a ninth, [a tenth day],   180
Enkidu's illness [grew worse].
An eleventh, a twelfth day, [Enkidu's illness grew worse].
Enkidu [sat up] in his bed,
He called for Gilgamesh, [roused him with his cry]:

My friend, [my god] has turned against me!   185
Like someone [who fell] in battle, [I am . . .],
I feared (this last) battle [. . .]
My friend, he who [falls] in battle [is glorious],
(But) I [. . . fell] in (this) battle . . .

[gap]

[*Enkidu dies.*]

Tablet VIII

[Gilgamesh mourns Enkidu. Line 18 refers to an episode that does not appear in the extant portions of the epic.]

At the first glimmer of dawn,
Gilgamesh [lamented] his friend:

Enkidu, my friend, your mother the gazelle,
Your father the wild ass brought you into the world,
Onagers raised you on their milk,   5
And the wild beasts taught you all the grazing places.
The pathways, O Enkidu, of the forest of cedars,
May they weep for you, without falling silent, night and day.
May the elders of the teeming city, ramparted Uruk,
    weep for you,
May the crowds who were blessing our departure
    [weep for you],   10
May the heights of highland and mountain [weep for you],
[. . .] pure [. . .]
May the lowlands wail like your mother,
May [the forest] of cypress and cedar weep for you,
Through which in our fury we forced our way.   15
May bear, hyena, panther, tiger, deer, jackal,
Lion, wild bull, gazelle, ibex, the beasts and creatures
    of the steppe, weep for you.
May the sacred Ulaya River weep for you, along whose
    banks we once strode proud,
May the holy Euphrates weep for you,
Whose water we libated from waterskins.   20
May the young men of ramparted Uruk weep for you,
Who watched us slay the Bull of Heaven in combat.
May the plowman weep for you [at his plow],
Who extolled your name in the sweet song of harvest home.[1]

1. Mesopotamian literature referred to work songs sung when the crops were brought in
   from the harvest as symbols of happiness and prosperity. A Sumerian composition in
   the style of such a song is in honor of Enkimdu, god of plowmen, so a play on the two
   names may be intended.

May he weep for you, the [orchardist] of the vast city
    of Uruk,   25
Who, at first [fruit], extolled your name.
May the shepherd and herdsman weep for you,
Who used to hold milk and buttermilk to your mouth,
May [the herd boy] weep for you,
Who used to hold butter to your lips.   30
May the brewer weep for you,
Who used to hold ale to your mouth.
May the harlot weep for you,
Who massaged you with sweet-smelling oil.
May [the groom] at the wedding weep for you,   35
Who [. . .] a wife [. . .] ring.[2]
May [foundlings and orphans] weep for you,
Like brothers may they weep for you,
Like sisters may they loosen their hair for your sake.
May they weep for Enkidu, your mother, your father [who
    adopted you],[3]   40
All the while I too shall be weeping for you!
Hear me, O young men, listen to me,
Hear me, O elders of [Uruk], listen to me!
I weep for my friend, Enkidu,
I wail as bitterly as a professional keener.   45
Oh for the axe at my side, oh for the one I trusted beside me!
Oh for the sword at my belt, oh for the shield before me,
Oh for my best garment, oh for the raiment that pleased
    me most!
An ill wind rose against me and snatched him from me!
O my friend, wild-running donkey, mountain onager,
    panther of the steppe,   50
O my friend Enkidu, wild-running donkey, mountain
    onager, panther of the steppe!
You who stood by me when we climbed the [highlands],
Seized [and slew] the Bull of Heaven,
Felled Humbaba who [dwelt] in the forest of [cedars],
What now is this sleep that has seized you?   55
You have faded from me and you cannot hear me!

But, as for him, he did not raise [his head].
He touched his heart but it beat no more.

---

2. This may mean that grooms are forever grateful to Enkidu for interfering with Gil-
gamesh's custom of taking brides on their wedding nights (Tablet II, lines 62–69).
3. This difficult passage may refer to Ninsun's adoption of Enkidu (Tablet III, line 112).
Foundlings and orphans, like Enkidu, shall forever mourn him as one of them.

Then he covered his friend's face, like a bride's.
He hovered round him like an eagle,   60
Like a lioness robbed of her cubs,
He paced to and fro, back and forth,
Tearing out and letting fall in a heap the locks of [his hair],
Ripping off and hurling away his fine clothes like
    something foul.

[*Gilgamesh commissions a memorial statue for Enkidu.*]

At the first glimmer of dawn,   65
Gilgamesh sent out a proclamation in the land:

    Hear ye, blacksmith, lapidary, metalworker, goldsmith,
        jeweler!
    Make my friend [in metals and gemstones],
    [Such as no one ever] made of his friend!
    The limbs of my friend [. . .]   70
    [. . .] your eyes of lapis, your chest of gold,
    Your skin of [. . .]

                        [*gap*]

    I will lay you out in a noble resting place,
    In a perfect resting place I will lay you out!
    I will settle you in peaceful rest in that dwelling sinister, 75
    Potentates of the netherworld will do you homage.
    I will have the people of [Uruk shed bitter tears for you],
    I will burden the [pleasure-loving] people with a task
        for you,
    And, as for me, after your death, I will let my hair grow
        matted,
    I will put on a lion skin and roam the steppe!   80

                        [*gap*]

[*From his treasury, Gilgamesh takes out and displays grave goods for Enkidu.*]

At the first glimmer of dawn, Gilgamesh arose,
[He went to the storehouse],
He broke its seal, he surveyed the treasure,
[Obsidian], carnelian,[4] [. . .], alabaster,
[. . .]   85
He set out [. . .] for his friend,

---

4. A reddish stone, prized in Mesopotamia for making beads and seals.

He set out [. . .] for his friend,
He set out [. . . made of] ten pounds of gold for his friend,
He set out [. . . made of ten] pounds of gold for his friend,
He set out [. . . made of ten] pounds of gold for his friend,   90
[. . .]
[. . .] between them, mounted in thirty pounds of gold.

[*In the fragmentary lines that follow, there is mention of splendid weapons,
perhaps a sword, bow, and quiver, together with fittings and ornaments of
gold, ivory, and iron. Next Gilgamesh displays gifts for various netherworld
deities to render them inclined to receive Enkidu's ghost with favor.*]

He slaughtered many fatted [cattle] and sheep, heaped them
    high for his friend, (saying):
"[. . . in the] open for my friend."
They carried off all the meat for the potentates of the
    netherworld.   95
[. . .] Ishtar, the great queen,
[A throw stick made of . . .], the sacred tree,
[He displayed in the open for] Ishtar, the great queen,
(Saying): "May Ishtar, the great queen, accept this,
May she welcome my friend [and walk at his side]."   100
[. . .]
He displayed in the open for Namrasit [. . .],
(Saying): "May Namrasit [. . .] accept this,
May he welcome my friend and walk at his side."
A jar of lapis [. . .]   105
He displayed in the open for Ereshkigal, [queen of the
    netherworld],
(Saying): "May Ereshkigal, [queen of the crowded nether-
    world], accept this,
May she welcome my friend and walk at his side."
A flute of carnelian [. . .],
He displayed in the open for Tammuz, the shepherd, beloved
    of [Ishtar],   110
Saying: "May Tammuz, the shepherd, beloved of [Ishtar],
    accept this,
May he welcome my friend and walk at his side."
A chair of lapis [. . .]
A staff of lapis [. . .]
He displayed in the open for Namtar, [courier of the
    netherworld],   115
Saying: "May Namtar, [courier of the crowded netherworld],
    accept this,
May he welcome my friend and walk at his side."

7. *He filled a lapis bowl with butter.* Lapis bowl and whetstone from a grave at Ur.

[gap]

He displayed in the open for [Hushbishag, housekeeper of the
   netherworld],
[Saying: "May Hushbishag, housekeeper of the crowded neth-
   erworld, accept this],
[May she welcome my friend and walk at his side]."   120
He had [. . .] make [. . .]
A bracelet(?) of silver, armlets(?) of copper,
[He displayed in the open] for Qassa-tabat, [sweeper for
   Ereshkigal],
Saying: "May Qassa-tabat, sweeper for [Ereshkigal], accept
   this,
May he welcome my friend and [walk at his side].   125
May my friend not be afraid, may he not become sick at
   heart."
[A box?] of alabaster, the inside inlaid with lapis and
   carnelian,
[Filled with incense from?] the forest of cedars,

[And a . . .] inlaid with carnelian,
He displayed for Ninshuluhhatumma, who keeps the house
    in order,   130
Saying: "May Ninshuluhhatumma, who keeps the house in
    order, accept this,
May she welcome my friend and walk at his side,
May she [intercede on behalf of?] my friend,
May my friend not be afraid, may he not become sick at heart."

A double-edged dagger, its hilt of lapis,   135
With a likeness of the holy Euphrates,
He displayed in the open for Bibbu, meat carver of the
    netherworld,
Saying: "May Bibbu, meat carver of the crowded netherworld,
    [accept this],
[May he] welcome [my friend] and walk at his side."
[. . . and] flask of alabaster,   140
He displayed in the open [for Tammuz-apsu], scapegoat of the
    netherworld,
Saying: "[May Tammuz]-apsu, scapegoat of the crowded nether-
    world, [accept this],
May he welcome my friend and walk at his side."

[*Fragmentary lines, with more offerings. Someone speaks to Gilgamesh,
then he decides to dam the Euphrates(?), in order to build Enkidu's tomb
in the riverbed. Once the dam is breached, the tomb will be forever safe
underwater, as described in the Sumerian poem "The Death of Gil-
gamesh" (below, pp. 155–56).*]

When Gilgamesh heard this,
He conceived [in his heart] the damming of the river.   145

At the first glimmer of dawn, Gilgamesh opened the [. . .],
He brought out a great table of precious wood.
He filled a carnelian bowl with honey,
He filled a lapis bowl with butter,
He adorned [the table] and displayed it in the open   150

[*gap*]

Tablet IX

[*Gilgamesh, distraught, roams the steppe. He then sets forth on a quest to find Utanapishtim, the survivor of the Flood, who was granted immortality by the gods.*]

Gilgamesh was weeping bitterly for Enkidu, his friend,
As he roamed the steppe:

> I shall die too! Shall I not then be like Enkidu?
> Oh sorrow has entered my heart!
> I have grown afraid of death, so I roam the steppe.   5
> Having come this far, I will go on swiftly
> Toward Utanapishtim, son of Ubar-Tutu.
> I have reached mountain passes at night,
> I saw lions and I felt afraid,
> I looked up to pray to the moon,   10
> To the moon, beacon of the gods, my prayers went forth:
> "[. . .] keep me safe!"

[At night] he lay down, then awoke, it was a dream.
[. . .] moon, he rejoiced to be alive.
He raised the axe at his side,   15
He drew the [sword] from his belt,
He dropped among them like an arrow,
He struck the lions, killed, and scattered them.

[*In a fragmentary passage, Gilgamesh evidently draws two pictures, perhaps of himself and Enkidu, gives them names, and prays to the moon god a second time, then the text breaks off. The following episode, found in an old version, may come next. As interpreted here, a god, perhaps the moon god, is telling Shamash what Gilgamesh is doing.*]

> [He kills lions], wild bulls, bison [of the uplands . . .],
> He has put on their skins, he eats their flesh.   20
> Gilgamesh [dug many] wells where they never were
>   before,
> He [drank] the water and went on, chasing the winds.

69

Shamash was distressed, he bent down over him,
He said to Gilgamesh:

> Gilgamesh, wherefore do you wander?   25
> The eternal life you are seeking you shall not find.

Gilgamesh spoke to him, the valiant Shamash:

> After my restless roaming in the steppe,
> There will be ample repose, deep in the earth,
> I shall surely lie asleep all the years (to come).   30
> For now, let my eyes see the sun, let me have all the light
>   I could ever want,
> Darkness is infinite, how little light there is!
> When may the dead see the radiance of the sun?

[*As the standard version resumes, Gilgamesh approaches in awe the fear-some scorpion monsters guarding the eastern portal of the vast tunnel under the earth, from which the sun emerges at sunrise. Each end of this passage is marked by a great mountain called Mashum, "the twin."*]

The twin peaks are called Mashum.
When he arrived at the (first) peak called Mashum,   35
Which daily watches over the rising [of the sun]—
Their peaks thrust upward to the vault of heaven,
Their flanks reach downward to the infernal regions—
Scorpion monsters guard its portal,
Their fearsome glories are stupefying, the sight of them is death,   40
Their ghastly radiance spreads over the mountain,
They watch over the sun at his rising and setting!
When Gilgamesh saw them, he hid his face in fear and dread.
He took hold of himself and approached them.
The scorpion monster called to his wife: 45

> The one who has come to us, his body is flesh of the gods!

The scorpion monster's wife answered him:

> Two-thirds of him is divine, one-third is human.

The scorpion monster, the male one, called out,
[To Gilgamesh the king], flesh of the gods, he said these
    words: 50

> [Who are you] who have come this long way,
> [How have you] come here, before me?

[How did you cross the seas], a perilous crossing?
I would learn of your [journey],
[The goal toward which] you make your way,   55
I would learn of [its purpose].

[gap]

[*When Gilgamesh explains his quest, the scorpion monster asserts that no one can traverse the tunnel between the twin mountains. When the sun sets, he enters the western portal of the tunnel, passes under the entire span of the earth in twelve hours, then re-emerges at the eastern portal, where Gilgamesh is standing, to begin his twelve-hour journey across the sky. In that short time, no other being could travel fast enough in the opposite direction through the tunnel before being burned up as the sun enters for his nighttime journey.*]

[I traversed all lands],
[I came over, one after another, wearisome mountains],
[Then I crossed, one after another, all the seas] . . .
[I seek the road to] my forefather, Utanapishtim, [whom
   they call the "Distant One"],   60
He who took his place among the gods [and found
   eternal life].
Life and death: [he will reveal to me the secret].

The scorpion monster made ready to speak, spoke to him,
Saying to Gilgamesh:

There was never, O Gilgamesh, [anyone like you . . .],   65
No one ever [entered the interior of the mountain].
Its passage is twelve double hours [. . .],
Dense is the darkness, [no light is there].
At the sun's rising, [they watch over him],
At the sun's setting, [they watch over him],   70
At the sun's setting, [they let him enter],
They let him come forth [at this rising].
[. . .] dug [this tunnel].
As for you, how [will you . . .]?
Will you enter [. . .]?   75

[gap]

[*In the intervening gap, something happens to persuade the scorpion monster to open the portal to the tunnel under the earth. To judge from the analogy of Utanapishtim and his wife, encountered later in the epic, the scorpion monster's wife intervenes on Gilgamesh's behalf and convinces her husband to admit him.*]

In sorrow [. . .]
[His features weathered] by cold and sun,
In distress [. . .]
Now then, will you [show him the road to his forefather,
    Utanapishtim]?

The scorpion monster made ready to speak, spoke to him,   80
Saying to king Gilgamesh, [scion of the gods]:

Go, Gilgamesh [. . .]
May Mount Mashum [. . .]
May the mountain ranges [. . .]
[Bring you] safely [. . .]   85

[He opened to him] the portal of the mountain,
Gilgamesh [entered the mountain . . .].
He heeded the words of the [scorpion monster],
[He set out on] the way of the sun.

[*Gilgamesh races through the tunnel, a heroic run equal to the sun's jour-
ney across the sky. It is so dark that he cannot reassure himself by looking
back to the light from the entrance behind him to know if the sun is still in
the heavens. At the same time, he knows that if he sees light ahead of him,
the sun has entered the western portal, and he is doomed.*]

When he had gone one double hour,   90
Dense was the darkness, no light was there,
It would not let him look behind him.
When he had gone two double hours,
Dense was the darkness, no light was there,
It would not let him look behind him.   95
When he had gone three double hours,
Dense was the darkness, no light was there,
It would not let him look behind him.
When he had gone four double hours,
Dense was the darkness, no light was there,   100
It would not let him look behind him.
When he had gone five double hours,
Dense was the darkness, no light was there,
It would not let him look behind him.
When he had gone six double hours,   105
Dense was the darkness, no light was there,
It would not let him look behind him.
When he had gone seven double hours,
Dense was the darkness, no light was there,

8. *Dense was the darkness, no light was there*. This episode was probably inspired by the Tigris tunnel, a stone passage in Armenia where the river flows under a mountain. This tunnel was several times visited by Mesopotamian kings. This relief shows men exploring it with torches.

It would not let him look behind him. 110
At eight double hours, he was rushing on, like a [. . .]
Dense was the darkness, no light was there,
It would not let him look behind him.
When he had gone nine double hours,
[He felt] the north wind, 115
[. . .] his face,
Dense was the darkness, no light was there,
It would not let him look behind him.
When he had gone ten double hours,
[The time for the sun's entry] was drawing near, 120
[When he had gone eleven double hours], just one double
    hour [was left],
[When he had gone twelve double hours], he came out ahead
    of the sun!
[Ahead of him . . .] there was a bright gleam,
When he saw the [. . .] of the trees of the gods, he went
    forward.
A carnelian tree bore its fruit, 125
Like bunches of grapes dangling, lovely to see,
A lapis tree bore foliage,
Fruit it bore, a delight to behold.

[The fragmentary lines that remain continue the description of the won-derful grove. Identification of most of the stones is conjectural.]

[. . .] cypress [. . .]
[. . .] cedar [. . .]   130
Its boughs were striped agate and [. . .],
Coral(?), [. . . and] rubies(?).
Instead of thorns and brambles there were [clusters] of
    crystal,
He touched a carob, it was [a lump of] costly stone!
Agates, hematite, [. . .],   135
[Lay about] like cucumbers [. . . on the] open ground.
Instead of [a sea . . .] there was turquoise,
Which [. . . pearls(?) instead of] shells,
They had [. . .]
[She . . .] Gilgamesh as he walked about,   140
She looked up to gaze at him.

Tablet X

[Gilgamesh approaches the tavern of Siduri, a woman who lives alone by the seashore at the western end of the earth. This interesting personage is unknown outside this poem, nor is it clear who her clientele might be in such a remote spot. Alarmed by Gilgamesh's appearance, she locks her door and hides on the roof. In contrast to his deference to the scorpion monster, Gilgamesh is aggressive. When he identifies himself, Siduri is skeptical and wants to know why anyone so splendid as Gilgamesh appears in such condition.]

Siduri the tavern keeper, who dwelt at the edge of the sea,
Dwelt there and [kept a tavern . . .]
She had cup racks, she had [vats of gold],
She was covered with a veil [. . .]
Gilgamesh strode toward her [. . .]   5
He was clad in a skin, [he was] frightful.
He had flesh of gods in [his body],
Sorrow was in his heart,
His face was like a traveler's from afar.
The tavern keeper eyed him from a distance,   10
Speaking to herself, she said these words,
She debated with herself:

    This I am sure is a slaughterer of wild bulls!
    Whence made he straight for my door?

At the sight of him, the tavern keeper barred her door,   15
She barred her door and went up to the roof terrace.
But he, Gilgamesh, could hear her [prattle],
He looked straight up and fastened [his eyes upon her].

Gilgamesh said to her, to the tavern keeper:

    Tavern keeper, when you saw me why did you bar your door,   20
    Bar your door and [go up to the] roof terrace?
    I will strike down the door, I will shatter [the doorbolt],

9. *The tavern keeper eyed him from a distance.* Ivory head of a woman. Taverns in Mesopotamia were often kept by independent businesswomen.

[. . .] my [. . .]
[. . .] in the steppe.

[The tavern keeper said to him, to] Gilgamesh: 25

[. . .] I barred my door,
[. . . I went up to] the roof terrace,
[. . .] I want to know.

Gilgamesh said to her, to the tavern keeper:

[I am he, who, with my friend Enkidu . . .]   30
[Who slew the guardian],
[Who caught and slew the bull that came down from heaven],
Who felled Humbaba who dwelt in the forest of cedars,
Who killed lions at the mountain passes.

The tavern keeper said to him, to Gilgamesh: 35

[If indeed you are he, who, with Enkidu], slew the guardian,
Who felled Humbaba who dwelt in the forest of cedars,
Who killed lions at the mountain passes,
Who caught and slew the bull that came down from heaven,
Why are your cheeks emaciated, your face cast down,   40
Your spirit wretched, your features wasted,
Sorrow in your heart,
Your face like a traveler's from afar,
Your features weathered by cold and sun,
Why are you clad in a lion skin, roaming the steppe?   45

Gilgamesh said to her, to the tavern keeper:

Why should my cheeks not be emaciated, nor my face cast
    down,
Nor my spirit wretched, nor my features wasted?
Why should there not be sorrow in my heart,
Nor my face like a traveler's from afar,   50
Nor my features weathered by cold and sun,
Nor I be clad in a lion skin, roaming the steppe?
My friend, swift wild donkey, mountain onager, panther of
    the steppe,
Enkidu, swift wild donkey, mountain onager, panther of
    the steppe,
My friend whom I so loved, who went with me through
    every hardship,   55
Enkidu, whom I so loved, who went with me through every
    hardship,
The fate of mankind has overtaken him.
Six days and seven nights I wept for him,
I would not give him up for burial,
Until a worm fell out of his nose.   60
I was frightened [. . .]
I have grown afraid of dying, so I roam the steppe,
My friend's plight weighs heavy upon me.
A distant road I roam over the steppe,
My friend Enkidu's plight weighs heavy upon me!   65
A distant road I roam over the steppe,
How can I be silent? How can I hold my peace?
My friend whom I loved is turned into clay.
Enkidu, my friend whom I loved, is turned into clay!
Shall I too not lie down like him,   70
And never get up forever and ever?

[*An old version adds the following passage.*]

> After his death I could find no life,
> Back and forth I prowled like a bandit in the steppe.
> Now that I have seen your face, tavern keeper,
> May I not see that death I constantly fear!   75

The tavern keeper said to him, to Gilgamesh:

> Gilgamesh, wherefore do you wander?
> The eternal life you are seeking you shall not find.
> When the gods created mankind,
> They established death for mankind,   80
> And withheld eternal life for themselves.
> As for you, Gilgamesh, let your stomach be full,
> Always be happy, night and day.
> Make every day a delight,
> Night and day play and dance.   85
> Your clothes should be clean,
> Your head should be washed,
> You should bathe in water.
> Look proudly on the little one holding your hand,
> Let your mate always be blissful in your loins,   90
> This, then, is the work of mankind,
> He who is alive [should be happy].

Gilgamesh said to her, to the tavern keeper:

> What are you saying, tavern keeper?
> I am heartsick for my friend.   95
> What are you saying, tavern keeper?
> I am heartsick for Enkidu!

[*gap*]

[*The standard version resumes.*]

Gilgamesh said to her, to the tavern keeper:

> Now then, what is the way to Utanapishtim?
> What is its landmark? Give it to me.   100
> Give, oh give me its landmark!
> If need be, I'll cross the sea,
> If not, I'll roam the steppe.

The tavern keeper said to him, to Gilgamesh:

> Gilgamesh, there has never been a way across,   105
> No one, from the dawn of time, has ever crossed this sea.
> The valiant Shamash alone can cross this sea,
> Save for the sun, who could cross this sea?
> The crossing is perilous, highly perilous the course,
> And midway lie the waters of death, whose surface is
>   impassable.   110
> Suppose, Gilgamesh, you do cross the sea,
> When you reach the waters of death, what will you do?
> Yet, Gilgamesh, there is Ur-Shanabi, Utanapishtim's boatman,
> He has the Stone Charms with him as he picks cedar
>   in the forest.[1]
> Go, show yourself to him,   115
> If possible, cross with him, if not, turn back.

[*Gilgamesh recklessly attacks Ur-Shanabi and smashes the Stone Charms, apparently to prevent their making off with the boat. The Hittite version (below, p. 167) calls these mysterious objects "images," so they may have been magic figurines who helped keep the boat afloat, immune to the waters of death. Part of this episode is known from an unpublished manuscript available only in translation.*]

When Gilgamesh heard this,
He raised the axe at his side,
He drew the sword from his belt,
He crept forward, went down toward them,   120
Like an arrow he dropped among them,
His battle cry resounded in the forest.
When Ur-Shanabi saw him, he put on his glory,
He raised his own axe and stood up tall as he could before
    him.
Then Gilgamesh, for his part, hit him on the pate, gripped
    him by the head,   125
Gripped his arm together with his chest.
And the Stone Charms were those who sealed the boat from
    leaking,
It was they who had no fear of the waters of death.
The ocean, the broad sea, [lapped?] toward Gilgamesh,
He held back the Stone Charms and the boat from the water.   130
He smashed the Stone Charms and threw them into a channel.
He [. . .] the boat's mooring rope
And sat down [. . .] on the shore.

1. Its seems that the boatman is cutting off branches to load on his boat; compare Tablet
V, lines 265–66.

[*An old version preserves the following, in which Sur-Sunabu is another form of the name Ur-Shanabi.*]

(Gilgamesh) turned back and stood before him.
Sur-Sunabu stared at him,   135
Sur-Sunabu said to him, to Gilgamesh:

    What is your name, pray tell?
    I am Sur-Sunabu, servant of Utanapishtim the Distant
        One.

Gilgamesh said to him, to Sur-Sunabu:

    Gilgamesh is my name.   140
    I am he who came from Uruk, the abode of Anu,
    Who traveled here around the mountains,
    The distant road where the sun comes forth.
    Now that I have seen your face, Sur-Sunabu,
    Show me Utanapishtim the Distant One.   145

[*The standard version resumes.*]

Ur-Shanabi said to him, to Gilgamesh:

    Why are your cheeks emaciated, your face cast down,
    Your spirit wretched, your features wasted,
    Sorrow in your heart,
    Your face like a traveler's from afar,   150
    Your features weathered by cold and sun,
    Why are you clad in a lion skin, roaming the steppe?

Gilgamesh said to him, to Ur-Shanabi:

    Why should my cheeks not be emaciated, nor my face cast
        down,
    Nor my spirit wretched nor my features wasted?   155
    Why should there not be sorrow in my heart,
    Nor my face like a traveler's from afar,
    Nor my features weathered by cold and sun,
    Nor I be clad in a lion skin, roaming the steppe?
    My friend, swift wild donkey, mountain onager, panther
        of the steppe,   160
    Enkidu, swift wild donkey, mountain onager, panther of
        the steppe,

My friend whom I so loved, who went with me through
    every hardship,
Enkidu, whom I so loved, who went with me through every
    hardship,
The fate of mankind has overtaken him.
Six days and seven nights I wept for him,   165
I would not give him up for burial,
Until a worm fell out of his nose.
I was frightened [. . .]
I have grown afraid of dying, so I roam the steppe,
My friend's plight weighs heavy upon me.   170
A distant road I roam over the steppe,
My friend Enkidu's plight weighs heavy upon me!
A distant road I roam over the steppe,
How can I be silent? How can I hold my peace?
My friend whom I loved is turned into clay.   175
Enkidu, my friend whom I loved, is turned into clay!
Shall I too not lie down like him,
And never get up forever and ever?

Gilgamesh said to him, to Ur-Shanabi:

    Now then, Ur-Shanabi, what is the way to Utanapishtim?   180
    What is its landmark? Give it to me.
    Give, oh give me its landmark!
    If need be, I'll cross the sea,
    If not, I'll roam the steppe.

Ur-Shanabi said to him, to Gilgamesh: 185

    Your own hands have foiled you, Gilgamesh,
    You have smashed the Stone Charms, you have [thrown
        them into a channel],
    The Stone Charms are smashed and the cedar [has not
        been picked].

[*An old version has the following here.*]

    The Stone Charms, Gilgamesh, are what carry me,
    Lest I touch the waters of death.   190
    In your fury you have smashed them,
    The Stone Charms, they are what I had with me to make
        the crossing!

[*The standard version continues. Gilgamesh cuts a heroic number of enormous punting poles. Then they set out across the sea. When they reach the waters of death, Gilgamesh pushes once with each punting pole, then lets it go, lest he touch the waters of death. For the last part of the journey, beyond the waters of death, Gilgamesh has used up his poles, so desperately holds up his clothing as an improvised sail. The numbers and distances in this passage have not been convincingly explained. Utanapishtim, surprised, sees them coming. The restorations of lines 224–27 are guesswork, but it seems that the sage recognizes the approaching hero.*]

Gilgamesh, raise the axe in your hand,
Go down into the forest, [cut me five times sixty] poles each
    five times twelve cubits long,
Dress them, set on knobs,   195
Bring them to me [and load them on the boat].

When Gilgamesh heard this,
He raised the axe at his side,
He drew the sword at his belt,
He went down into the forest, he cut him five times sixty poles
    each five times twelve cubits long,   200
He dressed them, set on knobs,
He brought them to him and [loaded them on the boat].
Gilgamesh and Ur-Shanabi embarked on the boat,
They launched the craft, it was they who manned it.
A journey of a month and a half they made in three days!   205
Ur-Shanabi reached the waters of death at last,
Ur-Shanabi said to him, to Gilgamesh:

Stand back, Gilgamesh! Take the first [pole],
Your hand must not touch the waters of death,
    you will [do yourself in]!
Take the second, the third, the fourth pole, Gilgamesh,   210
Take the fifth, sixth, and seventh pole, Gilgamesh,
Take the eighth, ninth, and tenth pole, Gilgamesh,
Take the eleventh and twelfth pole, Gilgamesh.

At twice sixty sea-miles Gilgamesh had used up the poles.
Then he, for his part, unfastened his belt [. . .],   215
Gilgamesh tore off the clothes from his body,
Made a tall mast with his arms.
Utanapishtim was watching him from a distance,
Speaking to himself, he said these words,

10. *Gilgamesh and Ur-Shanabi embarked on the boat.* Seal image showing two figures in a boat.

He debated with himself: 220

> Why have [the Stone Charms], belonging to the boat,
>   been smashed,
> And one not its master embarked [thereon]?
> He who comes here is no man of mine,
> But at his right [my man is standing].
> I can see that he is no [man] of mine, 225
> I can see that he is no [god . . .],
> I can see that [two-thirds of him is divine, one third is
>   human].

[gap]

[In the fragmentary lines that follow, Gilgamesh lands at Utanapishtim's wharf, greets him, and asks the sage how he achieved immortal life after the Flood. It seems that Utanapishtim already knows his name.]

Utanapishtim said to him, to Gilgamesh:

> Why are your cheeks emaciated, your face cast down,
> Your spirit wretched, your features wasted, 230
> Sorrow in your heart,
> Your face like a traveler's from afar,
> Your features weathered by cold and sun,
> Why are you clad in a lion skin, roaming the steppe?

[*Gilgamesh tells Utanapishtim his story, wallowing in the luxury of self-pity on the difficulties of his quest. Thanks to his sacrifices, he says, the outcome will be that the human race will never thereafter have to know the pain of mourning a loved one.*]

Gilgamesh said to him, to Utanapishtim: 235

    Why should my cheeks not be emaciated, nor my face cast
        down,
    Nor my spirit wretched nor my features wasted?
    Why should there not be sorrow in my heart,
    Nor my face like a traveler's from afar,
    Nor my features weathered by cold and sun,   240
    Nor I be clad in a lion skin, roaming the steppe?
    My friend, swift wild donkey, mountain onager, panther
        of the steppe,
    Enkidu, swift wild donkey, mountain onager, panther
        of the steppe,
    My friend whom I so loved, who went with me through
        every hardship,
    Enkidu, whom I so loved, who went with me through every
        hardship,   245
    The fate of mankind has overtaken him.
    Six days and seven nights I wept for him,
    I would not give him up for burial,
    Until a worm fell out of his nose.
    I was frightened [. . .]   250
    I have grown afraid of dying, so I roam the steppe,
    My friend's plight weighs heavy upon me.
    A distant road I roam over the steppe,
    My friend Enkidu's plight weighs heavy upon me!
    A distant road I roam over the steppe,   255
    How can I be silent? How can I hold my peace?
    My friend whom I loved is turned into clay.
    Enkidu, my friend whom I loved, is turned into clay!
    Shall I too not lie down like him,
    And never get up forever and ever?   260

Gilgamesh said to him, to Utanapishtim:

    I said to myself: I will go see Utanapishtim the Distant
        One, of whom they tell.
    I set forth, I traversed all lands,
    I came over, one after another, wearisome mountains,
    Then I crossed, one after another, all the seas.   265

Too little sweet sleep has smoothed my countenance,
I have worn myself out in sleeplessness,
My muscles ache for misery,
What have I gained for my trials?
I had not reached the tavern keeper when my clothes were
        worn out,   270
I killed bear, hyena, lion, panther, tiger,
Deer, ibex, wild beasts of the steppe,
I ate their meat, I made a butchery of their skins.
Let them close the gates of sorrow,
Let them seal [its portal] tight with pitch and tar!   275
Thanks to me, they shall never [have to leave off] dancing
        [in their days],
Thanks to me, joyful, they shall spend [their nights in bliss]!

[*Utanapishtim responds in a long speech, poorly known because of dam-
age to the manuscripts. He chides Gilgamesh for his self-pity and ostenta-
tious mourning, all the more unseemly because the gods had favored him.
The village idiot, he points out, wears rags and eats bad food, but no one
accords him merit for that.*]

Utanapishtim said to him, to Gilgamesh:

Why, O Gilgamesh, do you go in pursuit of sorrow,
You who are [formed] of the flesh of gods and mankind,   280
You for whom (the gods) acted like father and mother?
When was it, Gilgamesh, you [turned into] a fool?
They set a throne for you in the assembly of elders [and said
        to you], "Please to take your seat."
The fool is given beer dregs instead of butter,
Bran and crusts instead of [. . .].   285
He wears sacking instead of a [. . .],
He girds himself with a [. . .] as if it were a sash of honor,
Because he has no sense [nor reason],
He has no good advice [. . .]
Think on him, Gilgamesh, [. . .]   290

[*In the fragmentary lines that follow, Utanapishtim evidently tells Gil-
gamesh to act like a king and maintain the sanctuaries of the gods, as
ordained from earliest times. After a gap in the text, Utanapishtim is
found discoursing on the nature of death.*]

You strive ceaselessly, what do you gain?
When you wear out your strength in ceaseless striving,
When you torture your limbs with pain,

You hasten the end of your days.
Mankind, whose descendants are snapped off like reeds in
    a canebrake,   295
The handsome young man, the lovely young woman,
Death will rob them of their [. . .] all too soon.
No one sees death,
No one sees the face [of death],
No one [hears] the voice of death,   300
But cruel death cuts off mankind.
There is a time for building a house,
There is a time for starting a family,
There is a time for brothers to divide an inheritance,
There is a time for disputes to prevail in this world.[2]   305
There is a time the river, having risen and brought
    high water,
Mayflies are drifting downstream on the river,
Their faces gazing at the sun,
Then, suddenly, there is nothing![3]
The missing and the dead, how alike they are!   310
They limn not death's image,
No one dead greets a living being in this world.
The supreme gods, the great gods, being convened,
The goddess-mother Mammitum, she who created their
    (own) destiny, ordained (with them):
They established death and life,   315
The time of death they did not make known.

2. Utanapishtim says acerbically that the final stage in the life cycle of two generations of
a family is a dispute over inheritance.
3. This refers to the sudden appearance in springtime of insects that soon die off in the
heat of summer.

Tablet XI

[*Gilgamesh, whose search for Utanapishtim has been characterized by increasing violence, finds to his astonishment that there is no battle to be fought; heroics will bring him no further. Now he needs knowledge. He asks Utanapishtim, the wisest man who ever lived, his great question: how did he alone escape the universal fate of the human race?*]

Gilgamesh said to him, to Utanapishtim the Distant One:

As I look upon you, Utanapishtim,
Your limbs are not different, you are just as I am,
Indeed, you are not different at all, you are just as I am!
My mind was made up to do battle with you,   5
[But now], in your presence, my arm is stayed.
You then, how did you join the ranks of the gods and find
      eternal life?

[*In answer, Utanapishtim relates the story of the Flood. According to Tablet I, among Gilgamesh's main achievements was bringing back to the human race the hitherto unknown history of this event. As told here, it is abbreviated. In the fuller account, preserved in an earlier Babylonian narrative poem called "Atrahasis,"[1] the gods sent the Flood because the human race had multiplied to such an extent that their noise and complaining were unbearable to Enlil, the chief god ruling on earth. After two attempts to reduce the population of the earth by plague and famine were thwarted by Enki (Ea), the god of wisdom and fresh water, Enlil ordered a deluge to obliterate the entire human race. Here Utanapishtim's tale begins. He lived at the long-vanished city of Shuruppak and was a favorite of the god Ea, who warned him of the coming Flood. Although he had taken an oath not to reveal the gods' plans, Ea circumvented this by addressing the wall of a reed enclosure Utanapishtim had built near a watercourse, evidently as a place to receive dreams and commands from his god directly or through divine water creatures. Utanapishtim is ordered to tear down his house, presumably to use the wood to build a boat. When his fellow citizens ask him what he is about, he is to reply in ambiguous terms, saying that he can no longer live on dry land because Enlil dislikes him. He foretells an imminent "shower of abundance."*]

---

1. Translated in *Muses*, pp. 160–203. Atrahasis was the name of the flood hero in the earlier story incorporated into the epic, so appears in line 49 instead of Utanapishtim.

Utanapishtim said to him, to Gilgamesh:

I will reveal to you, O Gilgamesh, a secret matter,
And a mystery of the gods I will tell you.   10
The city Shuruppak, a city yourself have knowledge of,
Which once was set on the [bank] of the Euphrates,
That same city was ancient and gods once were within it.[2]
The great gods resolved to send the deluge,
Their father Anu was sworn,   15
Their counselor the valiant Enlil,
Their throne-bearer Ninurta,
Their canal-officer Ennugi,
Their leader Ea was sworn with them.
He repeated their plans to the reed fence: 20
"Reed fence, reed fence, wall, wall!
"Listen, O reed fence! Pay attention, O wall!
"O man of Shuruppak, son of Ubar-Tutu,
"Wreck house, build boat,
"Forsake possessions and seek life,   25
"Belongings reject and life save!
"Take aboard the boat seed of all living things.
"The boat you shall build,
"Let her dimensions be measured out:
"Let her width and length be equal,   30
"Roof her over like the watery depths."
I understood full well, I said to Ea, my lord:
"Your command, my lord, exactly as you said it,
"I shall faithfully execute.
"What shall I answer the city—the populace and the elders?"   35
Ea made ready to speak,
Saying to me, his servant:
"Then you shall speak to them thus:
'I am sure that Enlil has come to dislike me,
'I shall not dwell in your city,   40
'I shall not even set my foot on the dry land of Enlil!
'I shall descend to the watery depths and dwell with my
    lord Ea.
'Upon you he shall shower down in abundance,
'A windfall of birds, a surprise of fishes,
'He shall pour upon you a harvest of riches,   45
'In the morning, cakes in spates,
'In the evening, grains in rains.'"

2. This means that this vanished city once had temples.

[*The entire community helps to build the boat, shaped like an enormous cube. The hull is constructed before the interior framing, as was customary at that time, with cordage used to sew the planks together and to truss the hull for strength.*]

At the first glimmer of dawn,
The land was assembling at the gate of Atrahasis:
The carpenter carried his adze,   50
The reed-cutter carried his stone,
The [shipwright?] carried his broadaxe,
The young men [. . .],
The old men brought the coiled palm-fiber,
The wealthy carried pitch,   55
The pauper brought stores [. . .].
In five days I planked her hull:
One full acre was her deck space,
Ten dozen cubits, the height of each of her sides,
Ten dozen cubits square, her outer dimensions.   60
I laid out her structure, I planned her design:
I decked her in six,
I divided her in seven,
Her interior I divided in nine.
I drove the water plugs into her,[3]   65
I saw to the spars and laid in the stores.
Thrice thirty-six hundred measures of tar I poured into
    the oven,
Thrice thirty-six hundred measures of tar [I poured out]
    inside her.
Thrice thirty-six hundred measures basket-bearers brought
    aboard for oil,
Not counting the thirty-six hundred measures of oil that
    the offering consumed,   70
And the twice thirty-six hundred measures of oil that the
    boat builder held in reserve.

[*A middle version gives a different description of building the ark, according to which it resembles a coracle, a circular river boat made of coiled reed basketry ribbed with wood, in use in Iraq until recent times. Utanapishtim is speaking, quoting Ea's instructions.*]

"Draw a plan of the boat that you will build, a plan of
    a circle.
"Let her length and breadth be equal,

---

3. The "water plugs" have been explained in various ways, for example, as caulking, stabilizers, depth markers, water taps, bilge drains, and drains to let out rainwater when the boat was beached. None of these is supported by Mesopotamian evidence.

"Let her deck area be one acre, let her sides be ten
  cubits high,
"Let thongs, each 120 cubits long, be interwoven
  [inside] her.   75
"Let my household twist the palm-fiber for you,
"It will surely take four times 3,600 plus thirty measures
  of fiber."
I laid out thirty ribs within her, ten times ten cubits long,
  twenty fingers thick,
I fastened 3,600 stanchions within her, ten fingers thick,
  half ten cubits long,
I walled in her compartments, above and below.   80
I allowed sixty times sixty measures of bitumen for her
  outside,
I allowed sixty times sixty measures of bitumen for her
  inside,
I had sixty times sixty measures of bitumen poured out for
  her compartments,
I had my kilns loaded with 28,800 measures of tar,
Then I poured out 3,600 measures of bitumen into her.   85
The bitumen did not come all the way up,
Five times sixty measures of lard I added . . . [4]

[*In the fragmentary lines that follow, it appears that the boat is caulked
with a mixture of tar and additives. As the standard version resumes,
Utanapishtim is feeding his workmen royally. What he does next is not
clear. Utanapishtim may himself help to apply a final layer of oil with
rollers to the exterior of the hull, using the amount set aside in line 71,
until it is coated two-thirds of its height, or the boat may be put on rollers
and launched so it settles in the water two-thirds of its height. In any
case, the boat is now ready for loading. Utanapishtim, again referred to as
"Atrahasis," loads on his family, his possessions, and every type of animal,
as well as skilled craftsmen to keep alive knowledge of the arts.*]

For the workmen I slaughtered bullocks,
I killed sheep upon sheep every day.
Beer, ale, oil, and wine   90
[I poured out] for the workers like river water,
They were feasting as if it were New Year!
One sunrise I set my hand to coating her (outside) with oil,
By sunset the boat was completed.
[. . .] were very difficult,   95
We kept moving the rollers up and down

4. For the construction of the ark, see Irving Finkel, *The Ark before Noah: Decoding the
   Story of the Flood*. London: Hodder and Stoughton, 2014.

Until two-thirds of her [was coated].
[Whatever] I had I loaded upon her,
What silver I had I loaded upon her,
What gold I had I loaded upon her,   100
I sent up on board all my family and kin,
Beasts of the steppe, wild animals of the steppe, all types
    of skilled craftsmen I sent up on board.

[*A fragmentary middle version gives more detail about this episode. In these
lines, the animals board the ark and are provisioned.*]

As for the wild animals of the steppe [. . .]
Two by two [they went up into the boat].
I had five [. . .] of beer [. . .]   105
They were carrying eleven or twelve [. . .]
Three measures of [. . .]-plants I [. . .]
One-third measure of fodder [. . .]

[*As is known from "Atrahasis," Utanapishtim is miserable to think that all
those who will remain on earth after the boat is launched are doomed to
drown. In a middle version, it appears that he prays to the moon to slow
down the passage of time until morning, but the moon is inexorable. The
standard version resumes.*]

Shamash set for me the appointed time:[5]
"In the morning, cakes in spates,   110
"In the evening, grains in rains,
"Go into your boat and seal the door from leaking!"
That appointed time arrived,
In the morning, cakes in spates,
In the evening, grains in rains.   115
I gazed upon the face of the storm,
The weather was dreadful to behold!
I went into the boat and sealed the door from leaking,
To the one who sealed the boat from leaking, to Puzur-Enlil
    the boatman,
I gave over the edifice, with all it contained.[6]   120

5. The reference to Shamash suggests that in some version of the story, now lost,
Shamash, rather than Enki, warned Utanapishtim of the Flood and told him how much
time he had to build his ship. This substitution of one god for the other may have been
suggested by Shamash's role as protector of Gilgamesh in the epic. In the "Atrahasis"
version of the story of the Flood, Enki sets a timing device, ironically a water clock, to
tell Utanapishtim how much time he has before the coming of the deluge.
6. The name Puzur-Enlil means "secret of Enlil," so is a wordplay on the oath of secrecy
taken by the gods not to reveal the coming of the Flood. Perhaps it is here to be under-
stood as "secret from Enlil." The "edifice" refers to the enormous boat, not to Utana-
pishtim's house, which he had destroyed and emptied of its valuables.

[*The Flood, accompanied by thunder and a fiery glow, overwhelms the earth. The gods are terrified by its violence and what they have done.*]

At the first glimmer of dawn,
A black cloud rose over the horizon.
Inside it Adad was thundering,
While the destroying gods Shullat and Hanish went in front,
Advancing as his throne-bearers over hill and plain.   125
Errakal was tearing out the mooring posts
   (of the world),
Ninurta, as he went, made the dikes overflow.
The supreme gods held torches aloft,
Setting the land ablaze with their glow.
Adad's awesome power passed over the heavens,   130
Whatever was bright was turned into gloom.
He charged over the land like an ox, he smashed [it like a
   clay pot]!
For one day the storm wind [blew],
Swiftly it blew, [the flood came forth],
The [onslaught] passed over the people like a battle.   135
No one could see the one next to him,
People could not recognize each other in the downpour.
The gods became frightened of the deluge,
They shrank back, went up to Anu's highest heaven,
The gods cowered like dogs slinking in the open.   140
The goddess, screaming like a woman in childbirth,
Sweet-voiced Belet-ili wailed aloud:[7]
"Would that day had come to naught,
"When I was one to speak up for an evil deed in the assembly
   of the gods!
"How could I have spoken up for an evil deed in the assembly
   of the gods   145
"And spoken up for an attack to destroy my people?
"It is I who bring them into the world, they are my people!
"(Now), like so many fish, they choke up the sea!"
The supreme gods were weeping with her,
In tearful sorrow, they were weeping [with her],   150
Their lips were parched, taking on a feverish warmth.
Six days and seven nights
The wind continued, the flood and windstorm [leveled
   the land].
When the seventh day arrived,

7. Belet-ili was the mother goddess who created the human race, along with Enki-Ea, so comparing her in this passage to a woman giving birth is irony.

The windstorm abated, that flood abated in battle,   155
The sea, that had churned like a woman in labor, grew calm,
The tempest stilled, the deluge ceased.

[*As the floodwaters recede, Utanapishtim can see land on the far horizon.
The boat is aground on a mountain.*]

I looked at the weather, stillness reigned,
And the whole human race had turned into clay.
The landscape was flat as a rooftop.   160
I opened a hatch, sunlight fell upon my face.
Falling to my knees, I sat down weeping,
Tears streaming down my face.
I looked at the edges of the world, the borders of
    the sea,
At fourteen places a point of land arose.   165
The boat had come to rest on Mount Nimush,
Mount Nimush held the boat fast, not letting it move.
One day, a second day Mount Nimush held the boat fast,
    not letting it move,
A third day, a fourth day Mount Nimush held the boat fast,
    not letting it move,
A fifth day, a sixth day Mount Nimush held the boat fast,
    not letting it move.   170

[*Utanapishtim sends out three birds to see if land has emerged near the
boat. He then quits the boat and makes an offering to the gods, who crowd
around it, famished.*]

When the seventh day arrived,
I brought out a dove and set it free,
The dove soared off in search of food,
No landing place appeared to it, so it came back.
I brought out a swallow and set it free,   175
The swallow soared off in search of food,
No landing place appeared to it, so it came back.
I brought out a raven and set it free,
The raven soared off and saw the ebbing of the waters.
It ate, scratched, and bobbed (its head), so it did not
    come back.   180
I brought out an offering and offered it to the four
    directions,
I set up an incense offering on the summit of the mountain.
I arranged seven and seven cult vessels,
I heaped reeds, cedar, and myrtle in their bowls.
The gods smelled the savor,   185

11. *I brought out a dove and set it free.* Detail of a wall painting from a
Mesopotamian palace.

> The gods smelled the sweet savor,
> The gods crowded around the sacrificer like flies.

[*The mother goddess blames Enlil for the Flood, saying her glittering neck-
lace of fly-shaped beads, which may stand for the rainbow, will memorial-
ize the human race drowned in the Flood.*]

> As soon as Belet-ili arrived,
> She held up the great fly-ornaments that Anu had made for
>   her in his ardor:
> "O gods, these shall be my lapis necklace, lest I forget,   190

"I shall be mindful of these days and not forget, not ever!
"The gods should come to the incense offering,
"(But) Enlil should not come to the incense offering,
"Because he brought on the Flood without thinking,
"And marked my people for destruction!"   195
As soon as Enlil arrived,
Enlil saw the boat and flew into a rage,
He was filled with fury at the gods.
"[From] where has a living creature escaped?
"No man was to survive destruction!"   200
Ninurta made ready to speak,
Said to the valiant Enlil:
"Who but Ea could contrive such a thing?
"For Ea alone knows every artifice."

[*Ea urges future limits: punish but do not kill, diminish but do not annihi-
late, use less drastic means to reduce the human population. Enlil grants
Utanapishtim and his wife eternal life but removes them far from the rest
of the human race.*]

Ea made ready to speak,   205
Said to the valiant Enlil:
"You, O valiant one, the wisest of the gods,
"How could you have brought on the Flood without thinking?
"Punish the wrongdoer for his wrongdoing,
"Punish the transgressor for his transgression.   210
"'Ease up for no snap, pull tight for no slack.'[8]
"Instead of your bringing on a flood,
"Let the lion strike to diminish the human race!
"Instead of your bringing on a flood,
"Let the wolf strike to diminish the human race!   215
"Instead of your bringing on a flood,
"Let famine strike to wreak havoc in the land!
"Instead of your bringing on a flood,
"Let pestilence strike to wreak havoc in the land!
"It was not I who *told* the secret of the great gods,   220
"I let Atrahasis have a dream and so he *heard* the
     secret of the gods.
"Now then, think what to do about him."
Then Enlil came up into the boat,
Leading me by my hands, he brought me out,
He brought out my wife, had her kneel beside me.   225

---

8. As suggested by Andrew George, this may be a proverbial expression, referring to keep-
ing up just the right tension on a rope to pull a barge efficiently (*Babylonian Gilgamesh
Epic*, p. 892).

He touched our brows, stood between us to bless us:
"Hitherto Utanapishtim has been a human being,
"Now Utanapishtim and his wife shall become like us gods.
"Utanapishtim shall dwell far distant at the mouth of the
    rivers."9
Thus it was they took me far distant and had me dwell at
    the mouth of the rivers.   230
Now then, who will convene the gods for your sake,
That you may find the eternal life you seek?
Come now, try not to sleep for six days and seven nights.

[*Utanapishtim has challenged Gilgamesh to go without sleep for a week;
if he fails this test, how could he expect to live forever? Even as he speaks,
Gilgamesh drifts off to sleep. Thus passes from the scene the all-night
rowdy of Tablet I.*]

As he sat there on his haunches,
Sleep was swirling over him like a mist.   235
Utanapishtim said to her, to his wife:

    Behold this fellow who wanted eternal life!
    Sleep swirls over him like a mist.

[*Utanapishtim's wife, taking pity on Gilgamesh, urges her husband to
awaken him and let him go home. Utanapishtim insists on a proof of how
long he slept, lest Gilgamesh claim that he had only dozed. She is to bake
him fresh bread every day and set it beside him, marking the wall for each
day. The bread spoils progressively as Gilgamesh sleeps for seven days.*]

His wife said to him, to Utanapishtim the Distant One:

    Do touch him so the man wakes up,   240
    Let him return safe on the way whence he came,
    By the portal he came through, let him return to his land.

Utanapishtim said to her, to his wife:

    Since the human race is duplicitous, he'll endeavor to
      dupe you,
    Come now, bake his daily loaves, put them one after
      another by his head,   245
    Then mark the wall for each day he has slept.

---

9. "Mouth" in Babylonian may be either the rising or ending point of a river; to the Meso-
potamians, the sources of the Tigris and Euphrates were very remote places, unlike
their outlets in the Gulf, so this location was probably imagined to be far away to the
north and west.

She baked his daily loaves for him, put them one after another
   by his head,
And made known for him on the wall the days he had slept.
The first loaf was dried hard,
The second was leathery, the third soggy,   250
The crust of the fourth had turned white,
The fifth was gray with mold, the sixth was fresh,
The seventh was still on the coals when he touched him, the
   man woke up.

[*Claiming at first that he has scarcely dozed a moment, Gilgamesh sees the
bread and realizes that he has slept the entire time he was supposed to stay
awake for the test. He gives up in despair. What course is left for him?
Utanapishtim does not answer directly, but orders the boatman to take him
home. Further, the boatman himself is never to return. Thus access to
Utanapishtim is denied the human race forever. Gilgamesh is bathed and
given clothing that will stay magically fresh until his return to Uruk.*]

Gilgamesh said to him, to Utanapishtim the Distant One:

   Scarcely had sleep stolen over me,   255
   When straightaway you touched me and roused me.

Utanapishtim said to him, to Gilgamesh:

   [Up with you], Gilgamesh, count for me your daily loaves,
   [That the days you have slept] may be known to you.
   The first loaf is dried hard,   260
   The second is leathery, the third soggy,
   The crust of the fourth has turned white,
   The fifth is gray with mold,
   The sixth is fresh,
   The seventh was still on the coals when I touched you
     and you woke up.   265

Gilgamesh said to him, to Utanapishtim the Distant One:

   How should I carry on, Utanapishtim, wherever should I go,
   [Now that] the Bereaver has taken hold of my [flesh]?[1]
   Death lurks in my bedchamber,
   And wherever I turn, there is death!   270

---

1. "The Bereaver" is an epithet of death. It could also mean something like "kidnapper."

Utanapishtim said to him, to Ur-Shanabi the boatman:

> Ur-Shanabi, may the harbor cast you off, may the
>   crossing despise you,
> Be banished from the shore you shuttled to.
> The man you brought here,
> His body is matted with filthy hair,   275
> Hides have marred the beauty of his flesh.
> Take him in hand, Ur-Shanabi, bring him to the washing bowl,
> Have him wash out his filthy hair with water, clean as clean
>   can be,
> Have him throw away his hides, let the sea carry them off,
> Let his fine body be rinsed clean.   280
> Let his headband be new,
> Have him put on raiment worthy of his dignity.
> Until he reaches his city,
> Until he completes his journey,
> Let the raiment stay spotless, fresh and new.   285

Ur-Shanabi took him in hand and brought him to the
    washing bowl,
He washed out his filthy hair with water, clean as clean can be,
He threw away his hides, the sea carried them off,
His fine body was rinsed clean.
He renewed his headband,   290
He put on raiment worthy of his dignity.
Until he reached his city,
Until he completed his journey,
The raiment would stay spotless, fresh and new.

[*Gilgamesh and Ur-Shanabi embark on their journey to Uruk. As they
push off from the shore, Utanapishtim's wife intervenes, asking her dour
husband to give the hero something to show for his quest. Gilgamesh brings
the boat back to the shore and waits expectantly. Utanapishtim tells him of
a plant of rejuvenation. Gilgamesh dives for the plant by opening a shaft
through the earth's surface to the water below. He ties stones to his feet, a
technique traditionally used by pearl divers in the Gulf. When he comes
up from securing the plant, he is on the opposite side of the ocean, where
he started from.*]

Gilgamesh and Ur-Shanabi embarked on the boat,   295
They launched the craft, it was they who manned it.
His wife said to him, to Utanapishtim the Distant One:

> Gilgamesh has come here, spent with exertion,
> What have you given him for his homeward journey?

At that he, Gilgamesh, lifted the pole,   300
Bringing the boat back to the shore.
Utanapishtim said to him, to Gilgamesh:

> Gilgamesh, you have come here, spent with exertion,
> What have I given you for your homeward journey?
> I will reveal to you, O Gilgamesh, a secret matter,   305
> And a mystery [of the gods] I will tell you.
> There is a certain plant, its [shape] is like a thorn bush,
> Its thorns are like the wild rose and will prick [your hand].
> If you can secure this plant,
> [When you eat it, you will return to how you were in your
>   youth].   310

No sooner had Gilgamesh heard this,
He opened a shaft, [threw away his tools].
He tied heavy stones [to his feet],
They pulled him down into the watery depths [. . .]
He took hold of the plant and pulled it up, [it pricked his
    hand],   315
He cut the heavy stones [from his feet],
The sea cast him up on its shore.

[*Gilgamesh resolves to take the plant to Uruk to experiment on an old
man before eating it himself. While Gilgamesh is bathing on the home-
ward journey, a snake eats the plant and rejuvenates itself by shedding its
skin. He cannot get more of the plant because immense quantities of
water have flooded up through the shaft he dug and covered the place. He
has also thrown away his tools, so cannot dig another shaft. He gives up,
wishing that he had abandoned the quest before taking the boat to meet
Utanapishtim.*]

Gilgamesh said to him, to Ur-Shanabi the boatman:

> Ur-Shanabi, this plant is a cure for heartache,
> Whereby a man can regain his vitality.   320
> I will take it to ramparted Uruk,
> I will have an old man eat some and so test the plant,
> His name shall be "Old Man Has Become
>   Young-Again-Man."
> I myself will eat it and return to how I was in my youth.

At twenty double leagues they took a bite to eat,   325
At thirty double leagues they made their camp.
Gilgamesh saw a pond whose water was cool,

He went down into it to bathe in the water.
A snake caught the scent of the plant,
[Stealthily] it came up and carried the plant away,   330
On its way back it shed its skin.
Thereupon Gilgamesh sat down weeping,
His tears streaming down his face.
He said to Ur-Shanabi the boatman:

> For whom, Ur-Shanabi, have my arms been toiling?   335
> For whom has my heart's blood been poured out?
> For myself I have obtained no benefit,
> I have done a good deed for a reptile!
> Now, the floodwaters rise against me for twenty double
>   leagues,
> When I opened the shaft I threw away the tools.   340
> How shall I find my bearings?
> Had I only turned away, and left the boat on the shore!

[*At last reaching Uruk, Gilgamesh invites Ur-Shanabi to admire the city
and its great walls, using the same words as the narrator at the beginning of
the epic.*]

At twenty double leagues they took a bite to eat,
At thirty double leagues they made their camp.
When they arrived in ramparted Uruk,   345
Gilgamesh said to him, to Ur-Shanabi the boatman:

> boatman
> Go up, Ur-Shanabi, pace out the walls of Uruk.
> Study the foundation terrace and examine the brickwork.
> Is not its masonry of kiln-fired brick?
> And did not seven masters lay its foundations?   350
> One square mile of city, one square mile of gardens,
> One square mile of clay pits, a half square mile of Ishtar's
>   dwelling,
> Three and a half square miles is the measure of Uruk!

ANALOGUES TO
THE EPIC OF GILGAMESH

The Sumerian Gilgamesh Poems

Five Sumerian epic poems celebrate exploits of Gilgamesh. They have been reconstructed from tablets mostly dating to the nineteenth and eighteenth centuries B.C.E. The epics themselves may have been composed about three hundred years earlier, during the period of the Third Dynasty of Ur (ca. 2112–2004 B.C.E.). The Sumerian poems are short compared to the Babylonian epic, ranging from about 120 to 400 lines, and generally treat only what became individual episodes of its larger narrative. They also contain incidents not included in the Babylonian epic. Today, they often seem light-hearted yet eloquent, combining traditional story motifs with elements of the absurd, but important themes, such as Gilgamesh's valor and vainglory, as well as his fear of dying, lend the best of them a certain gravity, even a tone of somber resignation. There are also moments of ribald humor ("Gilgamesh and the Bull of Heaven," line 112) and biting irony ("Gilgamesh and Huwawa," line 133). Some passages may allude to contemporaneous personalities or political, religious, or social issues, but these lie beyond the ken of a modern reader.

The richness and variety of the Sumerian traditions about Gilgamesh can be gauged from two summaries of his deeds in "The Death of Gilgamesh" (lines 3–10, 35–44), which mention some dozen achievements, only four of which are recounted in the Sumerian poems now known. On the other hand, his victories over Akka of Kish and the Bull of Heaven, the subjects of two of these poems, are not mentioned there.

Some of these texts quote each other, for example, "Gilgamesh, Enkidu, and the Netherworld," lines 134–35 are found in "Gilgamesh and Huwawa," lines 184–85. The opening lines of "Gilgamesh and Huwawa" are used in "Gilgamesh and the Bull of Heaven," lines 166–69, and Gilgamesh's battle gear is described the same way in "Gilgamesh, Enkidu, and the Netherworld," lines 126–28 and "Gilgamesh and the Bull of Heaven," lines 131–34. These five poems do not, however, form a connected "series" like the Babylonian epic.

The Sumerian language is much less well understood than Babylonian, so substantially different renderings of these poems are possible. Most of the surviving manuscripts are the handiwork of advanced Babylonian-speaking students who were studying Sumerian as an essential component of their formal education. They contain many variants and show that the young scholars and their teachers could understand the same passages in quite different ways, just as modern philologists do. The compositions themselves were fluid; whole episodes could be added, deleted, reinterpreted, or expanded. These translations combine a choice of material from various manuscripts into coherent narratives.

Gilgamesh and Akka[†]

This short epic narrates an unsuccessful siege of Uruk by the army of King Akka of Kish. While the story of the siege does not have a counterpart in the later Babylonian *Epic of Gilgamesh*, the incident of Gilgamesh's seeking approval from the city elders and the young men of Uruk finds an echo in Tablet II of the Babylonian epic but in connection with the expedition to the cedar forest.

The narrative is set in the mid-third millennium B.C.E., when the powerful city-state of Kish, in northern Babylonia, competed with Uruk, the largest city in the south, for hegemony over the land.

[*The story begins abruptly with envoys from Kish arriving in Uruk. Nothing is said of their message, but they evidently demand Uruk's submission and threaten war. Gilgamesh seeks support for going to war, first from the city elders then from the city's men of fighting age. The elders advise submission; the young men call for defiance.*]

Akka, son of Enmebaragesi,
Sent envoys to Gilgamesh from Kish to Uruk.
Gilgamesh presented the matter before the elders of his city,
Seeking just the right words:

There are wells to be used up, many wells of the land to be
     used up,   5
Many shallow wells with bucket-sweeps of the land to be
     used up,
Many deep wells with rope-hoists to be used up![1]

---

† Translated by Douglas Frayne for the first Norton Critical Edition of *Gilgamesh*. These translations have been significantly revised and annotated by Benjamin R. Foster for this new Norton Critical Edition.

1. This debated passage is here understood, following a proposal of W. G. Lambert ("Akka's Threat," *Orientalia* 49 [1980]: 339–40), to mean that Uruk has wells enough to withstand any siege, so should defy Kish; the same expression is used in "Gilgamesh and Huwawa," line 254, when Huwawa has "used up" his direful radiances. Other translators, however, believe that the wells are to be dug at Kish by the forced labor of the citizens of Uruk or that the wells are at Uruk but have not been "finished" yet. Gilgamesh is boasting that there are many wells, no doubt thanks to him, some just holes in the ground, some deep enough to require a bucket attached to a pivoting pole with a counterpoise, like the Egyptian shadoof, and others so deep as to require a windlass.

(Shall we say): We will not submit to the house of Kish
(or) We will not go to war?

In the convened assembly, the elders of his city   10
Answered Gilgamesh:

(Though) there are wells to be used up, many wells of the
    land to be used up,
Many shallow wells with bucket-sweeps of the land to be
    used up,
Many deep wells with rope-hoists to be used up!
(Let us say): We will submit to the house of Kish!   15
We will not go to war!

Gilgamesh, lord of Kullab,
Trusting in the goddess Inanna,
Did not take the judgment of the elders of his city to heart.
Gilgamesh presented the matter a second time before the
    young men of his city,   20
Seeking just the right words:

There are wells to be used up, many wells of the land to be
    used up,
Many shallow wells with bucket-sweeps of the land to be
    used up,
Many deep wells with rope-hoists to be used up!
(Shall we say): We will not submit to the house of Kish   25
(or) We will not go to war?

In the convened assembly, the young men of his city
Made reply to Gilgamesh:

As the saying goes:
There are those who stand up tall, there are those who stay
    seated,   30
There are those who ride with princes, there are those who
    hobble donkeys.
Who of these will have the spirit for this?[2]
We will not submit to the house of Kish!
Shall we not go to war?
Uruk, the masterpiece of the gods,   35
Eanna, the house come down from heaven,

---

2. This means that some people, such as the young men, are energetic and show courage,
whereas others, such as the old men, do not wish to exert themselves.

It was the great gods who wrought their fabric!
You are entrusted with its great rampart, that cloudbank
    reposing on earth,
And its paramount dwelling, which An himself has founded,
You are the king their champion,   40
Man with a mane, prince beloved of An![3]
If (Akka) does come, how could he inspire fear?
That army is puny, it falls apart from the rear,[4]
Its men will never look you in the eye!

[*Gilgamesh, delighted with this flowery speech, prepares for war.*]

Then did the spirits of Gilgamesh, lord of Kullab, brighten,   45
The judgment of the young men of his city was pleasing to
    his heart.
He addressed his servant Enkidu:

    Now then, let the implements and gear of war be at the ready,
    Let the weapon of war be once again at your side,
    May they give off a fearsome radiance, a monstrous dread.   50
    As for him, when he comes, a monstrous dread of me will
        surely overwhelm him,
    His mind surely will confounded be, his judgment
        discomposed!

[*The army of Kish arrives with wonderful speed. Despite the young men's
bravado, Uruk is dismayed. Gilgamesh calls for a volunteer to parley with
Akka.*]

Not five days, not ten days, had gone by,
When Akka, son of Enmebaragesi, (and his men) laid siege to
    Uruk.
It was Uruk's mind that was confounded.   55
Gilgamesh, lord of Kullab,
Addressed its warriors:

    You, my chosen warriors!
    Let one stout-hearted man volunteer: "I will go to Akka."

Birhurturra, his royal retainer,[5]   60
Spoke up pleasingly to his king:

3. Gilgamesh's hair is compared to a lion's mane, anticipating the description of him in
   the epic, Tablet I, line 55, in which his lush hair is compared to a field of grain.
4. A valiant force would first break in the forward ranks, not the rear.
5. Some scholars see in this strange name the Sumerian word for "butterfly," so it may
   conceal a joke.

My king! I will strut my way to Akka.
His mind surely will confounded be, his judgment
   discomposed!

[*The troops of Kish treat Birhurturra disrespectfully. When he is brought
before Akka, he is unable to finish his speech because Akka is distracted
by the sight of the chief butler on the city wall.*]

Birhurturra went out through the city gate.
No sooner had Birhurturra gone out through the city gate   65
Than they seized him at the door,
They knocked off Birhurturra's cockaded helmet.
He was brought before Akka,
He began to address Akka.
He had not finished his speech when the chief butler of
   Uruk mounted the rampart, leaned out over the rampart.[6]   70
Akka caught sight of him, addressed Birhurturra:

   Varlet, is that man your king?

   That man is not my king!
   Were that man my king,
   His would be a terrifying brow,   75
   His would be a bison's stare,
   His would be a dark blue beard,
   His would be fingers magnificent!
   No multitudes fell,
   No multitudes rose up,   80
   No multitudes rolled in the dirt!
   All the world was not overwhelmed,
   The mouths of the land were not filled with dirt!
   He sheared off no prows of transport barges,
   He did not take Akka, king of Kish, prisoner amidst his troops!   85

They beat him, they thrashed him,
They knocked off Birhurturra's cockaded helmet.

[*Gilgamesh shows himself to the enemy. The predicted consequences come
to pass.*]

---

6. The personage translated here as "chief butler" had nominal charge of the metal uten-
   sils used in preparing, serving, and consuming palace food, though he may also be a
   high court official. That the butler could be mistaken for the king was presumably a
   humorous touch.

Gilgamesh mounted the rampart after the chief butler of Uruk,
His fearsome radiance overwhelmed all the old and young
  of Kullab.
He armed the young men of Uruk with weaponry for war,   90
He stationed them at the roadway through the door of the
  city gate.
Enkidu went out alone through the city gate,
Gilgamesh leaned out over the rampart.
Akka caught sight of him:

  Varlet, is that man your king?   95

  That man is indeed my king.

Just as he had said it, so it was.
Multitudes fell,
Multitudes rose up,
Multitudes rolled in the dirt.   100
All the world was overwhelmed,
The mouths of the land were filled with dirt,
He sheared off the prows of transport barges,
He took Akka, king of Kish, prisoner amidst his troops!

[*Gilgamesh and Akka exchange compliments.*]

Gilgamesh, lord of Kullab,   105
Addressed Akka:

  Shall Akka be my overseer? Shall Akka be my captain?
  Shall Akka be my governor? Shall Akka be general of my
    troops?
  Akka, you gave me breath, Akka, you gave me life,
  Akka took the fugitive into his embrace,   110
  Akka provided the fugitive bird with grain.[7]

[*Akka responds:*][8]

---

7. The meaning of this passage is debated. One ancient scribe apparently read lines 107–09
as questions, as taken here, suggesting that Akka deserves a better fate than being
impressed into the army of Uruk; other scribes understood them to be statements. In any
case, as in line 118 below, there is a clear implication that the king of Kish had once shel-
tered Gilgamesh, though this may be irony if he was actually a prisoner at some point.
8. The different scribes who copied the surviving manuscripts understood what is said
and who is speaking lines in 112–17 differently from each other, so the translator has
to make a choice among several possibilities. Some translators believe that the young
men sing Gilgamesh's praises during his colloquy with Akka, as they had in lines
35–41. As in Tablet V of the Babylonian epic, Gilgamesh's sparing the defeated enemy
is a sign of his innate nobility; compare also Enkidu's speech of submission. Tablet II,
lines 107–10.

Uruk, the masterpiece of the gods,
You are entrusted with its great rampart, that cloudbank
   reposing on earth,
And its paramount dwelling, which An himself has founded.
You are the king their champion,   115
A man with a mane, a prince beloved of An!
Will you grant me grace?

[*Gilgamesh releases him.*]

Before Utu, I hereby grant you grace, (as you did me) in
   time gone by.

He let Akka go free to Kish.

O Gilgamesh, lord of Kullab,   120
How sweet it is to sing your praises!

Gilgamesh, Enkidu, and the Netherworld

"Gilgamesh, Enkidu, and the Netherworld" predates the Babylonian
epic, but beginning at line 161, a version of it was translated into Baby-
lonian and appended to *The Epic of Gilgamesh* as Tablet XII (omitted in
this Norton Critical Edition). The Babylonian translator used a Sume-
rian original different from the older ones used here. This translation
follows the older versions where possible. Passages incorporated here
from the Babylonian translation are printed in italic.

Parts of this story are related to the Babylonian epic's account of
Gilgamesh's oppression of Uruk, Enkidu's death, and Gilgamesh's
mourning in Tablets I, VII, and VIII, respectively.

Beginning with primeval times when the universe was created, the
poem opens with Enki, the god of wisdom, journeying in his boat
toward the netherworld. He is battered by a storm that also buffets a
solitary tree growing by the Euphrates River. Inanna finds the tree and
plants it in her grove at Uruk. She plans to use its wood to make a chair
and bed for herself. After ten years the tree is ready to be cut, but a
snake, a monster-bird, and a demon-girl have made their homes in it.
When Inanna's brother, Utu, refuses to help her, Inanna turns to Gil-
gamesh, who drives away the creatures and cuts down the tree. Taking
part of the wood for himself, he has a ball and a stick made. Gilgamesh
and his friends play incessantly with them in the city square, riding
piggyback on the fatherless of Uruk as part of the game. The mothers
and sisters of the oppressed cry out to the gods for relief, and the ball
and stick drop down into the netherworld.

Enkidu volunteers to bring them back. He ignores Gilgamesh's advice
as to how to behave in the netherworld and so is trapped there. Gil-
gamesh, distraught at the loss of his friend, asks the gods Enlil and Sin

for help but in vain. Enki, however, arranges for Enkidu to come back.
Gilgamesh questions him about what happens to people after they die,
and Enkidu describes the grim lot in store for them. Gilgamesh, moved
by the eternal misery of the dead, makes offerings in Uruk to his dead
ancestors.

In one manuscript, "Gilgamesh and Huwawa" was considered a
direct continuation of this story, implying that Enkidu's account of the
dreariness and deprivation of the land of the dead motivated Gil-
gamesh's expedition to the cedar forest as a quest for immortal fame in
this world.

[*Prologue. A tempest.*]

In those days, in those far-off days,
In those nights, in those distant nights,
In those years, in those far-off years,
In most ancient times, when what was needful had first
    come forth,
In most ancient times, when what was needful had been
    tenderly cared for,   5
Bread had first been tasted in the shrines of the land,
Ovens in the land had first been stoked,
Heaven had been separated from earth,
Earth had been measured off from heaven,
The name "mankind" had been established,   10
When An had carried off the heavens for himself,
Enlil had carried off the earth for himself,
Whereas the netherworld they had given to Ereshkigal as
    their dowry gift,
He, having embarked, having embarked,
The father, having embarked for the netherworld,   15
Enki, having embarked for the netherworld,
Little things rained down on the king,
Big things rained down on Enki,
Those little things were like grinding stones,
Those big things were like smashing stones,   20
The hull of Enki's little boat went under, then under again,
    like a bobbing turtle,
The water at the prow snapped at the king like a wolf,
The water at the stern struck at Enki like a lion!

[*Inanna and her cherry tree.*]

At that time, there was a solitary tree, a solitary cherry tree, a
    solitary tree,
Growing on the bank of the gleaming Euphrates,   25

Watered by the Euphrates.
The force of the south wind uprooted it, stripped away its
    branches,
The Euphrates battered it with water.
The woman heedful of An's commands was walking along,
She who was heedful of Enlil's commands was walking along.   30
She picked up the tree, she brought it to Uruk,
There she brought it into Inanna's sacred grove.
The woman did not plant the tree with her hand, she planted
    it with her foot,
The woman did not water the tree with her hand, she watered
    it with her foot.[1]
She said: "How long till there is a gorgeous chair for me to
    sit on?"   35
She said: "How long till there is a gorgeous bed for me to
    lie on?"
Five years, ten years passed,
The tree had grown massive, its bark had no splits.
At its roots a snake immune to spells had built its nest,
In its branches the lion-headed monster-bird Anzu had
    placed its young,   40
In its trunk a demon-girl had made her home.
The smiling maiden with a happy heart,
She, radiant Inanna, wept and wept.

[*Inanna asks her brother, the sun god Utu, for help.*][2]

As dawn broke and the horizon brightened,
When, at daybreak, the little birds were twittering,   45
Utu having quit his chamber,
His sister, radiant Inanna,
Addressed the youthful warrior Utu:

> My brother, in those far-off days when destiny was decided,
> When abundance overflowed in the land,   50
> When An had carried off the heavens for himself,
> Enlil had carried off the earth for himself,
> Whereas the netherworld they had given to Ereshkigal as
>   their dowry gift,
> He, having embarked, having embarked,

1. This means that she took special care to give it abundant water; compare Deuteronomy
   11:10.
2. Sumerian manuscripts often did not adjust the grammatical person of repeated pas-
   sages or did not do so consistently, but this has been done in this translation for the
   sake of clarity. Inanna's speeches, unlike the main narrative, are in a dialect usually
   reserved for female speakers in literature but also more widely used in ritual laments.

The father, having embarked for the netherworld,   55
Enki, having embarked for the netherworld,
Little things rained down on the king,
Big things rained down on Enki,
Those little things were like grinding stones,
Those big things were like smashing stones,   60
The hull of Enki's little boat went under, then under again,
    like a bobbing turtle,
The water at the prow snapped at the king like a wolf,
The water at the stern struck at Enki like a lion!
At that time, there was a solitary tree, a solitary cherry tree,
    a solitary tree,
Growing on the bank of the gleaming Euphrates,   65
Watered by the Euphrates.
The force of the south wind uprooted it, stripped away its
    branches,
The Euphrates battered it with water.
I, the woman heedful of An's commands, was walking along,
I who was heedful of Enlil's commands was walking along.   70
I picked up the tree, I brought it to Uruk,
There I brought it into the lady's sacred grove.
I, the woman, did not plant the tree with my hand, I
    planted it with my foot,
I, the woman, did not water the tree with my hand, I
    watered it with my foot.
I said: "How long till there is a gorgeous chair for me to
    sit on?"   75
I said: "How long till there is a gorgeous bed for me to lie on?"
Five years, ten years passed,
The tree had grown massive, its bark had no splits.
At its roots a snake immune to spells had built its nest,
In its branches the lion-headed monster-bird Anzu had
    placed its young,   80
In its trunk a demon-girl had made her home.
The smiling maiden with a happy heart,
I, radiant Inanna, wept and wept.

Her brother, the youthful hero Utu, did not come to her aid in
    that matter.

[*Inanna asks Gilgamesh for help.*]

As dawn broke and the horizon brightened,   85
When, at daybreak, the little birds were twittering,
Utu having quit his chamber,

His sister, radiant Inanna,
Addressed the youthful warrior Gilgamesh:

My brother, in those far-off days when destiny was decided,   90
When abundance overflowed in the land,
When An had carried off the heavens for himself,
Enlil had carried off the earth for himself,
Whereas the netherworld they had given to Ereshkigal as
    their dowry gift,
He, having embarked, having embarked,   95
The father, having embarked for the netherworld,
Enki, having embarked for the netherworld,
Little things rained down on the king,
Big things rained down on Enki,
Those little things were like grinding stones,   100
Those big things were like smashing stones,
The hull of Enki's little boat went under, then under again,
    like a bobbing turtle,
The water at the prow snapped at the king like a wolf,
The water at the stern sprang at Enki like a lion!
At that time, there was a solitary tree, a solitary cherry tree,
    a solitary tree,   105
Growing on the bank of the gleaming Euphrates,
Watered by the Euphrates.
The force of the south wind uprooted it, stripped away its
    branches,
The Euphrates battered it with water.
I, the woman heedful of An's commands, was walking
    along,   110
I who was heedful of Enlil's commands was walking along.
I picked up the tree, I brought it to Uruk,
There I brought it into the lady's sacred grove.
I, the woman, did not plant the tree with my hand, I
    planted it with my foot,
I, the woman, did not water the tree with my hand, I
    watered it with my foot.   115
I said: "How long till there is a gorgeous chair for me to sit
    on?"
I said: "How long till there is a gorgeous bed for me to sleep
    on?"
Five years, ten years passed,
The tree had grown massive, its bark had no splits.
At its roots a snake immune to spells had built its nest,   120
In its branches the lion-headed monster-bird Anzu had
    placed its young,

In its trunk a demon-girl had made her home.
The smiling maiden with a happy heart,
I, radiant Inanna, wept and wept.

Her brother, Gilgamesh, came to her aid in that matter.   125

[*Gilgamesh expels the creatures from the tree.*]

He tied around his waist his fifty-pound belt,
He strapped on its fifty-pound weight (with ease).
He took up his bronze battle axe weighing seven talents and
     seven pounds.[3]
At its roots, he smote the snake immune to spells,
In its branches, the lion-headed monster-bird Anzu took its
     young, flew off to the mountains.   130
In its trunk, he forced the demon-girl to forsake her dwelling,
She made her escape to the open country.

[*Gilgamesh gives part of the tree to Inanna and keeps part to make a game stick and ball.*]

He uprooted the tree, stripped away its branches,
The men of his city who accompanied him
Lopped off its shoots, tied them up in bundles, heaped them
     into piles.   135
Giving some to his sister, radiant Inanna, for her chair,
Giving some to her for her bed,
He, for his part, had himself a ball made from its roots,
He had himself a game stick made from its branches.

[*Gilgamesh and the young men of the city bully the fatherless with his game. Their mothers and sisters pray successfully for the ball and stick to drop down into the netherworld.*][4]

Wanting to play with the ball, he did not stop playing ball in
     the city square,   140
Wanting to brag about himself, he did not stop bragging about
     himself in the city square.
The young men of his city who wanted to play ball,

---

3. The axe weighed well over 470 pounds (about 213 kilograms). Compare "Gilgamesh and the Bull of Heaven," lines 131–34.
4. The precise nature of this game is unknown except that it seems to involve a bat or mallet and a wooden ball or puck. Gilgamesh and the young men of the city evidently come up with a variation of it in which they play riding on the backs of boys who have no fathers to intervene on their behalf, though some manuscripts suggest that he is the only one playing.

Rode piggyback on teams of the fatherless,
"Oh, my neck, oh, my hips!" (the fatherless) moaned.
The one who had a mother, she brought food to her son,   145
The one who had a sister, she poured water for her brother.
As dusk was approaching,
He marked the place where the ball was standing,
Holding his ball up in front of him, he took it home.
At dawn, as he was ready to mount piggyback where the mark
    was made,   150
From the plaints of the widows,
From the pleas of the young girls,
His ball and his stick had fallen down to the bottom of the
    netherworld.
He tried with his hand, he could not reach them,
He tried with his foot, he could not reach them,   155
He sat himself down at the gate to the infernal regions, the
    entrance to the netherworld,
Gilgamesh burst into tears, set to weeping and weeping:

    Oh, my ball, oh, my stick!
    My ball, which still gave me pleasure,
    The game that had not bored me yet!   160
    Now if only my ball were there for me in the carpenter's
        shop,
    O carpenter's wife, like my very own mother, if only it were
        there for me!
    O carpenter's child, like my very own little sister, if only it
        were there for me![5]
    My ball has fallen down into the netherworld, who will
        bring it up for me?
    My stick has fallen down into the infernal regions, who will
        bring it up for me?   165

[*Enkidu offers to retrieve them. Gilgamesh gives him advice about how
to comport himself decorously in the netherworld. He should act as if he
is in mourning or dead and not attract attention to himself as someone
who has not yet died.*]

His servant, Enkidu, answered him:

    My king, why do you weep so? Why are you sick at heart?
    This very day I myself will bring your ball back up from the
        netherworld,

5. Gilgamesh may be saying that he wishes the ball were still being made, as he now
understands how to behave with it more responsibly, or he may have taken the ball to
return it to the carpenter for reworking prior to the next day's play and wishes it were
still there. The Babylonian translator understood: "If only I had left it in . . . ."

I myself will bring your stick back up from the infernal
  regions!

Gilgamesh answered Enkidu: 170

  If today you descend to the netherworld,
  Let me give you advice, be sure to take my advice to heart,
  Let me tell you some watchwords, be sure to take my watch-
    words to heart.
  Do not wear clean clothes,
  They will surely see it as the sign of an outsider.   175
  Do not anoint yourself with sweet-scented oil from a flacon,
  They will surely encircle you when they smell it.
  Do not fling a throw stick in the netherworld,
  Those killed by a throw stick will surely encircle you.[6]
  Do not hold a willow wand in your hand,   180
  The ghosts will be agitated because of you.[7]
  Wear no sandals on your feet,
  You should make no loud noise in the netherworld.
  Do not kiss your wife you loved,
  Do not strike your wife you hated,   185
  Do not kiss your son you loved,
  Do not strike your son you hated,
  An outcry in the netherworld will surely hold you fast.
  She who lies there, she who lies there, the mother of
    Ninazu who lies there,[8]
  Her radiant shoulders are not clothed,   190
  No linen garment is spread over her radiant bosom,
  She has fingers like trowels,
  She rips out her hair like leeks.

[*Enkidu ignores Gilgamesh's advice.*]

  He wore clean clothes,
  They saw it as the sign of an outsider.   195
  He anointed himself with sweet-scented oil from
    a flacon,
  They encircled him when they smelled it.
  He flung a throw stick in the netherworld,
  Those killed by a throw stick encircled him.

---

6. A throw stick was a curved wooden weapon resembling a boomerang, used in hunting
   and warfare.
7. Sticks of willow wood were used in exorcism, so would be offensive to ghosts (Gadotti).
8. This refers to Ereshkigal (above, line 13). Though she is queen of the netherworld, even
   she acts as if she is in mourning.

He held a willow wand in his hand,   200
The ghosts were agitated because of him.
He wore sandals on his feet,
He made a loud noise in the netherworld.
He kissed his wife he loved,
He struck his wife he hated,   205
He kissed his son he loved,
He struck his son he hated,
An outcry in the netherworld held him fast.
The mother of Ninazu who lay there,
Her radiant shoulders were not clothed,   210
No linen garment was spread over her radiant bosom,
She had fingers like trowels,
She ripped out her hair like leeks.

[*Gilgamesh mourns Enkidu, trapped in the netherworld.*]

From that ill-omened day to the seventh day thereafter,
His servant Enkidu did not ascend from the netherworld.   215
The king wailed and wept bitterly:

My beloved servant, my faithful companion, the one who
    advised me, the netherworld has seized him!
The messenger of death did not seize him, the demon of
    disease did not seize him, the netherworld seized him!
The merciless agent of the plague god did not seize him, the
    netherworld seized him!
He did not fall in the field of manly battle, the netherworld
    seized him!   220

[*Gilgamesh, saying that Enkidu is not really dead but trapped in the neth-
erworld, seeks help from the gods Enlil and Sin, to no avail.*]

All alone the warrior Gilgamesh, son of Ninsun,
Made his way to Ekur, the house of Enlil.
Before Enlil he wept:

O father Enlil, my ball has fallen into the netherworld,
    my stick has fallen into the infernal regions.
Enkidu went to bring them back up, the netherworld
    seized him!   225
The messenger of death did not seize him, the demon of
    disease did not seize him, the netherworld seized him!
The merciless agent of the plague god did not seize him,
    the netherworld seized him!

He did not fall in the place of manly battle, the netherworld
seized him!

Father Enlil did not come to his aid in that matter, *he went off*
to Ur.
All alone the warrior Gilgamesh, son of Ninsun,   230
Made his way to Ur, to Sin.
Before Sin he wept:

O *father Sin, my ball has fallen into the netherworld, my*
stick has fallen into the infernal regions.
Enkidu went to bring them back up, the netherworld seized
him!
The messenger of death did not seize him, the demon of
disease did not seize him, the netherworld seized him!   235
The merciless agent of the plague god did not seize him, the
netherworld seized him!
He did not fall in the field of manly battle, the netherworld
seized him!

Father Sin did not come to his aid in that matter, he went off
to Eridu.
All alone the warrior Gilgamesh, son of Ninsun,
Made his way to Eridu, to Enki.   240
Before Enki he wept:

O father Enki, my ball has fallen into the netherworld, my
stick has fallen into the infernal regions.
Enkidu went to bring them back up, the netherworld seized
him!
The messenger of death did not seize him, the demon of
disease did not seize him, the netherworld seized him!
The merciless agent of the plague god did not seize him, the
netherworld seized him!   245
He did not fall in the field of manly battle, the netherworld
seized him!

[*What happens next is not clear. The Babylonian translator understood*
that Enkidu returned as a ghost, though he could be embraced, just as he
himself embraced his dead relatives in the netherworld. In "The Death of
Gilgamesh," Enkidu is already dead (line 100), and the elders say that no
one has ever returned from the netherworld (line 224). But, according to
one manuscript, the direct continuation of this poem is "Gilgamesh and
Huwawa," in which Enkidu is very much alive. Therefore it may be that
Sumerian scholars understood that Enkidu returned alive, because he
had not yet died when he descended to the netherworld.]

Father Enki came to his aid in that matter.
He addressed the youthful warrior Utu, son of Ningal:

If you would open a hole in the netherworld now,
You could bring his servant up from the netherworld.   250

He opened a hole in the netherworld,
By means of his dream zephyr Sisig, he brought his servant up
    from the netherworld.[9]
They embraced and kissed each other,
They wore each other out with questions.

[*Gilgamesh (G.) questions Enkidu (E.) about the netherworld. The first
grim news, which hits Gilgamesh hard, is that there is no sex there.*]

(G.) Did you see the way things are in the netherworld?   255
If only you could tell me, my friend, if only you could tell me!
(E.) If I tell you the way things are in the netherworld,
You will be sitting there weeping, I will be sitting there
    weeping too.
The penis that when you felt it, you were thrilled,
That penis is there like a rotten timber, vermin eat it.   260
The sweet spot that you said of it, "Where is it? Let me
    at it!"
That sweet spot is there like a crack in parched ground, full
    of dust.

"Woe is me!" cried the lord, he sat down in the dust.

(G.) Did you see him who had one son?
(E.) I saw him.   265
(G.) How does he fare?
(E.) He weeps bitterly at the peg driven into his wall.[1]

(G.) Did you see him who had two sons?
(E.) I saw him.
(G.) How does he fare?   270
(E.) He is sitting on two bricks eating bread.[2]

---

9. This mysterious being was a puff of air sometimes associated with dreaming. To judge
   from "The Death of Gilgamesh," line 69, it glittered with motion but without light.
1. This means that his house has been mortgaged or sold instead of passed on to
   descendants.
2. His two sons, symbolized by the two bricks, maintain his funerary offerings.

(G.) Did you see him who had three sons?
(E.) I saw him.
(G.) How does he fare?
(E.) He drinks water from a waterskin on his saddle.   275

(G.) Did you see him who had four sons?
(E.) I saw him.
(G.) How does he fare?
(E.) He is happy as a man hitching up a team of four asses.

(G.) Did you see him who had five sons?   280
(E.) I saw him.
(G.) How does he fare?
(E.) His hand is adept as a master scribe's, he can enter the
        palace directly.[3]

(G.) Did you see him who had six sons?
(E.) I saw him.   285
(G.) How does he fare?
(E.) He is happy as a man hitching up his plow.

(G.) Did you see him who had seven sons?
(E.) I saw him.
(G.) How does he fare?   290
(E.) He sits on a throne with the lesser gods hearing legal
        proceedings.

(G.) Did you see him who had no heir?
(E.) I saw him.
(G.) How does he fare?
(E.) He eats bread hard as a kiln-dried brick.   295

(G.) Did you see the courtier?
(E.) I saw him.
(G.) How does he fare?
(E.) He leans in a corner, like a useless(?) baton.[4]

(G.) Did you see the woman who never gave birth?   300
(E.) I saw her.
(G.) How does she fare?
(E.) She is thrown away callously like a hollow-sounding(?)
        pot, no man takes pleasure in her.

---

3. The five sons equal the five fingers of a skilled hand that brings prestige and remunerative
   employment to a scribe who enters government service immediately after his training.
4. The Sumerian is obscure. The Babylonian translation has "fine staff." The point may
   be that once at the center of things, the courtier is now of no importance.

(G.) Did you see the able-bodied young man who never
    undressed his wife?
(E.) I saw him.   305
(G.) How does he fare?
(E.) He made an entire reed mat by hand, he weeps over the
    mat he made.[5]

(G.) Did you see the able-bodied young woman who never
    undressed her husband?
(E.) I saw her.
(G.) How does she fare?   310
(E.) She braided an entire rope by hand, she weeps over the
    rope she braided.

(G.) Did you see him who was devoured by a lion?
(E.) I saw him.
(G.) How does he fare?
(E.) He is wailing bitterly, "Oh my hand! "Oh my foot!"   315

(G.) Did you see him who fell from a roof?
(E.) I saw him.
(G.) How does he fare?
(E.) They cannot mend his bones.

(G.) Did you see him who was drowned by the storm
    god's flood?   320
(E.) I did.
(G.) How does he fare?
(E.) He bloats big as an ox while vermin eat him.

(G.) Did you see the leper?
(E.) I saw him.   325
(G.) How does he fare?
(E.) His food is separate, his drink is separate.
        He eats plants he uproots,
        He drinks putrid water,
        He lives outside the city.   330

(G.) Did you see him who fell in battle?
(E.) I saw him.
(G.) How does he fare?
(E.) His mother cannot hold his head there, his wife weeps
    over him.

---

5. Because he never untied his wife's clothes, he is doomed to weave mats forever.

(G.) *Did you see the one whose corpse was left lying in
        the open?*   335
(E.) *I saw him.*
(G.) *How does he fare?*
(E.) *His ghost finds no rest in the netherworld.*

(G.) Did you see the ghost of him who has no one to make
        funerary offerings?
(E.) I saw him.   340
(G.) How does he fare?
(E.) He eats pot scrapings and bread crusts thrown out into
        the street.

(G.) Did you see him who was struck by a boat's plug?
(E.) I saw him.
(G.) How does he fare?   345
(E.) He must say, "Alas, my mother!"
        If he pulls the plug out, the waters rush over him,
        (If he leaves it), when he eats bread, the head of the
        plug pulverizes the bread into crumbs.[6]

(G.) Did you see him who did not heed the words of his
        mother and father?
(E.) I saw him.   350
(G.) How does he fare?
(E.) He never stops wailing, "Oh for myself! Oh for my
        body!"

(G.) Did you see him who was cursed by his mother and
        father?
(E.) I saw him.
(G.) How does he fare?   355
(E.) He is deprived of an heir, his ghost wanders.

(G.) Did you see him who made light of the name
        of his god?
(E.) I saw him.
(G.) How does he fare?
(E.) His ghost eats putrid food and drinks putrid water.   360

(G.) Did you see him who died a natural death?
(E.) I saw him.

6. Obscure. It seems that the man has been impaled by a ship's plug. If he pulls it out, the
   boat sinks; if he leaves it in, he cannot eat. Thus he has no choice but to wail. Plugs
   were part of building the ark in the Babylonian epic, Tablet XI, line 65.

(G.) How does he fare?
(E.) He lies on the bed of the gods and drinks clean water.

(G.) Did you see my little stillborn babies who never knew
        who they were?   365
(E.) I saw them.
(G.) How do they fare?
(E.) They play at tables of silver and gold, (set) with honey
        and butter.

[*Some versions skip from here to line 385 and end at line 388.*]

(G.) Did you see him who swore an oath outrageous to a god?
(E.) I saw him.   370
(G.) How does he fare?
(E.) He tries to drink at the libation place at the top of the
        netherworld but cannot [get near it(?)].

(G.) Did you see the man of Girsu who used to bring (liba-
        tions of) water to his mother and father?
(E.) I saw him.
(G.) How does he fare?   375
(E.) He faces alone a thousand Amorites, his ghost cannot
        beat them back, nor can it resist them, Amorites grab
        a place in front of it at the libation place at the top of
        the netherworld.[7]

(G.) Did you see the Sumerians and Akkadians?
(E.) I saw them.
(G.) How do they fare?
(E.) They drink filthy water at a place of carnage.   380

(G.) Did you see my father and mother, wherever they were?
(E.) I saw them.
(G.) How do they fare?
(E.) Both of them drink filthy water at a place of carnage.

(G.) Did you see him who was set on fire?   385
(E.) I saw him.

7. At the time this poem was written, it seems that rulers of another Sumerian city, Girsu,
in rivalry with the kings of Ur, claimed Gilgamesh and Lugalbanda as ancestors and
made funerary offerings to them in Uruk. Amorites in Sumerian literature were
depicted as barbaric nomads who lived in tents in the countryside and did not bury
their dead properly. According to Enkidu, as punishment for appropriating Gilgamesh's
lineage as their own, the deceased rulers of Girsu are blocked by hordes of Amorites
from getting their own funerary offerings.

(G.) How does he fare?
(E.) His ghost does not exist, it went up in smoke to
    the sky.[8]

[*One version of the story ends here and continues directly to "Gilgamesh and Huwawa," line 5 of which is the same as line 391 here.*]

(Gilgamesh) was sore at heart, overcome by despair,
The king was searching for a way to live,   390
The lord turned his thoughts to the mountain of the living.

[*In another, longer, version, there may have been an episode in which Gilgamesh, having given up on his game, presides over a proper athletic event in honor of the dead and sets up funerary statues, as in "The Death of Gilgamesh," lines 70–74. When the text of that version resumes, Gilgamesh, conscience-stricken that he has neglected caring for his deceased ancestors, mourns them and makes libations for them to drink.*]

They [returned(?) to Uruk],
They [returned(?) to their city].
He brought in his equipment and armament, axe and spear, to
    secure it,
He put on a celebration in his palace.   395
The young men and women of Uruk, the notables and
    matrons of Kullab,
Celebrated when they saw those statues.
When Utu, the sun, rose from his chamber, (Gilgamesh)
    raised his head and said:

    O my father, O my mother, do you drink this clear water!

The day was no more than half over when they put aside their
    diadems,
Gilgamesh threw himself down at the place of mourning,   400
For nine days he threw himself down at the place of mourning,
The young men and women of Uruk, the notables and
    matrons of Kullab wept,
He repulsed the man of Girsu.

[*Gilgamesh says*]:

    O my father, O my mother, do you drink this clear water!

---

8. One manuscript inserts an interesting additional exchange here: "Why, my friend, did you not forbear to ask this?" "I have now asked it, my friend." Death by fire was evidently regarded with particular horror.

[*Invocation.*]

O warrior Gilgamesh, son of Ninsun, how sweet it is to praise
   you!

Gilgamesh and Huwawa

Several closely related epic poems describe an expedition that Gil-
gamesh, Enkidu, and a party of adventurers undertake from Uruk to
the cedar forest to cut a great cedar tree and establish eternal fame for
Gilgamesh. They encounter the monster Huwawa and, after a lengthy
colloquy, Enkidu kills him (in one manuscript, both he and Gilgamesh
kill him). This story finds a counterpart in the second half of Tablet II
and Tablets III–V of the Babylonian *Epic of Gilgamesh*. One version of
it, known as "Gilgamesh and Huwawa A," is the basis for this transla-
tion; a choice of passages, printed in italic, that complete or supple-
ment that version have been interpolated from a shorter one, "Gil-
gamesh and Huwawa B." Furthermore, additional lines taken from
other versions or manuscripts have been inserted here and there to fill
out the story. Most manuscripts elide repetitive passages, given here in
full, and some have additional episodes and arrange or understand the
material differently with different wording. All this suggests that there
were various ways of telling this tale, elaborating from a core adven-
ture by inserting, deleting, or expanding episodes and dialogue. It was
evidently a favorite among ancient students.

[*Prologue.*]

Hail the anointed one, with scepter graced,[1]
Of princely birth, pride and glory of the gods,
Massive bull, standing tall in battle,
Youthful lord adored in Uruk!

[*Gilgamesh is found pondering his mortality. He proposes a quest to win
eternal fame.*]

The lord turned his thoughts to the mountain of the living,   5
The lord Gilgamesh turned his thoughts to the mountain of
   the living![2]
He addressed his servant Enkidu:

1. Some scholars believe that the difficult and disputed original implicitly compares
   Gilgamesh to a vigorous tree sending out branches, perhaps in ironic anticipation of
   his role as a tree cutter in the poem. According to the metaphor as used in later times,
   the king may have been compared to a tree trunk and his wooden staff of authority, or
   scepter, to a branch.
2. Or "land of the living," because the Sumerian word can mean either "land" or "moun-
   tain." "Land of the living" is the opposite of "land of the dead," the subject of the previ-
   ous poem. Some scholars believe that "the living" refers to Huwawa.

Enkidu, since even an able-bodied man cannot go beyond
  the final moment of his life,
I will mount that mountain,[3] I will make a name
  for myself.
Wherever renown may be established, there will I establish
  my renown,   10
Wherever no renown may be established, there will I
  establish the renown of the gods.

His servant Enkidu answered him:

My lord, if you mean anon to mount that mountain, Utu
  should know of it from us,
If you mean to mount that mountain where cedars are cut,
  Utu, youthful Utu should know of it from us.
Any plan about that mountain is Utu's concern,   15
Any plan about that mountain where cedars are cut is
  Utu's concern!

[*Gilgamesh asks Utu for permission to go to the mountain land. When his
response is discouraging, Gilgamesh pleads with him to allow the quest.
Utu relents.*]

Gilgamesh prepared a white kid (as an offering),
He clasped a brown kid to his breast as a greeting gift.
Holding a sacred scepter prayerfully to his face,
He addressed Utu in heaven: 20

O Utu, let me mount that mountain, please be the one to
  help me,
Let me mount that mountain where cedars are cut, please
  be the one to help me!

Utu answered him from heaven:

Young man, you are indeed noble on your own, but on that
  mountain, what would you be?

[*Gilgamesh responds:*]

O Utu, let me speak a word to you, give ear to my word,   25
Let me persuade you, please consider!

---

3. "Mount" here reflects a play on the word for "enter" (*kura*) and "mountain" (*kur*). The
  same verb occurs as a kind of motif throughout the poem, variously translated as
  "bring" (line 180) and "join" (line 183).

When someone dies in my city, my heart is apprehensive,
When someone is no more, my heart is full of foreboding.
I have looked over the city rampart,
I have caught sight of a corpse floating in the water.   30
It will be the same for me, surely this is what is in store
    for me!
No man, however tall, can stretch to heaven,
No man, however long his reach, can span the earth.
Since even an able-bodied man cannot go beyond the final
    moment of his life,
I will mount that mountain, I will make a name
    for myself.   35
Wherever renown may be established, there will I establish
    my renown,
Wherever no renown may be established, there will I estab-
    lish the renown of the gods.

Utu accepted his tears as if they were a gift,
Like the compassionate being he was, he treated him with
    compassion.

[*Utu gives Gilgamesh seven wondrous warriors to protect and guide him
on the way to the mountain.*]

Seven are they, those heroes, sons of one mother.   40
The first, the eldest, has lion's paws and eagle's claws,
The second is a slithering snake with [gaping] jaws,
The third is a dragon with a serpent's head [. . .],
The fourth spews fire [. . .],
The fifth is a fork-tongued viper that [. . .],   45
The sixth is a springtime flood battering mountains,
The seventh flashes like lightning, none can withstand his
    power,
These seven heroes did the youthful Utu give to Gilgamesh,
    (saying):

[*gap of three lines*]

They will shine like stars in heaven,
They will stand high in the sky like planets.   50
On earth they know the roadway to Aratta,[4]
They know the byways as trading parties do,
Like pigeons, they know the mountain clefts,

---

4. Aratta was, in Sumerian epic literature, a legendary city far to the east, somewhere in
the Iranian highlands, rich with precious metals and stones.

They will surely bring you to the mountain range, where
   boats can go no further.

This made the cedar cutter jubilant,   55
This made the lord Gilgamesh jubilant!
He had the heralds' horns sounded citywide in unison,
He had them proclaim in harmony like a duo:

   He who has a household, to his household!
   He who has a mother, to his mother!   60
   Single young fellows like me, fall in at my side!

[*Version B has a different text here.*]

   He who has a wife, to your wife!
   He who has a child, to your child!
   Warrior or no warrior,
   He who has no wife, he who has no child,   65
   Let such men fall in by my side, with Gilgamesh!

He who had a household, (went) to his household,
He who had a mother, (went) to his mother,
Single young fellows like him, fifty of them, fell in at his side.
He made his way to the smithy,   70
He had them cast there a hatchet and a broadaxe, his heroic
   weapons.
The king went out from the city,
Gilgamesh went out from Kullab.
He made his way through the tree-shaded steppe,
There he felled ebony, cherry, apple, and boxwood,[5]   75
[. . .] to the men of his city who accompanied him.
He took the road to the mountain where cedars are cut, (saying):

   Seven are they, those heroes, sons of one mother.
   The first, the eldest, has lion's paws and eagle's claws,
   The second is a slithering snake with [gaping] jaws,   80
   The third is a dragon with a serpent's head [. . .],
   The fourth spews fire [. . .],
   The fifth is a fork-tongued viper that [. . .],
   The sixth is a springtime flood battering mountains,
   The seventh flashes like lightning, none can withstand
      his power,   85

5. The open plains of Mesopotamia were not forested with such trees, nor could, of
   course, the heroes take the felled logs with them, so this episode exemplifies the enjoy-
   ment of the fantastic characteristic of Sumerian epic.

These seven heroes did the youthful Utu give to
  Gilgamesh!

                    [*gap of three lines*]

They will shine like stars in heaven,
They will stand high in the sky like planets.
On earth they know the roadway to Aratta,
They know the byways as trading parties do,   90
Like pigeons, they know the mountain clefts,
They will surely bring us to the mountain range, where boats
  can go no further.

[*The expedition enters the mountain land. Gilgamesh finds a suitable
cedar tree and cuts it down. Huwawa is disturbed by the noise and knocks
the hero out with one of his deadly radiances. As in the epic, Tablet IX,
lines 90–122, great distance is conveyed by repetition.*]

He crossed the first mountain range,
  he did not find the cedar he hoped for.
He crossed the second mountain range,
  he did not find the cedar he hoped for.
He crossed the third mountain range,
  he did not find the cedar he hoped for.   95
He crossed the fourth mountain range,
  he did not find the cedar he hoped for.
He crossed the fifth mountain range,
  he did not find the cedar he hoped for.
He crossed the sixth mountain range,
  he did not find the cedar he hoped for.
Having crossed the seventh mountain range,
  he found the cedar he hoped for!
He inquired no further, he sought no other spot.   100
While Gilgamesh was chopping at the cedar,
His servant Enkidu lopped off the limbs,
The men of his city who accompanied him heaped them
  into piles.
[By this hubbub], Gilgamesh disturbed Huwawa in his sleeping
  place,
He let loose a direful radiance against him *like a spear.*   105
[Gilgamesh], [. . .] was overcome, as if in deep sleep,
[Enkidu] was beset, as if in a stupor.
The men of his city who accompanied him cowered like
  puppies at his feet.

[*Enkidu rouses the unconscious hero.*]

Enkidu started awake, as if from a dream, he was dazed, as if
   from deep sleep.
He rubbed his eyes, all was deathly still,   110
He nudged (Gilgamesh), he could not wake him.
He addressed him, he made no reply:

> You who sleep, you who sleep,
> Gilgamesh, youthful lord of Kullab, how long will you sleep?
> He has let the mountains darken, he has let the shadows fall,   115
> The glimmer of twilight has descended upon them,
> Utu has gone majestically to the embrace of his mother
>   Ningal!
> Gilgamesh, how long will you sleep?
> The men of your city who accompany you
> Must not be left standing in a mountain cleft,   120
> Their mothers must not be left to twist ropes in your city's
>   square.[6]

This he shouted into his right ear.

[*Gilgamesh is roused to action. Enkidu now tries to dissuade him.*]

His call to heroism enveloped him like a linen garment,
(Gilgamesh) adjusted his gear, making it cover his chest.
He stood up like a bull on a pedestal,   125
He lowered his head and bellowed:

> By the life of Ninsun, mother mine, and my father, blessed
>   Lugalbanda,
> Shall I play the sleeping baby in the embrace of Ninsun,
>   mother mine?

A second time withal he said to him:

> By the life of Ninsun, mother mine, and my father, blessed
>   Lugalbanda,   130
> Until I determine if that being is mortal or divine,
> I will never turn back my steps from that mountain home-
>   ward toward my city!

The servant gladdened his spirit, sweetened his life, (saying):

> My lord, having never laid eyes on that being, you feel no
>   dread of it,

---

6. This menial and tedious task, referred to in the epic, Tablet XI, line 76, was presumably
a recourse only for the destitute.

I, having laid eyes on that being, do feel dread of it! 135
O Hero, his maw is a dragon's maw,
His face is a lion-monster's face,
His chest is an onrushing torrent,
His brow is a (conflagration) that consumes a reed thicket,
    none can escape it,
He is a man-eating lion that wipes not the blood from his
    slaver(ed mouth). 140
My king! Ride on to the mountain, I will ride on home.
I will tell your mother how you lived, she will smile,
Afterwards I will tell her that you have died, she will weep
    bitterly.

[*Gilgamesh quotes sayings to the effect that a person with a companion
or protection can come to no harm. He taunts Enkidu by saying that he
can always turn back once they have reached their goal.*]

(Gilgamesh) answered him:

Drop it, Enkidu! Two men together will not die, rafts lashed
    together will not sink, 145
No one can cut a three-strand rope,
No water can drown a man on a rampart,
A fire in a reed hut cannot be blown out.
If you help me and I help you, what could befall either one?
When it sank, when it sank, 150
When the seafaring boat sank,
When the river barge sank,
The raft lashed together was a lifeboat, it did not sink.
Come on, let us go forward together, let us see him face
    to face!
If when we go forward to him together, 155
If something frightful awaits, something frightful awaits,
    you turn back,
If something crafty awaits, something crafty awaits, you
    turn back!
Whatever your thoughts, come on, let us go forward to him
    together!

[*They meet Huwawa at last.*]

No man can approach sixty times six paces,
Without Huwawa stationing himself in his cedar house! 160
He stared at them, it was the gaze of death.

He shook his head at them, it was the sign of utter doom,
When he spoke, his words were very few:

> Young man who has come here with him, you will never
>   return to the city where you were born!

As for Gilgamesh, though fear and dread of him took hold of
    his muscles and limbs,   165
He did not turn his feet in place to flee,
He prodded one foot with the nail of his big toe,
[. . .] his side.

[*It seems that the poet, apostrophizing Gilgamesh, urges him not to waver
but to crouch down with his hands on the ground.*]

> Hail the anointed one, with scepter graced,[7]
> Of princely birth, pride and glory of the gods,   170
> Massive bull, standing tall in battle,
> Youthful lord adored in Uruk!
> Your mother was best at bearing a son,
> Your wet nurse was best at nursing a son,
> Do not be afraid, put your hands on the ground!   175

[*Gilgamesh seeks by trickery to persuade Huwawa to give up his seven
deadly auras, pretending that he has come with an offer of marriage that
will bring the monster fame and promising him gifts. It seems that with
each exchange, he creeps closer to the monster while maintaining a sup-
plicating position, perhaps squatting or on his hands and knees.*]

He put his hands on the ground, he said to Huwawa:

> By the life of Ninsun, mother mine, and my father, blessed
>   Lugalbanda,
> Nobody knows where you dwell in the mountain land,
> People should know where you dwell in the mountain land.
> Please let me bring to you Enmebaragesi, my big sister,
>   that she become your wife in the mountain land.[8]   180
> May I not get close to you and your family?
> Give me a direful radiance of yours,
> It is your family I wish to join.

---

7. Some scholars understand lines 169–75 to be part of Huwawa's speech, but this has
   not been followed here because of the change of grammatical person in line 165 and
   because, unusually for a Sumerian epic, he is described as a creature of few words. The
   ancient scribes who copied the manuscripts may likewise have had different views
   about who is speaking in this passage.
8. Enmebaragesi was a warrior king of Kish and the father of Akka (see "Gilgamesh and
   Akka," line 1), so a Sumerian audience probably understood this as a joke.

Huwawa gave him a first direful radiance.
The men of his city who accompanied him lopped off its
    shoots, tied them up in bundles,   185
They laid them to rest in the cleft of the mountain.
A second time he addressed him so:

> By the life of Ninsun, mother mine, and my father, blessed
>   Lugalbanda,
> Nobody knows where you dwell in the mountain land,
> People should know where you dwell in the mountain land.   190
> Please let me bring to you Peshtur, my little sister, that she
>   become your concubine in the mountain land.[9]
> May I not get close to you and your family?
> Give me a direful radiance of yours,
> It is your family I wish to join.

Huwawa gave him a second direful radiance.   195
The men of his city who accompanied him lopped off its
    shoots, tied them up in bundles,
They laid them to rest in the cleft of the mountain.
A third time he addressed him so:

> By the life of Ninsun, mother mine, and my father, blessed
>   Lugalbanda,
> Nobody knows where you dwell in the mountain land,   200
> People should know where you dwell in the mountain land.
> Please let me bring to you in the mountain land
> Ceremonial flour, the meal of the great gods, and a water
>   skin full of cool water.
> May I not get close to you and your family?
> Give me a direful radiance of yours,   205
> It is your family I wish to join.

Huwawa gave him a third direful radiance.
The men of his city who accompanied him lopped off its
    shoots, tied them up in a bundle,
They laid them to rest in the cleft of the mountain.
A fourth time he addressed him so: 210

> By the life of Ninsun, mother mine, and my father, blessed
>   Lugalbanda,
> Nobody knows where you dwell in the mountain land,
> People should know where you dwell in the mountain land.

---

9. Peshtur means "little fig" or the like. She is mentioned in "Gilgamesh and the Bull of
Heaven," line 143, so, unlike Enmebaragesi, really was Gilgamesh's unmarried sister.

Please let me bring to you big sandals for your big feet.
May I not get close to you and your family?   215
Give me a direful radiance of yours,
It is your family I wish to join.

Huwawa gave him a fourth direful radiance.
The men of his city who accompanied him lopped off its
    shoots, tied them up in bundles,
They laid them to rest in the cleft of the mountain.   220
A fifth time he addressed him so:

    By the life of Ninsun, mother mine, and my father, blessed
        Lugalbanda,
    Nobody knows where you dwell in the mountain land,
    People should know where you dwell in the mountain land.
    Please let me bring to you tiny sandals for your tiny feet.   225
    May I not get close to you and your family?
    Give me a direful radiance of yours,
    It is your family I wish to join.

Huwawa gave him a fifth direful radiance.
The men of his city who accompanied him lopped off its
    shoots, tied them up in bundles,   230
They laid them to rest in the cleft of the mountain.
A sixth time he addressed him so:

    By the life of Ninsun, mother mine, and my father, blessed
        Lugalbanda,
    Nobody knows where you dwell in the mountain land,
    People should know where you dwell in the mountain land.   235
    Please let me bring to you yellow calcite, chalcedony, and
        lapis.
    May I not get close to you and your family?
    Give me a direful radiance of yours,
    It is your family I wish to join.

Huwawa gave him a sixth direful radiance.   240
The men of his city who accompanied him lopped off its
    shoots, tied them up in bundles,
They laid them to rest in the cleft of the mountain.
A seventh time he addressed him so:

    By the life of Ninsun, mother mine, and my father, blessed
        Lugalbanda,
    Nobody knows where you dwell in the mountain land,   245
    People should know where you dwell in the mountain land.

Please let me bring to you in the mountain land [. . .]
May I not get close to you and your family?
Give me a direful radiance of yours,
It is your family I wish to join.   250

Huwawa gave him a seventh direful radiance.
The men of his city who accompanied him lopped off its
    shoots, tied them up in a bundle,
They laid them to rest in the cleft of the mountain.

[*Gilgamesh has gotten close enough for a surprise blow.*]

When Huwawa had used up his seventh direful radiance, Gil-
    gamesh was close to his doorway,
He crept up toward him, as if he were a groggy snake.   255
Feigning to kiss him, Gilgamesh punched him on the cheek!
Huwawa bared his glittering fangs and grimaced.
Huwawa addressed Gilgamesh:

Warrior, you have lied, you have assaulted me, you swore an
    oath
By your mother who bore you, Ninsun, and your father,
    blessed Lugalbanda,   260
You have forsworn your own god, Enki, lord Nudimmud!

The two of them [. . .],
Gilgamesh threw a halter over him, like a captured wild bull,
He trussed his arms, like a captured soldier.
He [dragged] the warrior from his doorway, he said to him,
    "Sit down!"   265
He [dragged] Huwawa from his doorway, [he said] to him, "Sit
    down!"
The warrior sat down, he burst into sobs, set to weeping and
    wailing,
Huwawa sat down, he burst into sobs, shedding tear upon
    tear!
He clutched Gilgamesh by the hand.

[*Huwawa laments to Utu, patron god of promises and of people without*
families, that Gilgamesh has broken his plighted word. Gilgamesh is
moved, Enkidu implacable.]

To you, O Utu, I would say this!   270
O Utu, I have known no mother who bore me, I have
    known no father who raised me,
I was born in the mountain land, it was you who raised me!

My mother who bore me was a cavern in the mountain,
My father who begot me was a peak in the mountain,
O Utu, let me live by myself, alone in the mountain!   275
Gilgamesh vowed by heaven, vowed by the earth, vowed by
    the netherworld!

Huwawa clutched Gilgamesh's hand, threw himself down
    before him.
Then was Gilgamesh moved to take pity on him, a noble
    creature,
He addressed his servant, Enkidu:

Enkidu, surely the captive bird should go home,   280
Surely the captive youth should be sent back to his mother's
    embrace!
Let him be our guide, against any watching for us on the
    road, let him be our guide!
Let him be our guide, let him carry my pack.

Enkidu, his servant, replied to Gilgamesh:

Hail the anointed one, with scepter graced,   285
Of princely birth, pride and glory of the gods,
Massive bull, standing tall in battle,
Youthful lord adored in Uruk!
Your mother was best at bearing a son,
Your wet nurse was best at nursing a son,   290
Exalted ever so high, if he have no sense,
Fate will swallow him up, he will not even recognize fate!
If the captive bird goes home,
If the captive youth be sent back to his mother's embrace,
You will never return to the city where you were born.   295
A captive warrior set free? A captive high priestess
    [restored] to her residence?
A captive priest restored to his bewigged finery?
Who has ever seen the like?
Huwawa will lead us astray on the road in the mountain land,
He will confound us on the path in the mountain land!   300
You will never return to the city where you were born.

Huwawa addressed Enkidu:

Against me, Enkidu, you have spoken wicked words to him,
You hireling, signed on for a dole of chow, lagging well
    behind your opponent, why have you spoken wicked
    words to him?

No sooner had he said this   305
Than Enkidu, in a fit of rage, cut off his head,
He dropped it into a leather sack.

[*Gilgamesh and Enkidu go to Nippur, where Enlil berates them for their deed, decreeing that Huwawa shall enjoy the same honor as Gilgamesh in later generations and that Huwawa-heads (see figure 4, above, p. 41) shall ornament temples ever after.*]

Off they went to Enlil,
They brought the head before Enlil and Ninlil.
After kissing the ground before Enlil,   310
He dropped the leather sack, he took out the head,
They set it down before Enlil.
When he approached Enlil, he rushed off,[1]
Then Ninlil went out [after him].
When Enlil and Ninlil had returned,   315
Enlil, at the sight of Huwawa's head,
Spoke angrily to Gilgamesh:

   Why have you acted so?
   Has it been decreed that his name should vanish from the
      earth?
   He shall take a seat before you,   320
   He shall eat the bread you eat,
   He shall drink the water you drink,
   (His head) shall adorn the temples of the great gods!

[*Enlil apportions Huwawa's radiances.*]

Enlil, from his throne, distributed his sublime radiances.[2]
His first sublime radiance he gave to the field,   325
His second sublime radiance he gave to the river,
His third sublime radiance he gave to the reed thicket,
His fourth sublime radiance he gave to the lion,

---

1. Text has: "he went out the window." Enlil and Ninlil are evidently horrified by the sight of the monster's head. Only one manuscript has lines 312–14.
2. It is not clear if Huwawa's radiances are additional ones that came to Nippur with his severed head or are the original seven tied up on the mountain like tree branches. Each recipient now has, according to the poem, something uncanny and dangerous that may serve to protect it. At the same time, the potency of the radiances, as argued by M. Civil ("Reading Gilgamesh II: Gilgamesh and Huwawa," in W. Sallaberger, K. Volk, and A. Zgoll, eds., *Literatur, Politik Und Recht in Mesopotamien: Festschrift für Claus Wilcke.* Wiesbaden: Harrassowitz, 2003, pp. 77–86), has been diminished by a process, known from Mesopotamian magic, of banishment from civilization to remote places or jail. The list of recipients varies among the manuscripts. Some give a radiance to Nungal, goddess of prisons and manager of Enlil's household. In others, it is Gilgamesh rather than Enlil who receives the last of the radiances.

His fifth sublime radiance he gave to the forest,
His sixth sublime radiance he gave to the prison,   330
His seventh sublime radiance he took himself.

Praise be to mighty Gilgamesh!
Praise be to Nisaba!

Gilgamesh and the Bull of Heaven

"Gilgamesh and the Bull of Heaven" finds a counterpart in Tablet VI
of the Babylonian *Epic of Gilgamesh*. Opening with a short hymn to
Gilgamesh celebrating his triumph, the story begins with Gilgamesh's
mother, the goddess Ninsun, giving him instructions. Gilgamesh
accordingly bathes, has his hair cut, and embarks on a boat. He gathers
materials in the marshes, perhaps to make a pavilion for Inanna. He
next enters the courtyard of Inanna's sanctuary and builds the pavil-
ion there. She is delighted with it and impetuously entreats him to set
aside his kingly judicial and administrative duties to give himself up
to her embraces. On his mother's advice, he says that Inanna should
not interfere with his role as royal warrior, whereby he can bring her
wealth.

In a fury, Inanna goes to her father, the sky god An, to demand that
the Bull of Heaven kill Gilgamesh. At first An refuses to hand over the
bull for fear of disastrous consequences for Uruk, but he gives in
when Inanna lets loose a world-shaking scream. In Uruk, the bull
devours all green plants, mows down the orchards, and drinks up the
water of its canals. The royal minstrel informs Gilgamesh, but, with
heroic insouciance, he responds that he prefers to drink and listen to
the minstrel's singing. Gilgamesh arms himself, talks at some length
with his mother and sister, then challenges the bull. He and Enkidu
kill it while Inanna looks on. As they butcher the fallen beast, Gil-
gamesh laments that he cannot butcher Inanna as well, even as she
flees from the scene.

The fragmentary manuscripts now known for this poem have been
combined here. They contain many gaps, obscurities, and variants, to
the extent that a coherent translation must be based on considerable
guesswork. As a Sumerian saying puts it, "If a scribe does not know how
to grasp the meaning, how will a translator bring it out?"

[*Opening paean.*]

Let me sing the song of the hero of the combat, hero of
    the combat,
Let me sing the song of lord Gilgamesh, hero of the combat,
Let me sing the song of the dark-bearded one, hero of the
    combat,

Let me sing the song of the fair-limbed one, hero of
   the combat,
Let me sing the song of the youthful lord, hero of the combat,   5
Let me sing the song of the champion boxer and wrestler,
   hero of the combat,
Let me sing the song of the seductive one, hero of
   the combat,
Let me sing the song of the one who struck down the evil
   thing, hero of the combat!

[*Gilgamesh's mother, Ninsun, evidently tells him to gather materials in the marsh to build a pavilion for Inanna; he complies, bathes, and grooms himself.*]

O lord, go down to the river, [. . .] the dust, bathe
   in the river,
O lord, do you enter the garden of Zabala,[1]   10
O king, be clipped like a splendid sheep maturing in the
   temple dwelling.
Sit down on the thwart at the prow of a boat,
What is in the marsh, my king,
You should gather bundles for her of what is in the marsh,
   the water staves,[2]
Lord, you should moisten the staves with water for her,
   like the lushest of reeds,   15
You should moisten their filling for her, like marvelous
   condiments.
In the wide courtyard of Inanna's temple,
Gilgamesh, you should take a wattle spike [in hand],[3]
My lord, go into the garden of Zabala to do your task,
The lady will see the water in the temple dwelling [. . .].   20

The lord went down to the river, [. . .] the dust, bathed
   in the river,
The lord entered the garden of Zabala,
The king was clipped like a splendid sheep maturing in the
   temple dwelling.
He sat down on the thwart at the prow of a boat,
The king gathered bundles for her of what was in the marsh,
   the water staves,   25

---

1. A Sumerian town with an important temple of Inanna.
2. Obscure. The word means "narrow, woody reed" or "oar" and is understood here to mean a sapling growing in the marsh that can be used to make a frame for the pavilion.
3. Gilgamesh uses some sharp tool to build his pavilion.

The lord moistened the staves with water for her, like the
   lushest of reeds,
He moistened their filling for her, like marvelous condiments.
In the wide courtyard of Inanna's temple,
Gilgamesh took a wattle spike [in hand],
The lord went into the garden of Zabala to do his task.   30
In the wide courtyard of Inanna's temple,
In the wide courtyard, where never was there combat [. . .],
[He built] a pavilion, she [saw] the pavilion,
Radiant Inanna [saw] the pavilion,
From the palace in the watery depths she [saw] the pavilion!   35

[*Inanna is so smitten by Gilgamesh and his pavilion that, like a prosti-
tute, she waits for him at the city wall. She begs him to dally with her and
forget his royal duties.*]

She [. . .] at the doorway of the great gate [. . .],
[Inanna . . .] at the rampart battlements, (saying):[4]

   My wild bull, my man, where else should we be?[5] I will
      never let you go,
   Lord Gilgamesh, my wild bull, my man, where else should
      we be? I will never let you go!
   I will not let you go to render verdicts in Eanna,   40
   I will not let you go to make decisions in the sacred temple
      dwelling,
   I will not let you go to render verdicts in the Eanna that
      An loves!
   O Gilgamesh, you shall be [lord], I shall be [lady]!

[*Gilgamesh informs his mother. She tells him not to succumb to Inanna's
blandishments lest he diminish his strength and hinder his progress.*]

The king [listened] to her words,
The king [told] his mother who bore him,   45
Gilgamesh [said] to Ninsun:

   O mother mine, how [. . .]!
   She [. . .] at the doorway of the great gate [. . .],
   [Inanna . . .] at the rampart battlements, (saying):

---

4. Compare the Babylonian epic, Tablet VII, line 83.
5. Obscure, perhaps, with Andrew George, emend to read "You should be our man"; com-
   pare the Babylonian epic, Tablet VI, line 9.

"My wild bull, my man, where else should we be? I will
    never let you go,   50
"Lord Gilgamesh, my wild bull, my man, where else should
    we be? I will never let you go!
"I will not let you go to render verdicts in Eanna,
"I will not let you go to make decisions in the sacred temple
    dwelling,
I will not let you go to render verdicts in the Eanna that
    An loves!
"O Gilgamesh, you shall be [lord], I shall be [lady]!   55

When he had so spoken to the mother who bore him,
His mother who bore him [answered Gilgamesh]:

    You must not let what Inanna would give into your temple
        dwelling!
    Our Lady of the Palace must not [stifle] your heroism,
    Our Lady Inanna must not hinder you!   60

               [gap]

[Gilgamesh answers Inanna, promising that if he acts as king rather than as
full-time lover, he can fill her temple pens with tribute livestock, her treasury
with wealth, and, perhaps, sustain her with good things. She is furious.]

    I must not let what Inanna would give into my temple
        dwelling!
    Our Lady of the Palace, you must not [stifle] my heroism,
    O Lady Inanna, you must not hinder me!
    I will summon the cattle of foreign lands, I will fill these
        pens with them,
    I will summon the sheep of foreign lands, I will fill these
        folds with them,   65
    I will [lavish on you] silver and carnelian, unguents and
        food, I will fill [. . .] with them.

[Inanna] addressed him, spluttering her words:

    Gilgamesh, how could you say this to me?
    Gilgamesh, how could you say this to me!?

               [gap]

[Inanna goes to her father, An, demanding that his monstrous bull, the Bull
of Heaven, kill Gilgamesh. When the text resumes, An is remonstrating.]

It will [eat] their entrails,   70
It will drink their blood,
[It will drink] their blood, as if from a water jar.
Inanna, it will churn up the waters, it will spew out masses
    of dung,
My beloved (bull) must not [. . .].

He let her hold its restraining cord, (saying):   75

    My child, why do this? It will churn up the waters, it will
        spew out masses of dung,
    If the great bull is set loose, [. . .] in Uruk,
    If the great bull is set loose against Gilgamesh, Uruk . . . ,
    I will not raise up against him that which bears my name.

[*Inanna answers:*]

    Let it churn up the waters, let it spew out masses of dung,   80
    My father, please give it to me!
    I want to kill the lord, I want to kill the lord,
    I want to kill Gilgamesh, I want to kill the lord!

Great An answered radiant Inanna:

    My child, the bull would have no pasture, its pasture
        is the horizon,   85
    My girl Inanna, it grazes at the horizon, where the sun
        comes up,
    I will not set loose the Bull of Heaven for you.

Radiant Inanna answered him:

    Then I will let loose a scream, it will reach both heaven and
        netherworld!

Her scream reached heaven, her scream reached the
    netherworld,   90
[Inanna's] scream reached heaven, her scream reached the
    netherworld!
It overspread [heaven and netherworld] like a [woolen cloak],
    it unrolled over them like a sheet of linen.
Who ever used a voice like that?
Who ever used a voice like that?
She spread terror, she spread terror,   95

Inanna spread terror [in heaven and netherworld]!
Great An answered radiant Inanna:

  I will give up the Bull of Heaven against him!

[*The Bull of Heaven devastates Uruk.*]

The girl Inanna manfully took hold of the sky-blue lead rope,
Radiant Inanna brought the Bull of Heaven down from
  heaven.   100
The bull was eating the green plants of Uruk,
The bull was drinking up the canals in gulps,
Though it gulped a double league at a time, its thirst was not
  quenched.
It was eating up the green plants, it was stripping the earth
  bare,
It was eating the date palm orchards of Uruk, crunching them
  in its teeth,   105
As the bull stood there, it filled Uruk,
The terror of the Bull of Heaven filled Kullab.

[*Gilgamesh's minstrel, Lugalgabagal, tells Gilgamesh about the bull.*]

At that time, he was drinking beer in the house of his god,
Lord Gilgamesh was drinking beer in the house of his god,
His minstrel, Lugalgabagal, was throwing up outside.   110
Looking up, he beheld the Bull of Heaven,
Hunched over, he came back inside the house:

  You drink, you drink, how long will you drink?
  O lord Gilgamesh, you drink, how long will you drink?
  Inanna has brought the Bull of Heaven down from heaven,   115
  The bull is eating the green plants of Uruk,
  The bull is drinking up the canals in gulps,
  Though it gulps a double league at a time, its thirst is not
    quenched.
  It is eating up the green plants, it is stripping the earth bare,
  It is eating the date palm orchards of Uruk, crunching
    them in its teeth,   120
  As the bull stands there, it fills Uruk,
  The terror of the Bull of Heaven fills Kullab.

[*Gilgamesh professes to be unconcerned.*]

Gilgamesh [said] to his minstrel, Lugalgabagal:

> My minstrel, tune your strings, sing your song,
> [Fill] your bronze cup, I wish to drink.   125

Lugalgabagal [answered] Gilgamesh his king:

> My king, you may eat, you may [drink],
> If I may ask, what [will you do] about this?

[*Gilgamesh responds by arming himself.*]

For him to slay the bull [. . .],
For Gilgamesh to slay the bull [. . .],   130
[He tied around his waist] his belt weighing fifty pounds,
[He strapped on its fifty-pound weight (with ease)].
[He wore at his side his] sword weighing seven talents and
   thirty minas,
[He took up his bronze] battle axe [weighing seven talents and
   seven pounds].[6]

[*In the fragmentary and obscure episode that follows, Gilgamesh may tell
his mother and sister about securing cattle and sheep in the temple of
Enki, his patron god. The purpose may be to feed the population of the
devastated city if the bull kills him, counterpart to the Babylonian epic,
Tablet VI, lines 103–04. If he slays the bull, he will feed the city with its
butchered remains.*]

[gap]

Gilgamesh [. . .]   135

> O mother mine [. . .],
> O my sister [. . .],
> They will bring(?) cattle to secure them,
> They will bring(?) the sheep to secure them,
> Let them [bring] beer to secure them.   140

Gilgamesh [. . .]
The mother who bore him, [Ninsun . . .]
His little sister, Peshtur [. . .]
Gilgamesh [. . .]

---

6. See above, p. 114, note 3.

Mother mine, [. . .] the temple of Enki,[7]   145
Peshtur, little sister, [. . .] in the temple,
They will bring(?) cattle to tie them up,
They will bring(?) the sheep to tie them up,
Let them [bring] beer to secure them.
Bull of Heaven, yes you, yes you! [. . .]   150
Either you will . . . [. . .]
Or I will . . . [. . .]
I will toss your carcass into the alley,
I will toss your enormous entrails into the main street,
I will give your hide to the tanner,   155
I will dole out your meat by the bushel to the fatherless
    of the city,
I will donate your two horns as oil vessels before Inanna
    in the Eanna temple!

[*Gilgamesh and Enkidu attack the Bull of Heaven.*]

Inanna watched from the rampart,
The bull bellowed in the dust.
Lord Gilgamesh stood in front of it,   160
Enkidu went around behind the bull.
The men of his city who accompanied him,
It covered with dust like a calf not trained to the yoke.
When Enkidu got behind the bull, he seized its tail,
He called out to his king, lord Gilgamesh: 165

    Hail the anointed one, with scepter graced,
    Of princely birth, pride and glory of the gods,
    Massive bull, standing tall in battle,
    Great lord Gilgamesh, adored in Uruk!
    Your mother was best at bearing a son,   170
    Your wet nurse was best at nursing a son.
    Lord, noble one among the gods,
    Have no fear, a warrior has no strength on his own,
    Where the ground is firm [. . .]
    The people [. . .]   175
    The people of the city [. . .]

No sooner had Enkidu so spoken to Gilgamesh
[Than Gilgamesh] smote the bull on the head with his seven-
    talent axe.

---

7. Mesopotamians believed that they had individual patron gods; it seems that Enki, god
of wisdom, was patron of Gilgamesh.

The bull reared up and up till it fell over backwards,
It splattered everywhere like slime, it blanketed (the ground)
   like a crop ripe for the harvest.   180
The king, though no great cook, wielded his knife,
He struck at Inanna with a haunch, she fluttered off like a
   pigeon whose wall he was wrecking,
The king took a stand by the bull's head, shedding bitter tears,

    Even as I am destroying this, so would I do to you!

[*Gilgamesh carries out his threat to the bull.*]

Just as he had said, he tossed its carcass into the alley,   185
He tossed its enormous entrails into the main street,
He gave its hide to the tanner,
He doled out its meat by the bushel to the fatherless of the city,
He donated its two horns as oil vessels before radiant Inanna
   in the Eanna temple.

[*Closing invocation.*]

The Bull of Heaven is dead!   190
O radiant Inanna, how sweet it is to praise you!

The Death of Gilgamesh

Although the events related in the Sumerian poem "The Death of Gilgamesh" do not occur in the Babylonian epic, certain elements may be found in the death, funeral, and burial of Enkidu in Tablets VII–VIII. The Sumerian poem, in which Enkidu is already dead, begins with Gilgamesh lying mortally ill. He dreams that he is taken before the gods. There he learns that despite his heroic deeds and his mother's divinity, he cannot escape death. Once in the netherworld, Gilgamesh will, however, enjoy special status as a judge and be numbered among the lesser gods. After he awakens, Gilgamesh evidently understands what is in store for him and that Enki, his personal god, intended his dream to ease his fear of death while accepting its inevitability. It seems that his son builds him a rich tomb in the Euphrates riverbed, where he is interred with members of his royal court and magnificent grave goods. The people mourn him. Even if he is gone, his name and fame abide in the land.

    The manuscripts for this poem are fragmentary, with important inconsistencies, making the sequence of episodes and the speeches often difficult to understand, so this version combines and harmonizes the best-preserved passages of each.

[*Opening lament.*]

The great wild bull has lain down, he will never stand
  up again,
Lord Gilgamesh has lain down, he will never stand up again,
The one who fetched away that tree like no other[1] has lain
  down, he will never stand up again,
The hero (who put on) the baldric has lain down,[2] he will
  never stand up again,
He who had strength like no other has lain down, he will
  never stand up again,   5
He who reduced the evil thing to bits and pieces[3] has lain
  down, he will never stand up again,
He who was champion boxer and wrestler has lain down,
  he will never stand up again,
He who told of sacrosanct lore has lain down,[4] he will never
  stand up again,
The despoiler of foreign lands has lain down, he will never
  stand up again,
He who knew the way up into mountain lands has lain
  down, he will never stand up again,   10
The lord of Kullab has lain down, he will never stand up
  again,
He has lain down on his deathbed, he will never stand up again,
He has lain down on the bed of mourning, he will never stand
  up again!

[*Gilgamesh is deathly ill.*]

He could not stand, he could not sit up, he spent the time
  in sighs,
He could not eat, he could not drink, he spent the time
  in sighs.   15
Fate's door bolt held him fast, he could not stand up again.
Like a fish harpooned in a pond, he was in the toils of decline,
Like a gazelle caught in a snare, he tossed about in bed.
Fate, who has no hands, who has no feet, but who [snatches]
  a man in the dark,
Demon Fate had hold of him.   20

[*gap*]

1. This refers to the great cedar tree that Gilgamesh felled and brought back from the
   seventh mountain, as in "Gilgamesh and Huwawa," line 99, and in this poem, line 36.
2. This refers to Gilgamesh arming himself for battle by putting on a heavy strap or belt to
   hold his weapons, as in "Gilgamesh and the Bull of Heaven," line 131.
3. Compare "Gilgamesh and the Bull of Heaven," lines 8 and 178–80.
4. This refers to the role of Gilgamesh as mediator of sacred knowledge, as in the Babylo-
   nian epic, Tablet I, line 7; in "Gilgamesh, Enkidu, and the Netherworld," lines 255–
   388; and in this poem, lines 41–44.

The physician took [. . .] in hand,
Before heaven he [. . .] the holy first-fruit offerings.
For six days Gilgamesh lay ill [. . . like?] a potsherd,
[Tears (?) flowed] over his body like sweat.
"Lord Gilgamesh is ill!" [. . .]   25
Uruk and Kullab were distraught [. . .],
Report [of his illness spread . . .] in the land.

                          [*gap*]

Then did the youthful lord Gilgamesh lie down on his deathbed,
The king fell into a deep sleep, (he saw a dream).

[*The dream of Gilgamesh begins, with the gods talking about his exploits.*]

In that dream, [his] god [Enki escorting him],   30
At the sacred place where the gods assemble,
As lord Gilgamesh came near,
They said of him, "(It is) Lord Gilgamesh!"
He took his place there.

[*A god speaks, perhaps An or Enlil, evidently addressing Gilgamesh.*]

In your case, having ventured upon each and every road,   35
(Having vowed), "I will bring down that cedar, like no other,
    from the mountain,"
You smote Huwawa in his forest,
And, having set up steles for distant days, forever,[5]
Having founded temples for the gods,
You reached Ziusudra in his abode.   40
Having brought back the venerable and ancient ways of
    Sumer, long forgotten,
The observances and ceremonies of the land,
Having executed flawlessly the rites of purification,
Having learned [about] the Flood [that wiped out] the popu-
    lation of the land,

                          [*gap*]

Gilgamesh should not now in such a way be taken off!   45

Thus did they inform Enki of Enlil's measures.
To An and Enlil did Enki make reply:

---

5. A stele was an upright stone slab, sometimes placed as a monument near the limit of a
   military campaign, normally engraved with a depiction of the king and a god (or gods)
   on the top and a commemorative inscription below. Setting up a stele may be referred
   to in "Gilgamesh and Huwawa," line 10.

In those days, in those distant days,
In those nights, in those distant nights,
In those years, in those distant years,   50
After a convocation of the gods let the Flood sweep over,
We being about to cause the human race to disappear,
Among us a single, solitary creature indeed remained alive,
Ziusudra, a human being, indeed remained alive!
From that day forth, we swore by the life of heaven, the life
     of earth,   55
From that day forth, we swore that no one of the human
     race would live forever.
Now Gilgamesh is brought here before (the convocation).
Despite the standing of his mother, we cannot spare him.
Gilgamesh, as a ghost among the dead in the netherworld,
Let him act as general of the netherworld, let him be chief
     of the shades.   60
He should hand down decisions, he should decide legal cases,
His word should be as weighty as that of Ningishzida and
     Dumuzi.

[*Gilgamesh's reaction, in his dream.*]

Then was the heart of the youthful lord, lord Gilgamesh sor-
     rowed, [realizing] that human life must end,
His spirit languished, his heart was aching.
[When] the living [shall commemorate] the dead,   65
[When] the young and able-bodied men [hold games] at the
     new moon,
For him, no longer there, there would be no light at all.
The dream zephyr Sisig, son of Utu,
Would be his (only) light in the netherworld, the place of
     gloom.
Men, those who are remembered by name,   70
When, in the future, their mortuary statues are fashioned,
When the young and able-bodied men do the "doorjamb"[6] at
     the new moon,
Box and wrestle before (the mortuary statues),
In the month of Ab, the festival of shades,
For him, no longer there, there would be no light.   75

[*Enlil evidently addresses Gilgamesh, in his dream.*]

---

6. Obscure; possibly an athletic event in which contestants prevented other contestants
   from entering a doorway.

Great mountain Enlil, father of the gods,
[Spoke] to lord Gilgamesh in the dream:

> Gilgamesh, you were destined for kingship, you were not
>   destined for eternal life.
> Your heart should not sorrow that human life must end,
> Your spirit should not languish nor your heart be aching.   80
> The misfortune of mankind that has come for you, for you
>   too I did decree it,
> What was determined at the cutting of your umbilical cord
>   and which has come for you, for you too I did decree it.
> The darkest day of mankind has overtaken you,
> The loneliest place of mankind has overtaken you,
> The inexorable flood wave has overtaken you,   85
> The combat with no rescue has overtaken you,
> The unequal battle has overtaken you,
> The fight with no reprieve has overtaken you.
> Do not descend to the "Great City"[7] with an anguished heart,
> One should say before Utu, "He released me!"   90
> Let (your anguish) be unraveled like the strands of a rope,
>   let it be peeled off as if it were an onionskin.[8]
> Go to the head of the funerary banquet where the great
>   netherworld gods are seated,
> There where the high priest lies, there where the assistant
>   priest lies,
> There where the chief priest and the high priestess lie,
> There where the anointed priest lies, there where the linen-
>   clad priestess lies,   95
> There where the "god's sister" lies, there where the "faithful
>   one" lies,
> There where your father is, where your grandfather is,
> There where your mother, sister, and sweetheart(?) lie,
> There where your best friend and companion are,
> There, where is your friend Enkidu, your comrade in battle.   100
> In the "Great City" where governors and kings are
>   summoned,
> There where the commanders of armies lie,
> There where the heads of battalions lie,
> When a man has entered the "Great City" of the world
>   below [. . .],
> From your sister's house, your sister will come toward you,   105

7. A euphemistic term for the netherworld.
8. This may mean that Gilgamesh should take comfort from the fact that even if he must
   die, special favor awaits him in the netherworld. It is likewise Utu (Shamash) who
   comforts Enkidu when he complains of dying in the Babylonian epic, Tablet VII, lines
   96–110, by saying that after his death he will have a splendid funeral.

From your sweetheart's(?) house, your sweetheart(?) will
    come toward you,
Your confidant will come toward you, your best friend will
    come toward you,
Your city elders will come toward you!
Your spirit should not ebb nor your heart ache,
Now you will be reckoned as one of the netherworld gods,   110
You will be counted as one of the lesser gods.
You will hand down decisions, you will decide legal cases,
Your word shall be as weighty as that of Ningishzida and
    Dumuzi.

[*Gilgamesh wakes up and accepts his destiny.*]

Then the youthful lord, lord Gilgamesh, woke up, it had been
    a dream!
He shuddered, it had been a deep sleep!   115
He rubbed his eyes, all was deathly still.
The dream [. . .]
The dream [. . .]
[Gilgamesh, lord of] Kullab,
[. . .] hero of the gem-studded(?) mountain,   120
[. . . Uruk], handiwork of the gods:

> *By the life of Ninsun, mother mine, and my father, blessed*
>   *Lugalbanda,*
> *Shall I play the sleeping baby in the embrace of Ninsun,*
>   *mother mine?*[9]
> Fate, who has no hands, who has no feet, but who [snatches]
>   a man in the dark, Demon Fate has hold of me,
> My [. . .]   125
> Lord Nudimmud let me have this dream.

[*Gilgamesh recounts his dream, evidently to the elders of Uruk.*]

> In that dream, [my] god [Enki escorting me],
> At the sacred place where the gods assemble,
> As I, lord Gilgamesh, came near,
> They said of me, "(It is) Lord Gilgamesh!"   130
> I took my place there. (They said):

> "In your case, having ventured each and every road,
> "(Having vowed), 'I will bring down that cedar, like no other,
>   from the mountain,'

---

9. One version evidently has this passage here, restored from "Gilgamesh and Huwawa,"
lines 127–28; another version has a different one that is too fragmentary to translate.

"You smote Huwawa in his forest,
"And, having set up steles for distant days, forever,   135
"Having founded temples for the gods,
"You reached Ziusudra in his abode.
"Having brought back the venerable and ancient ways of
    Sumer, long forgotten,
"The observances and ceremonies of the land,
"Having executed flawlessly the rites of purification,   140
"Having learned [about] the Flood [that wiped out] the
    population of the land,

[gap]

"Gilgamesh should not now in such a way be taken off !"

Thus did they inform Enki of Enlil's measures.
To An and Enlil did Enki make reply:

"In those days, in those distant days,   145
"In those nights, in those distant nights,
"In those years, in those distant years,
"After a convocation of the gods let the Flood sweep over,
"We being about to cause the human race to disappear,
"Among us a single, solitary creature indeed remained
    alive,   150
"Ziusudra, a human being, indeed remained alive!
"From that day forth, we swore by the life of heaven, the life
    of earth,
"From that day forth, we swore than no one of the human
    race would live forever.
"Now Gilgamesh is brought here before (the convocation).
"Despite the standing of his mother, we cannot spare him.   155
"Gilgamesh, as a ghost among the dead in the netherworld,
"Let him act as general of the netherworld, let him be chief
    of the shades.
"He should hand down decisions, he should decide legal
    cases,
"His word should be as weighty as that of Ningishzida and
    Dumuzi."

[*Gilgamesh's reaction, in his dream.*]

Then was my heart of me, the youthful lord, lord
    Gilgamesh, sorrowed, [realizing] that human life
    must end,   160
My spirit languished, my heart ached.
[When] the living [shall commemorate] the dead,

[When] the young and able-bodied men [hold games] at the
    new moon,
For me, no longer there, there would be no light at all.
The dream zephyr Sisig, son of Utu,   165
Would be my (only) light in the netherworld, the place of
    gloom.
Men, those who are remembered by name,
When, in the future, their mortuary statues are fashioned,
When the young and able-bodied men do the "doorjamb" at
    the new moon,
Box and wrestle before (the mortuary statues),   170
In the month of Ab, the festival of shades,
For me, no longer there, there would be no light.
Great mountain Enlil, father of the gods,
[Spoke] to me, lord Gilgamesh, in the dream:

"Gilgamesh, you were destined for kingship, you were not
    destined for eternal life.   175
"Your heart should not sorrow that human life must end,
"Your spirit should not languish nor your heart ache.
"The misfortune of mankind that has come for you, for you
    too I did decree it,
"What was determined at the cutting of your umbilical cord
    and which has come for you, for you too I did decree it.
"The darkest day of mankind has overtaken you,   180
"The loneliest place of mankind has overtaken you,
"The inexorable flood wave has overtaken you,
"The combat with no rescue has overtaken you,
"The unequal battle has overtaken you,
"The fight with no reprieve has overtaken you.   185
"Do not descend to the "Great City" with an anguished heart,
"One should say before Utu, "He released me!"
"Let (your anguish) be unraveled like the strands of a rope,
    let it be peeled off as if it were an onionskin.
"Go to the head of the funerary banquet where the great
    netherworld gods are seated,
"There where the high priest lies, there where the assistant
    priest lies,   190
"There where the chief priest and the high priestess lie,
"There where the anointed priest lies, there where the linen-
    clad priestess lies,
"There where the "god's sister" lies, there where the "faith-
    ful one" lies,
"There where your father is, where your grandfather is,
"There where your mother, sister, and sweetheart(?) lie,   195

"There where your best friend and companion are,
"There, where is your friend Enkidu, your comrade in battle.
"In the "Great City" where governors and kings are
    summoned,
"There where the commanders of armies lie,
"There where the heads of battalions lie,   200
"When a man has entered the "Great City" of the world
    below [. . .],
"From your sister's house, your sister will come toward you,
"From your sweetheart's(?) house, your sweetheart(?) will
    come toward you,
"Your confidant will come toward you, you best friend will
    come toward you,
"Your city elders will come toward you!   205
"Your spirit should not languish nor your heart ache,
"Now you will be reckoned as one of the netherworld gods,
"You will be counted as one of the lesser gods.
"You will hand down decisions, you will decide legal cases,
"Your word shall be as weighty as that of Ningishzida and
    Dumuzi."   210

[*The elders of Uruk(?), amazed, respond to Gilgamesh's report of his dream.*]

[After the youthful lord, the lord] Gilgamesh,
[The lord of Kullab], had related that [dream],
[The elders] to whom he had related it
Answered him,
[. . .] they were crying: 215

[. . .] why was this done (for him)?
The birth goddess Nintu has never borne [a man]
[Who, seized by Demon Fate], escaped [alive].
[. . .] there is no [such man].
A mighty man may be caught in a battle net,   220
A bird of the sky, snared in a trap, cannot escape,
A fish of the depths, seeing no reed haven,
The young fisherman casts his net and catches it.
No man whatsoever can go down to the netherworld and
    come back up again,
From days of old, who ever saw the like?   225
No other king has ever been decreed a fate like yours.
Of men, those who are remembered by name,
Where is he that [. . .] like you?

You will act as general of the netherworld, you will be chief
    of the shades.
You will hand down decisions, you will decide legal cases,   230
Your word shall be as weighty as that of Ningishzida and
    Dumuzi.

[gap]

[In a missing episode, one may surmise that Enki gave instructions in a
dream to Gilgamesh or to his son, Ur-lugal, how to build his tomb. Ur-
lugal evidently relates or explains the dream on his father's behalf. When
the text resumes, the architect has begun work, with a heavy heart.]

[. . .] a propitious day
[. . .]
His architect laid out his tomb as if that was a punishment
    for him.
What had been turning in the mind of that god, Enki,   235
He let him see in a dream how to relate it,
Ur-lugal related that dream, no one else could relate it!

[Uruk is mobilized to divert the Euphrates and build the tomb in the
riverbed.]

The lord called for a mobilization in his city,
The herald sounded his horn throughout the land:

    O Uruk, mobilize! Open the Euphrates channel!   240
    O Kullab, mobilize! Let the Euphrates channel flood!

Uruk's mobilization was (fast and furious), like a deluge,
Kullab's mobilization was (steady), like a fog that does not
    dissipate.
Within a single month elapsing,
In not five days, nor ten,   245
The Euphrates channel was opened, its high water poured out,
So the pebbles in its bed could gaze in wonder at the sun.

[Constructing the tomb of Gilgamesh.]

When the Euphrates bed was drained of its water, cracked
    and dry,
He built that tomb of stone,
He built its walls of stone,   250

He set its doors in frames of stone,
The bolt and sill were adamantine diorite,
Its pivot stones were adamantine diorite,
Its roof beams were cast of gold,
At its [. . .] he dragged a massive millstone.   255
He covered it all with black earth,
[So that . . .] in future days
No one could find it,
No searcher could find its sacred precinct.
[Thus did the youthful lord, lord] Gilgamesh,   260
Establish his vault within Uruk.

[*Gilgamesh's family and royal court are sacrificed after his death and buried in his tomb.*]

His favorite wife, his favorite child,
His favorite lesser wife and concubine,
His favorite minstrel, cupbearer, and [. . .],
His favorite barber, [. . .],   265
His [favorite] courtiers and palace retainers,
They were interred with him in Uruk, in his palace enclosure,
    just as [in his lifetime].[1]

[*Gilgamesh prepares gifts to put in the tomb for the various netherworld deities he will meet.*]

Gilgamesh, son of Ninsun,
Set out its greeting gift for Ereshkigal,
Set out its present for the demon Fate,   270
Set out its marvel for Dimpiku,
Set out its gift for Pitti,
Set out its gifts for Ningishzida and Dumuzi,
For Enki and Ninki, Enmul and Ninmul,
For Endukuga and Nindukuga,   275
For Endshurima and Nindashurima,
For Enutila and Enmeshara,
For the ancestors of Enlil,

---

1. The early Sumerian practice of killing family and retinue to accompany a deceased ruler is well known from tombs discovered at Ur, made of brick or stone, dating some centuries before the time this poem was composed. One such burial held the remains of six men and sixty-eight women, including musicians, dressed in court finery, who had been systematically killed and laid out in a sixty-five-square-meter pit, the walls and floor of which had been covered by reed mats, accessed by a shaft with plastered walls. In a comparable pit each victim carried a small cup. The pits were covered with a dark layer of ashes and dirt (as in line 256). "Enclosure," translating a Sumerian word that normally meant something like "sheepfold," may here refer to these mortuary pits prepared for mass human sacrifice.

For Shulpa'e, master of the table,
For Sumuqan and Ninhursag, 280
For the Anunna gods of the Holy Mound,
For the Igigi gods of the Holy Mound,
For the dead high priest, for the dead assistant priest,
For the chief priest, for the high priestess,
For the anointed priest, for the linen-clad priestess, 285
He set out greeting gifts.
He set out fine [. . .],
He set out these gifts for [. . .].

[*In the fragmentary lines that follow, Gilgamesh lies down, evidently pours out a liquid, and dies. Food is provided for his interment. Ur-lugal closes and floods the tomb.*]

He lay down in the [. . .] of Ninsun.
Gilgamesh, son of Ninsun, 290
Poured out the liquid of the place of handing over(?) someone
    who has . . . [. . .],[2]
[. . .] he struck [. . .]
[. . .] he counted out for him first-rate [loaves . . .] and good
    victuals,[3]
[. . . he counted out] for him good . . . ,
[. . .] bringing him in, he [set stones(?)] in its door. 295
He reopened the Euphrates channel, he let its waters [flow
    over],
He surrounded his [tomb] with water.

[*The people of Uruk mourn Gilgamesh.*]

Then for the youthful lord, the lord Gilgamesh,
They gnashed their teeth,[4]
They tore out their [hair], 300
The people of his city put no [. . .],
They rubbed their mouths(?) and [. . .] in the dust.
Then for the young lord, the lord Gilgamesh,
Their spirits languished, their hearts were aching.
Men, those who are remembered by name, 305

2. This line, apparently describing Gilgamesh's last act, is fragmentary and obscure. "Place of handing over" could also mean "place of burial."
3. Sumerian burials sometimes included food and drink. A later Babylonian comment on the loss of wealth after death goes, "The loft of your house, as well as the storehouse, is full of grain, but on the day of your death they will count out but nine loaves as a grave offering and put them by your head," *Muses*, p. 419.
4. The manuscript for this passage has "he" and "his" in lines 299–304, possibly referring to Ur-lugal but taken here as impersonal for plural, hence "they" and "their."

For whom mortuary statues have been made since days of old,
Placed in shrines in the temples of the gods,
May their names once spoken never be forgotten!
The birth goddess Aruru, great sister of Enlil,
Gave them offspring to perpetuate their names,   310
Their mortuary statues, made since days of old, have spoken
   for them in the land.

[*Closing invocations.*]

O Ereshkigal, mother of Ninazu, how sweet it is to praise you!
or
O Gilgamesh, [lord] of Kullab, how sweet it is to praise you!

The Hittite Gilgamesh

The tale of Gilgamesh was well known at Hattusha, capital of the Hittite empire, which dominated what is today central Turkey and northern Syria during the latter half of the second millennium B.C.E. Not only have archaeologists recovered from the city's ruins pieces of two different Akkadian-language versions of the epic, one of which has been used in this volume to fill a gap in the Babylonian text, but at least two Hurrian-language tablets dealing with Gilgamesh have also been found. Since these texts are badly preserved and Hurrian remains little understood, it is not yet possible to translate this material. For the most part the sources composed in the Indo-European Hittite language are also fragmentary. The translation from the Hittite that follows is based on a text reconstructed from approximately thirty tablet pieces, some of which are themselves made up of a number of yet smaller scraps. Another fifteen fragments remain unplaced and have not been included here.

The author of the Hittite Gilgamesh cycle has simplified what is known from the Mesopotamian sources, omitting many details. Little attention is paid to the city of Uruk, and none at all to its layout or fortifications. Characters such as Gilgamesh's parents and the father of the hunter have been eliminated. Of primary interest to the Hittite scribes was the expedition to the cedar forest, here called "the mountains of Huwawa." This is probably due to the supposed location of this fabled realm within the later Hittite domain. The third tablet treats Gilgamesh's grief at the death of Enkidu and his consequent wanderings in the world's wild regions. We learn that, as in the Babylonian epic, Gilgamesh visits an ancient hero now residing beyond the "waters of death," but neither the motivation for his quest nor its outcome are stated in the preserved lines.

Tablet I[†]

[*Although the writer begins by stating his intention to sing of the exploits of his hero and one of the tablets is labeled "Song of Gilgamesh," the Hittite text is composed in prose, not poetry. In contrast to the Mesopotamian tradition, in which Gilgamesh is the son of a goddess and a king of Uruk, here he is specially created—not born—and endowed by the gods with great*

---

† "The Hittite Gilgamesh" has been translated by Gary Beckman for the first edition of this Norton Critical Edition.

159

size and outstanding qualities. Uruk is not his native city, but he takes up residence and rules there after a period of roaming the world. His bullying of the city's young men and deflowering of its virgins lead the gods to bring Enkidu into being as a counterweight to Gilgamesh and as a focus for his energies. Enkidu first comes to the attention of Gilgamesh through the complaint of a hunter whose activities he has frustrated in the interest of the animals that had nurtured him in the wilderness.]

§1 [Of Gilgamesh], the hero, [I will sing his praises . . .]

§2 The hero [Ea(?) fashioned] the frame of the creature Gilgamesh. [The great gods] fashioned the frame of Gilgamesh. The sun god of heaven lent him [manliness]. The storm god lent him heroic qualities. The great gods [created] Gilgamesh: His body was eleven yards [in height]; his breast was nine [spans] in breadth; his . . . was three [. . .] in length.

§3 He wandered around all the lands. He came to the city of Uruk and he [settled] down. Then every day he overpowered the [young] men of Uruk. And the mother goddess [. . .] Then she [. . .] in the winds(?) of Gilgamesh. The mother goddess looked down(?) [. . .], and she [became angry] in her heart [. . .]

§4 Then all the gods [summoned the mother goddess] over to [the place] of assembly. She entered and [said], "This [Gilgamesh] whom you created, and [whom] I created [. . .]—he [. . . I(?)] mixed in." [And] all the [gods . . .] Gilgamesh, [the hero, . . . said, "Gilgamesh is continually overpowering the young] men [of Uruk." When she] heard this, then the mother [goddess] took the power of growth from [the river(?)] and went off to create the hero Enkidu in the steppe.

§5 The hero Enkidu was in the steppe, [and] the wild beasts raised [him. They made . . .] for him [. . .] And in whatever direction the wild beasts went [for] grazing, Enkidu [went with] them. [In whatever direction they went] for watering, Enkidu [went] with them.

§6 The [young] man Shangashu, [a hunter], used to prepare pits [and traps in the steppe] for the wild beasts, [but Enkidu] went out [before him] and kept stopping up [the pits with earth]. And he [kept throwing] into the river [the traps which he had set]. Shangashu went and spoke [to Gilgamesh], "A young man is going around before [me]. He possesses [. . .], and [he knows] the steppe. [He always stops up] with earth the pits which I [prepare], and he [takes] up and keeps throwing [into the river] the traps which [I have set]."

§7 Gilgamesh replied to Shangashu, [the hunter], "Lead out a harlot [to him], so that he might sleep [with the harlot. Let Enkidu] kneel [. . . !" . . . Then] Shangashu [led] the harlot [out to Enkidu. And he] slept [with the harlot].

[*short gap*]

[*The prostitute, here named Shanhatu, meaning "whore," dresses Enkidu in fine clothes and suggests that they go into Uruk. She motivates him by telling of Gilgamesh's outrageous conduct.*]

§8 [. . . The harlot] spoke to Enkidu, [" . . . to Uruk] let us go, and [. . . " . . .]

[short gap]

§9 [. . .] And Enkidu [. . .] had the festive [garments . . .] to him [. . .]

[gap]

§10 [Then Enkidu] replied [to Shanhatu, " . . . "] And Shanhatu replied [to Enkidu], "They keep taking away [the young women. When a woman] is given in marriage to a young man, before [her husband] has yet drawn near to her, [they] discreetly [take that woman] to Gilgamesh."

§11 [When] Enkidu heard this report, [anger] came over [him]. And <to> Gilgamesh [. . .] back and forth [. . .] he went(?) [. . . Gilgamesh] and [Enkidu . . . One] grabbed [the other . . .] immediately [. . .]

[short gap]

[*Gilgamesh bests Enkidu in wrestling, and the pair immediately become friends. Sharing a meal, they decide to confront the monstrous Huwawa, whom Enkidu had seen during his time in the steppe. Gilgamesh informs the popular assembly of Uruk of this plan.*]

§12 [. . .] Gilgamesh [and Enkidu] grappled with one another, and Gilgamesh [cast Enkidu] out. [Then] they [kissed(?)] one another. [And] when they had eaten and drunk, [then Gilgamesh] spoke to Enkidu, "Because the trees(?) have grown tall, [. . .] You wandered about [in the steppe(?) . . .] in the steppe(?)." Then Enkidu spoke [to Gilgamesh, " . . . Huwawa . . . " And Gilgamesh], the king, replied [to Enkidu, " . . .] in the future [. . . let us . . .]"

§13 The fighting men [of Uruk] gathered [to] Gilgamesh [. . .] They [. . .] And he prepared a feast, summoning all [the soldiers to the place of assembly . . . . Gilgamesh] spoke [to] the soldiers, "[. . .] I want to see Huwawa!"

[gap]

[*Gilgamesh and Enkidu trek to the mountain of cedars. On the way they cross the Mala River, the upper Euphrates or one of its tributaries. Once in the mountains, they are awestruck at the trees, the dense vegetation, and the forbidding terrain. After Gilgamesh finds evidence of the presence of Huwawa, Enkidu must fortify his comrade's resolve to continue their mission. Huwawa observes them secretly and realizes that the pair have come to carry off his cedars.]*

§14 [. . .] Gilgamesh [and Enkidu] went [to . . .] At twenty double leagues [they took a meal. At thirty] double leagues [they . . . And] when they [arrived] at the bank of the Mala River, they made an offering [to the gods]. And from there [they set out and], in sixteen(?) days they arrived in the heart of the mountains.

§15 [And when] they arrived [. . .] in the heart of the mountains, they [looked at] the mountains and stared at the cedars. [And] Huwawa stared down [at them from . . . , saying to himself], "Seeing that [they have reached] the place of the god, have they finished [cutting down . . .] the god's cedars?" [Then Enkidu] and Gilgamesh said to one another, "[The deity . . . has . . .] these inhospitable mountains and has made the mountains thick [with cedars]. They are covered in brambles(?), [so that it is not possible for a mortal] to cross. [. . .] hold the [. . .] limbs of the cedars, and [they are] within the [evil(?)] mountains [. . .]." But [. . .] falls on them(?) from Huwawa [. . .] They kept striking [the . . .] like musicians.

§16 And when Gilgamesh saw the track [of Huwawa], then he came to [. . .] And [he . . .] it. Then Enkidu [said to Gilgamesh], "Why [. . .], and why against [him do you . . . ?] Won't [you] stand with [Huwawa . . . ? If] Huwawa [. . .] against me, then a man would [. . .] much. And if he [. . .], then he will [. . .] us. [. . .] by means of a heroic spirit [. . .]"

§17 [And] whoever [. . .] to them [. . .] Enkidu [. . .]

[*short gap*]

[*The adventurers begin to harvest timber and are encouraged by the sun god to attack the guardian of the forest before he can prepare himself. As battle is joined, Huwawa issues a threat to Gilgamesh and Enkidu but is unable to carry it out. The struggle raises a great cloud of dust, through which Gilgamesh can barely see the sun god. He appeals to the deity, pointing out that he is merely fulfilling a fate preordained when the mother goddess(?) sent Enkidu to Uruk. Gilgamesh also reminds the sun god that he had sought the god's approval before setting out on the quest. The god responds by sending eight winds to disable Huwawa. When the monster begs for mercy, Enkidu dissuades Gilgamesh from granting it.]*

§18 [Then Enkidu] took an axe in his hand [. . .] And when Gilgamesh saw [this], he too took an axe [. . . in his hand, and] he cut down the cedars. [But when Huwawa] heard the noise(?), anger came over him, "Who has come and cut down the cedars [which] have grown up for me [among] the mountains?"

§19 Then down from the sky the sun god of heaven spoke to them, "Proceed! Have no fear! Go [in] while he has not yet entered the house, [has not yet . . .], and has not [yet donned(?)] his cloaks(?)." [When] Enkidu heard [this, rage] came [over him]. Enkidu and Gilgamesh went in against him and fought Huwawa in the mountains. [Huwawa] said to them, "[I will . . .] you up, and I will carry you up to heaven! I will smash you on the skull, and I will bring you [down] to the dark [earth]!" He [. . .] them up, but he [did] not [carry] them [up] to heaven. He [smashed] them on the skull, but he did not bring them down to the dark [earth. They grabbed] Huwawa, and by the hair they [. . .] in the mountains. [. . .] Then he [stripped(?) . . .] away their . . . They . . . the horses . . . The dust clouds which were raised in . . . [were so thick] that heaven was not visible [. . .] Then Gilgamesh looked up at the [. . .] of the sun god of heaven and cried out. He looked into the [. . .] of the sun god of heaven, and his tears [flowed] like canals.

§20 Gilgamesh [said] to the sun god of heaven, "This is the very day that in the city [. . .], because she(?) resettled [Enkidu(?)] in the city.

§21 "But I [prayed(?)] to the sun god of heaven, and then I set out on my journey and by means of battle [I . . . him.]" Then [the sun god] of heaven heard Gilgamesh's appeal, and raised up(?) the great winds against Huwawa: the South Wind, the North Wind, [the East Wind, the West Wind], the Gale-force Wind, the Freezing Wind, [the Storm Wind], and the Destructive Wind. Eight winds blew up and battered [Huwawa] in the eyes so that he was unable to advance and unable to retreat. Then Huwawa gave up.

§22 Huwawa said to Gilgamesh, "Release me, O Gilgamesh! You shall be my lord and I shall be your slave. [Take(?)] the cedars which I have raised for you. I will fell mighty beams(?) [for you in . . .] And a palace [. . .]." Enkidu [said] to [Gilgamesh], "Don't [listen to the plea] which Huwawa [makes to you! . . .] Don't [release] Huwawa!" [. . . in] the mountains [. . .]

[*short gap*]

§23 [And] Enkidu answered [Gilgamesh], "[. . .] likewise [. . .] your, [Gilgamesh's, . . .] While [he has] not yet [entered the house(?) . . .]"

[*short gap*]

§24 [. . . mountains . . .] from the [mountains] of Huwawa [. . .] they hold him down low.

Tablet II

[Enkidu suggests that they placate the god Enlil, whom their exploits have presumably angered, by taking cedar logs to his temple.]

§1 [Enkidu] replied [to Gilgamesh], "[When(?)] we came [forth . . .] to the mountains, then [we . . .]. What will we take back for [Enlil . . .]? Should we really fell the cedars? Whoever [. . .] the gate of Enlil's temple from one direction [. . .]. They have shut you out(?). Let them be likewise!" [. . .] They felled the cedars and [arrived] at the Mala River. And when the populace gazed upon them (that is, the cedars), they rejoiced over them. [. . .] Then Gilgamesh [and] Enkidu threw off their [filthy], if splendid, garments and cleaned themselves up. [. . .] And [. . .] them [. . . But] when [. . .]

[gap]

[Gilgamesh offers to construct a fine palace for the goddess Ishtar, who is more interested in taking the hero as a lover. His rejection of her over-tures has been lost, but an Akkadian text from Hattusha and several frag-ments too scanty to be included here mention the Bull of Heaven, which she commandeers to take her revenge.]

§2 [Then Gilgamesh said] to Ishtar, "[I will build] a palace for you [. . . I will set up(?)] . . . I will lay the threshold [of the gate with lapis lazuli] and porphyry(?)."[1] [Ishtar] replied [to] Gilgamesh, "[Don't] you know, O Gilgamesh, [that] there is no [. . .]? And for [it . . .] not with silver [and gold(?)]?" He replied, "I will lay] the threshold [of the gate . . . with] lapis lazuli [and] porphyry(?)."

§3 [Ishtar replied] to Gilgamesh, "[Come], O Gilgamesh, [be] my [husband . . . !]" Then Gilgamesh [replied to Ishtar, " . . .] let it [become(?) . . .]"

Tablet III

[After their return to Uruk, Enkidu has a troubling dream foretelling his death as decreed by the gods in retribution for the murders of Huwawa and the Bull of Heaven. Only the sun god, protector of Gilgamesh and Enkidu, speaks against this decision. Gilgamesh is distraught at the thought of losing his friend.]

§1 "[. . .] we will sleep." It dawned, [and] Enkidu said to Gil-gamesh, "Oh my brother—the dream which [I saw] last night! Anu,

1. A hard red rock with red and white crystalline inclusions.

Enlil, Ea, and the sun god of heaven [were seated in council]. And Anu spoke before Enlil, 'Because they have killed the Bull of Heaven, [and because] they have killed Huwawa, who [made] the mountains thick with cedars'—so said Anu—'between them [one must die]!' And Enlil said, 'Enkidu shall die, but Gilgamesh shall not die!'

§2 "Then the sun god of heaven responded to heroic Enlil, 'Didn't they kill them(!) at my(!) behest—the Bull of Heaven and Huwawa? And should innocent Enkidu now die?' Enlil became angry with the sun god of heaven, 'Why do you accompany them daily like a comrade?'" [Enkidu] lay down to sleep before Gilgamesh, and his tears [flowed] forth like canals. He said, "Oh my brother, you are indeed my dear brother. I will [not] be brought up again to my brother from the netherworld. I will take my seat with the shades. [I will cross] the threshold of [the dead], and I will never [see] my dear brother again with my eyes!"

§3 [. . .] Gilgamesh to [. . .] sets something. And he will announce him [. . .] He will make him his vizier. [. . .] Afterwards he will become afraid.

§4 But when Gilgamesh heard [the words of Enkidu], then [his tears flowed] forth like [canals . . .] His eyes [. . .]

§5 But when [. . .]

[gap]

[*Reacting to the sight of his dead comrade, Gilgamesh recites a proverb, which seems to mean that it is sometimes necessary to flee a bad situation. Gilgamesh sets out into the wilderness, where he kills many wild beasts, including two lions.*]

§6 While for him the city of Itiha [. . .] he threw off. But when he saw [Enkidu(?) . . .], then Gilgamesh [. . .] He ran off into the mountains, and he [. . .] wailed without cease, "[Whenever] they [must eat(?)] chaff, they will [go] forth from the house of a woman." [Then] Gilgamesh treated him/her likewise. He [abandoned(?)] the land, [and] he departed from the country. He roamed the mountains continually. [No] mortal [knows] the mountains which [he crossed or the rivers] which he forded.

§7 [And] he slew many wild beasts: the wild cow, [the . . .] he [. . .] But when he [arrived] in the heart of the mountains, he [slew] two . . . lions. [And] Gilgamesh arrived in the heart of the mountains [. . .] a bird [. . .]

[gap]

[*Gilgamesh arrives at the seashore, where he greets the personified Sea with a blessing upon him and his retainers. For unknown reasons the Sea responds with a curse upon Gilgamesh and the Fates.*]

§8 [And] he wandered around(?) [. . . He didn't say] anything. [. . .] . . . away.

§9 But [when] Gilgamesh [arrived] at the Sea, he bowed down to the Sea, [and said to the Sea], "Long may you live, O Great [Sea, and long may] the minions who belong [to you] live!" The Sea cursed Gilgamesh, [. . .], and the Fate-deities.

§10 [. . .] the sea [. . .] beside [the sea . . .] afterwards [. . .] with his hand(?) [. . .]

[*gap*]

[*The moon god demands that Gilgamesh render the lions he had killed earlier into images for his temple. Gilgamesh visits the tavern keeper Siduri, but the text of their conversation has been lost.*]

§11 [. . .] the hero moon god [said to Gilgamesh], "Go and [make] these two [lions] which you slew into two images for me! Transport them into the city! Take them into the temple of the moon god!"

§12 But at dawn Gilgamesh, like a [. . .] . . . When he arrived at [the sea(?) . . .], Siduri the tavern keeper was seated upon [a golden stool], and a vat of gold [stood before her].

§13 He . . . and good [he . . .] for himself. [He did] not [come(?)] near [. . .]. Then Naḥmizulen [saw Gilgamesh . . .] and [thought] to herself.

§14 [Thus thought] that woman, "The one who [. . .] the young men [and] destroyed [the guardian, destroyed] Huwawa, and destroyed [the Bull of Heaven . . . , and] destroyed [the lions in the heart of the mountains(?)]—now [he is . . .] they will come(?). With [. . .] he will [. . .]."

[*short gap*]

§15 [" . . . .] the sea [. . .] him. Not [. . . " The tavern] keeper replied [to him, (saying), " . . .] to him. The road that [you are traveling(?) . . .] Ur-Shanabi [. . .] away [. . .]"

[*gap*]

§16 [. . . "] Only [the sun god] of heaven [crosses the sea. No one else crosses the sea]." Then Gilgamesh [said to Naḥmizulen, " . . .] not with me [. . . the sea(?)." And Naḥmizulen] answered: "[. . . Ur-Shanabi], the boatman [of Ullu(?)], has [. . .] from [the journey(?) . . .] the boat [away(?) . . . "]

[*short gap*]

§17' [. . . Gilgamesh] ran down [. . .] And to [. . . he said], "Enkidu [and] I [. . .] for a life of (many) years [. . .] His day (of death) [arrived(?) . . . do not] believe!" And(?) [. . .]

[*gap*]

[*short gap*]

[*Gilgamesh argues with Ur-Shanabi about crossing the sea. The boatman informs him that this had been possible only with the aid of the stone images, which according to Mesopotamian sources, Gilgamesh had destroyed. Ur-Shanabi instructs Gilgamesh to cut long punting poles for the voyage. This accomplished, the two of them traverse the sea in a month and a half.*]

§18 [. . .] someone [. . . " . . .] you cross [. . . " Thus said Gilgamesh] to Ur-Shanabi, "[. . .] You are the one who crosses it every day and every night." Thus said Ur-Shanabi, "Those two stone images used to bring me across!" Thus said Gilgamesh, "Why are you quarreling with me?" And Gilgamesh [. . . Ur-Shanabi] replied, "[. . .] your [. . .] up to you [. . .] before [. . .] I planted." [. . .] with wood, down [. . .] they ate. Then Ur-Shanabi replied to Gilgamesh, the king, "What [is this], O Gilgamesh? Will you go [across] the sea? What will you do when you come to the waters of death? Take an axe in your hand [and cut] poles of forty or fifty yards."

§19 And when Gilgamesh heard the words of Ur-Shanabi, he [took] an axe in his hand and cut poles of fifty yards. He stripped and [trimmed(?)] them and placed them up into the boat. Then both of them, Gilgamesh and Ur-Shanabi, [went] up into the boat. Ur-Shanabi took the rudder(?) in his hand, [while] Gilgamesh <took> [the poles] in his hand. Their journey lasted one month and fifteen days [of . . .].

[*The remaining text is too fragmentary for translation. The mutilated final portion of Tablet III mentions Ullu, whose name means literally "the Distant One." This is certainly the same figure as the primordial hero Utanapishtim, who bears the epithet "Distant One" in the Babylonian text. Unfortunately, too little is preserved for us to reconstruct the course of the story here. None of the extant Hittite-language Gilgamesh material deals with the deluge, with the protagonist's contest with sleep, with his receipt and loss of the plant of rejuvenation, or with his final return to Uruk.*]

The Gilgamesh Letter[†]

Mesopotamian students during the first millennium B.C.E. enjoyed this humorous parody of Tablet VIII of *The Epic of Gilgamesh*. The person the letter is addressed to is unknown.

Say to Ti[. . .], king of [. . .]ranunna, thus says [Gilgamesh], king of Ur,[1] citizen of Kullab, created by Anu, [Enlil], and Ea, favorite of Shamash, beloved of Marduk,[2] who holds all lands from the horizon to the zenith as with a cord [. . .], whose feet daised monarchs kiss, the king your lord who has put all lands, from sunrise to sunset, under control, as with a cord, this [according to the com]mand of Enlil-of-Devastation:

[I have formed up] and sent you 600 good work-troops. I wrote to you concerning the great [blocks] of obsidian and lapis, overlaid with the finest gold, to attach to the [statue] of my friend Enkidu, but you said, "There are none."

Now I write to you once again! As soon as you see this letter, [make re]ady and go to the land of Erish,[3] take with you a caravan of horses, send ahead of you(?) [. . .] vicious dogs that attack like lions, [. . .] white horses with black markings, 70,000 black horses with white markings, 100,000 mares whose bodies have markings like wild tree roots, 40,000 miniature calves that gambol untrammeled, 50,000 teams of dappled mules, 50,000 fine calves with well-turned hooves and horns intact, 20,000 jars of honey, 30,000 jars of ghee, 80,000 jugs of wine, 80,000 bundles of crocuses, 90,000 great tabletops of dark rosewood, 100,000 donkeys laden with leeks and juniper, and then come yourself.

I intend to fasten one nugget of raw gold ore, it should weigh 30 minas, to the chest of my friend Enkidu. I intend to fashion [. . .] thousand chunks of moonstone, lapis, every sort of exotic stone there is, into necklaces for him.

[†] Translated by Benjamin R. Foster for this Norton Critical Edition.
1. Gilgamesh was, of course, king of Uruk, not Ur.
2. Marduk was the national god of Babylon and had nothing to do with Gilgamesh.
3. Possibly a joke, interpreting the name of an ancient Sumerian city, Eresh, as Babylonian *erish*, "I asked for."

40,000 (ingots) of . . . white tin for the treasury of the great lord Marduk, 90,000 talents of iron: pure, excellent, choice, select, tested, precious, first-rate, hammered, flawless, so the smith can make a stag.

120,000 talents of pure, good [copper(?)], with all the requisite goods, so the smith can make a project for the temple from it.

A new coffin, unique, something precious, exotic, such as I have never seen, occupied or empty, see to it that [. . .] thousand troops [br]ing it in close formation.

Fill new barges with silver and gold and float them down the Euphrates with the silver and gold. You should send them(?) to the port of Babylon that my gods bear witness and my heart rejoice.

If I do not meet you in the gate of my city Ur on the fifteenth day of the seventh month, then I swear by the great gods, an oath on whom cannot be undone, and I swear by my gods Lugalbanda, Sin, Shamash, Palil, Lugalgirra, Meslamtaea, Zababa,[4] and (my personal?) god that I will send my lord "Attacker-in-My-Vanguard"(?), whose name you often hear, and he will pulverize your cities, loot your palaces, uproot your orchards, and put wickets(?) in your canal mouths. I, Gilgamesh, the one who tells his dreams,[5] will enter your capital city and I will take up residence therein. Whatever [mothers are there] should not entrust their [daughters] to me![6]

[I will . . .] . . . your children, your possessions, and your descendants . . . at the gate of Ur, I will make you and your household go into guardhouse and smithy . . . I will make you stand with the protective statues at the outermost gate, . . . as the people of Ur pass by you they will lord it over you.[7]

Quickly send me an answer and come here, and you will not have to bear any punishment from me.

Letter of Gilgamesh, the mighty king, who had no rival.

---

4. This list includes little-known deities for an antique effect, as well as Gilgamesh's father.
5. Compare the Babylonian epic, Tablet I, line 253.
6. Compare Tablet I, line 74.
7. Compare Tablet I, line 66.

The Birth of Gilgamesh According to the Roman Historian Aelian†

In his book *On the Characteristics of Animals*, the Roman historian Aelian (ca. 170–235 C.E.) tells a story of Gilgamesh being rescued as a baby by a flying eagle. Some scholars have suggested that Aelian took his story from Berossus, supposed to have been a Babylonian priest, who wrote a history of Babylonia in Greek entitled *Babyloniaca* around 281 B.C.E.

Now a further characteristic of animals is love of human beings. For instance an eagle reared a baby. But I want to tell you the whole tale, in order to furnish evidence for what I have proposed. When Seuechoros was king of the Babylonians, the Chaldeans said that the child born of his daughter would deprive his grandfather of his kingdom.[1] He was frightened by this, and if I may put it that way in jest, he played Akrisios to the girl,[2] for he kept watch over her most strictly, but secretly the girl bore a child (for fate was more clever than the Babylonian), since she had become pregnant by some obscure man. So the guards, out of fear for the king, threw the child from the citadel, for there the aforementioned girl had been imprisoned. Now when an eagle, due to its keen sight, saw the child while still falling, it went beneath the infant before he was dashed to the ground, and put its back under him, brought him to some garden and put him down with utmost care. But when the guardian of the place saw the beautiful child, he fell in love with him and reared him. He was called Gilgamos and became king over the Babylonians.

---

† The translation from the Greek given here is by A. Pietersma of the University of Toronto; the accompanying notes are by D. Frayne.
1. "Seuechoros" may be a corruption of Enmerkar, Gilgamesh's grandfather. "Chaldeans" was a general term for Babylonian astrologers in Classical sources.
2. Akrisios was an ancient Greek king who, fearing a prophecy that his daughter would bear a son who would kill him, placed his daughter and her newborn baby (the hero Perseus) in a chest and sent them out to sea to perish.

CRITICISM AND RESPONSE

Critical Approaches to
The Epic of Gilgamesh

Scholars who reconstruct the often fragmentary literature from ancient Mesopotamia concern themselves primarily with piecing together the extant witnesses to the text and carefully analyzing their language. Those who engage in this arduous process usually offer an individual understanding and interpretation based on their personal experience with the text in question, influenced by their particular background, training, and tastes. Not only are Mesopotamian texts such as *The Epic of Gilgamesh* remote from us in time, there is no continuous tradition of reading them from antiquity onward, as is the case with the Homeric epics or the Bible, so a barrier of oblivion stands between us and the cultures that produced their various versions, which philologists strive to surmount using the techniques and approaches of their discipline. This means that good critical writing about the epic takes into account philological and textual details that usually do not engage the attention of the modern scholar of literature.

Three of the critical essays reprinted here, by Thorkild Jacobsen, William Moran, and Andrew George, exemplify interpretations of *The Epic of Gilgamesh* by philologists, deeply versed in the languages and cultures of ancient Mesopotamia, who did not bring a specific critical approach to their analyses. The fourth, by Susan Ackerman, exemplifies the use of a specific critical approach, that is, liminality. Her notes lead the reader to more interpretations of the epic by philologists (Abusch, Foster), as well as to approaches based in comparison (Bird, Mobley, Niditch), sociology and anthropology (Harris), and queer theory (Walls). Additional critical approaches to the epic are discussed by Andrew George, "*The Epic of Gilgamesh*: Thoughts on Genre and Meaning," in J. Azize and N. Weeks, ed., *Gilgamesh and the World of Assyria: Proceedings of the Conference Held at the Mandelbaum House, the University of Sidney, 21–23 July 2004*. Leeuven: Peeters, 2007, pp. 37–66. There is far less critical writing on the Sumerian Gilgamesh poems; see Piotr Michalowski, "Maybe Epic: The Origins and Reception of Sumerian Heroic Poetry," in

David Konstan and Kurt A. Raaflaub, eds., *Epic and History*. Malden, MA: Blackwell, 2010, pp. 7–25. The poem by Hillary Major is an example of modern response to the epic, for which see Theodore Ziolkowski, *Gilgamesh among Us: Modern Encounters with the Ancient Epic*. Ithaca, NY: Cornell UP, 2011.

   As for liminality, the term has its origin in the study of human societies in which individuals withdraw from the social unit to a secret or remote location, are subjected to some sort of trial or ordeal, often under the supervision of a person with special knowledge of certain rites, and then, if they succeed, return to the social unit ("reaggregate") with a new, higher status as an initiate. Literary criticism of the epic uses the term more broadly, drawing attention to thresholds of place, such as settlements, doors, gates, or walls, versus uninhabited regions; thresholds of time, such as dawn, days, or weeks; and thresholds of being and awareness, such as life and death, sleeping and waking. According to this usage, some characters in the poem are "liminal" insofar as they act beyond or across conventional boundaries of human habitation, experience, and society. The excerpt from Ackerman's study included here focuses on the role of women in *The Epic of Gilgamesh*.

THORKILD JACOBSEN

"And Death the Journey's End": The Gilgamesh Epic[†]

* * *

Gilgamesh, as far as one can judge, was a historical figure, the ruler of the city of Uruk (the biblical Erekh) around 2600 B.C. It stands to reason that stories about him would have been current long after his death, but they only become graspable to us around 2100 B.C. when they were taken up by the court poets of the Third Dynasty of Ur. The kings of that dynasty counted Gilgamesh as their ancestor. We possess a number of short epical compositions in Sumerian, the originals of which must date to that revival of interest, but the Gilgamesh Epic proper, with which we are here concerned, dates from around 1600 B.C., at the end of the Old Babylonian period, and was composed in Akkadian. Strictly speaking, we should perhaps not say the "epic" but the "contours of the epic," since what we have of Old Babylonian date are fragments, and may represent only separate songs of a loosely-

---

[†] From *The Treasures of Darkness: A History of Mesopotamian Religion*. New Haven, CT: Yale UP, 1976, pp. 195–219. Reprinted by permission of Yale University Press. Line numbers in square brackets refer to this Norton Critical Edition. Notes are by the editor of this Norton Critical Edition unless otherwise indicated.

connected Gilgamesh cycle. These fragments do, however, cover all the essential—largely internally dependent—episodes that make up the tale in its later version. This version, made probably toward the end of the second millennium by one Sîn-liqi-unninnī, is preserved for the most part in copies from around 600 B.C. from the famous library of Ashurbanipal in Nineveh.[1] It contains much that is extraneous to the tale, and it lacks the freshness and vigor of the Old Babylonian fragments. In our retelling of the story here we shall therefore quote the older fragments whenever possible.

The Story

The story begins in the high style of "romantic epic," by introducing the hero to us. As the *Odyssey* begins with a characterization of Odysseus:

> Tell me, Muse, of that man, so ready at need,
> who wandered far and wide, . . .
> and many were the men whose towns he saw and whose
>   minds he learnt.
> yea, and many the woes he suffered in his heart upon the deep,
> striving to win his own life and the return of his company . . .

so the Gilgamesh Epic opens with lines calculated to whet the listener's interest in its hero as a man who has had strange and stirring experiences and who has seen far-off regions:

> He who saw all, throughout the length of the land
> came to know the seas, experienced all things . . . . [= I, 1–2][2]

But there is a special note to the Gilgamesh Epic introduction not found in the *Odyssey*, a stress on something beyond mere unusual, individual experience, a focus rather on lasting tangible achievements, typified by the walls of Uruk, still extant, still a cause for wonder when the introduction was written:

> He built the town wall of Uruk, (city) of sheepfolds,
> of the sacred precinct Eanna, the holy storehouse.
> Look at its wall with its frieze like bronze!
> Gaze at its bastions, which none can equal!
> Take the stone stairs that are from times of old,
> approach Eanna, the seat of Ishtar,
> the like of which no later king—no man—will ever make.

1. Ashurbanipal was an Assyrian king of the seventh century B.C.E. who caused many Mesopotamian literary and scholarly works to be collected and copied for his library.
2. In this and other passages, Jacobsen's interpretation and translation of *The Epic of Gilgamesh* differ from those found in this Norton Critical Edition. His proposals have been considered, along with many others, but for various reasons have not always been accepted by the translator.

Go up on the wall of Uruk, walk around,
examine the terrace, look closely at the brickwork:
Is not the base of its brickwork of baked brick?
Have not seven masters laid its foundations? [= I, 11–21]

From our first meeting with the young Gilgamesh he is character-
ized by tremendous vigor and energy. As ruler of Uruk he throws him-
self into his task with zeal. He maintains a constant military alert,
calls his companions away from their games, and harasses the young
men of the town to the point where it gets black before their eyes and
they faint from weariness, and he leaves them no time for their fami-
lies and sweethearts.

The people of Uruk are understandably not very happy at this, and
they begin to pester the gods with complaints and entreaties to do
something about it. The gods divine with remarkable insight what is
at the root of the trouble: Gilgamesh's superior energy and strength
set him apart and make him lonely. He needs a friend, someone who
measures up to him and can give him companionship on his own
extraordinary level of potential and aspiration. So they call the creator
Aruru and ask her to create a counterpart of Gilgamesh:

You, Aruru, created the wild bull (Gilgamesh)
now create his image, in stormy heart let it equal Gilgamesh,
let them vie with each other, and Uruk have peace. [= I, 103–06]

Aruru forms a mental image of the god of heaven as a model, washes
her hands, pinches off clay, throws it down in the desert, and thus
creates Enkidu.

Enkidu is, as it were, man in a state of nature. He is enormously
strong, goes naked, and hair covers all of his body; his locks are
long like a woman's and grow as luxuriantly as grain. He knows
nothing about the country and people but roams with the gazelles
in the desert, eating grass and slaking his thirst in the evening with
the animals at the drinking places. As their friend he helps protect
them by filling in pits dug to catch them and destroying traps set for
them. This brings him into contact with man. A trapper in the neigh-
borhood finds his livelihood severely threatened by Enkidu's actions,
but since Enkidu is so big and strong, there is nothing he can do.
Dejected, he goes home to his father and tells about the newcomer
and how he prevents him from carrying on his trade. The trapper's
father advises him to go to Gilgamesh in Uruk and ask for a harlot
who will go along and try to seduce Enkidu away from his animals.
The trapper makes his way to Uruk and appeals to Gilgamesh. Gil-
gamesh listens to his story and tells him to take along a harlot to
use her wiles on Enkidu.

So the trapper finds a harlot and together they walk out into the
desert, until, on the third day they reach the watering place where

Enkidu likes to come with the animals, and here they sit down to wait. One day passes, then a second, and on the third Enkidu and the animals appear and go down to drink. The trapper points Enkidu out to the harlot and urges her to take off her clothes and try to attract Enkidu's attention. In this she is eminently successful. For six days and seven nights Enkidu enjoys himself with her, oblivious to everything else. When at last satisfied, after the seventh night, he wants to go back to his animals. But they shy away. He runs after them, only to find that he no longer has his old power and speed and can no longer keep up with them.

In part, of course, that may be simply because he is by then a bit tired; but almost certainly the author of the story saw more in it. Something magical and decisive has happened. The easy, natural sympathy that exists between children and animals had been Enkidu's as long as he was a child, sexually innocent. Once he has known a woman he has made his choice, from then on he belongs to the human race, and the animals fear him and cannot silently communicate with him as they could before. Slowly, Enkidu comprehends some of this. "He grew up," says the author, "and his understanding broadened." [= I, 210]

So Enkidu gives up trying to catch up with the animals and returns to the harlot, who is very kind to him, saying:

> I look at you Enkidu, you are like a god!
> Why do you roam
> the desert with animals?
> Come, let me lead you
> into Uruk of the wide streets,
> to the holy temple, the dwelling of Anu,
> Enkidu, rise, let me take you
> to Eanna, the dwelling of Anu,
> where Gilgamesh is administering the rites.
> You could do them too, instead of him, installing yourself!
>
> [= II, 6–13]

This speech pleases Enkidu, and he takes her suggestions very much to heart. She then undresses, clothes him in the first of her garments, herself in the second, and, holding him by the hand, leads him through the desert until they come to a shepherd's camp where they are kindly and hospitably received. Here Enkidu has his first meeting with civilization and its complications. The shepherds set food and drink before him, something he has never seen before.

> He was wont to suck
> the milk of the wild beasts only;
> they set bread before him.
> He squirmed, he looked,

and he stared.
Enkidu knew not
how to eat bread,
had not been taught
how to drink beer.
The harlot opened her mouth
and said to Enkidu:
"Eat the bread, Enkidu,
it is the staff of life!
Drink the beer, it is the custom of the land!"
Enkidu ate bread,
until he was full up,
drank beer—
seven kegs—
he relaxed, cheered up,
his insides felt good,
his face glowed.
He washed with water
his hairy body,
rubbed himself with oil,
and became a man.
He put on a garment,
was like a young noble.
He took his weapon
and fought off the lions,
and the shepherds slept at night. [= II, 26–46]

For some days Enkidu stays with the shepherds. One day, however, as he is sitting with the harlot, he sees a man hurrying by and asks the harlot to bring the man to him that he may hear why he has come. The man explains that he is bringing wedding cake to Uruk, where Gilgamesh is about to be married. This upsets Enkidu: he grows pale, and immediately sets out for Uruk with the harlot. Their arrival creates a stir. The people gather around them gaping at Enkidu, noting his tremendous strength and stature. He is slightly shorter than Gilgamesh but equally as strong.

As they admire him, Gilgamesh approaches with his nuptial procession, going to the house of his father-in-law for his wedding, but as he nears the door Enkidu bars the way and does not let him in to his bride. The two seize each other, fighting like young bulls, destroying the threshold and shaking the walls. Eventually, Enkidu gains the upper hand, and Gilgamesh sinks down on one knee; but as the defeated Gilgamesh subsides and turns his back, Enkidu speaks to him—not gloatingly as a victor, but full of admiration and respect:

Matchless your mother
bore you,

> the wild cow of the corral
> Ninsûna,
> raised above men is your head,
> kingship over the people
> Enlil assigned to you! [= II, 107–10]

Enkidu's magnanimity wins Gilgamesh's heart, and out of their battle grows a lasting friendship. Gilgamesh takes Enkidu by the hand, leads him home to his mother, and she accepts Enkidu as a son, a brother for Gilgamesh.

Thus all problems are solved. Enkidu is happy in Uruk, Gilgamesh has found a friend but—as so often—the happiness does not last. In his new life Enkidu is going soft. The hardness of his muscles is disappearing; he feels flabby, out of condition, no longer fit as in the old days in the desert. Gilgamesh comes upon him one day weeping and instantly divines what to do. What they both need is a good strenuous expedition with lots of hardship and high adventure. They ought, he proposes, to set out together to kill a terrible monster called Huwawa, who lives far away in the cedar forest in the west.

Much as Enkidu may deplore the loss of his old hardihood, this way of regaining it seems rather more than he bargained for. For while Gilgamesh has only heard of Huwawa, Enkidu has actually seen him in the days he was roaming the desert, and he has acquired a healthy respect for him:

> Huwawa, his roar is a floodstorm,
> his mouth very fire,
> his breath death.
> Why do you want
> to do this?
> An irresistible onrush
> is the trampling of Huwawa! [= II, 164–66]

But Gilgamesh is not to be dissuaded. He chides Enkidu for lack of courage and shames him into going along. They have mighty weapons forged for them, take leave of the elders of the town, who give them much paternal advice about how to travel, and say goodbye to Gilgamesh's mother.

Their trip is told in great detail, and we especially hear of Gilgamesh's dreams, all of which are terrifying warnings of disaster. But Enkidu is headstrong and with unconscious impiety interprets every one of them to mean that they will overcome Huwawa. The section of the story that deals with their actual encounter with Huwawa is unfortunately badly preserved in all the versions we have, but it seems clear that in one way or other Huwawa loses out, begs for his life, which Gilgamesh is inclined to spare, and is eventually killed at Enkidu's insistence. The most complete account of the episode we have is earlier than the epic, a Sumerian tale which probably was among the sources that the author of the epic had at his disposal. It tells how Gilgamesh at first succumbs to the terror encompassing Huwawa and is unable to move. From that perilous situation he saves himself by pretending to Huwawa that he has not come to fight him but to get to know the mountains where he lives and to offer him his older sister as wife and his younger sister as handmaiden. Huwawa is taken in, divesting himself of his armor of rays of terror. Thus defenseless, he is set upon by Gilgamesh, who smites and subdues him. Huwawa pleads for his life and Gilgamesh—as a gentleman—is inclined to spare him, until Enkidu, with a peasant's distrust, speaks thus:

> "The tallest who has no judgment
> Namtar (death) swallows up, Namtar who acknowledges
>   no (excuses).
> Letting the captured bird go home,
> the captured lad return to his mother's lap,
> you will never make it back to your (own) city and mother
>   who bore you." ["Gilgamesh and Huwawa," 292–95]

Huwawa, furious at this interference, cuttingly asks whether Enkidu, "a hireling who, to the detriment of the food supply, walks behind his companions," is thus to put him in the wrong, at which Enkidu, stung by the insult, cuts off Huwawa's head.

When Gilgamesh and Enkidu return to Uruk—we are now back with the epic—Gilgamesh washes the grime of battle and travel off his body and dresses in fresh clothes. Thus arrayed he is so attractive that the goddess of Uruk herself, Ishtar, becomes enamored of him and proposes marriage: If he will become her husband she will give him a chariot of gold and lapis lazuli, kings will kneel before him, his goats will have triplets, his sheep twins. Gilgamesh though, will have none of it and seems to rather panic at the thought. Instead of quietly and calmly refusing, he heaps insults upon her: she is an unfinished door which does not keep out wind and drafts, pitch that dirties the one who carries it, a water skin which leaks on the one who carries it, a shoe that pinches the foot of its owner, and so on. Worse yet, all her previous lovers have come to a bad end. There was Dumuzi, or Tammuz, the love of her youth, for whom she instituted laments year after year. There was the varicolored bird she loved, only to break its wing so that it now runs round in the forests and cries "*kappee! kappee!*" ("my wing! my wing!"). There was the lion, for which she dug pits, and the war-horse, for which she destined whip and spurs. There was the shepherd whom she loved and then turned into a wolf so that his own dogs set upon him, and there was her father's gardener, Ishullānu, who came to grief at her hand when he refused her advances.

At this catalogue of her shortcomings, Ishtar—never very patient—rushes to her father, Anu, the god of heaven, tells him that Gilgamesh has insulted her, and begs him to let her have the "bull of heaven" to kill him. Anu is not eager to comply, suggesting that probably Ishtar herself has invited the scolding, but Ishtar is so incensed that she threatens to break the gates of the netherworld and let the dead up to eat the living if Anu does not let her have her way. Anu points out that the bull of heaven is such a destructive animal that, if let loose, there will be seven years of famine. But Ishtar assures him that she has stored enough grain and hay for man and beast for seven years, and in the end, Anu gives in to her.

As Ishtar takes the bull of heaven down to Uruk it shows itself a terrible threat. Its first snort blows a hole in the ground into which fall a hundred men, its second traps two hundred more. But Gilgamesh and Enkidu prove old hands at handling cattle. Enkidu gets behind the bull and twists its tail—an old cowboy trick—while Gilgamesh like a matador plunges his sword into the neck of the bull.

The death of the bull of heaven shocks Ishtar. She mounts the city wall, treads a mourning measure,[3] and curses Gilgamesh. At this Enkidu tears off a hind leg of the bull and hurls it up at her, shouting: "You! Could I but get at you I would make you like unto it." Ishtar and her women set up a wail over the shank of the bull, while Gilgamesh calls together the craftsmen so that they can admire the size of the bull's horns before he presents them as a votive offering to his father, the god Lugalbanda. Then he and Enkidu wash themselves in the Euphrates and return to Uruk in triumph. The entire population of the city come out to gaze at them and Gilgamesh exultantly sings out to the maids of the palace: "Who is noblest of youths? / Who, most renowned of swains?" and they answer: "Gilgamesh is noblest of youths! / Enkidu most renowned of swains!" [= VI, 172–75]

At this point in the story the two friends stand at the pinnacle of power and fame. They have killed the terrible Huwawa in the remote and inaccessible cedar forest, in their arrogance they have treated a great goddess with disdain, and in killing the bull of heaven they have proved they could get the better of her. There seems to be nothing they cannot do.

Now, however, things begin to catch up with them. Huwawa was appointed guardian of the cedar forest by Enlil, and in killing him Gilgamesh and Enkidu have incurred Enlil's anger. In a dream that night Enkidu sees the gods assembled to pass judgment on him and Gilgamesh for killing Huwawa. Enlil demands the death penalty but the sun god—god of fairness and moderation—intercedes and is able to save Gilgamesh. Enkidu, however, perhaps as the more palpably

---

3. Jacobsen thinks that Tablet VI, line 151, refers to a dance of mourning.

guilty one, has to die. And so Enkidu falls ill. Horror-stricken at what he knows is happening to him, he wishes he had never come to Uruk and curses the trapper and the harlot who brought him. The sun god, again speaking up for fairness, points out to Enkidu how much he has gained in his new life of luxury with Gilgamesh for a friend, and Enkidu then balances the harlot's curse with a long blessing. But, reconciled or not, Enkidu is doomed and dies.

Up to this point, it will have been noted, Gilgamesh has lived by the heroic values of his times. Death was a part of the scheme of things, so, since you had to die anyway, let it be a glorious death in battle with a worthy foe so that your name and fame would live. Thus, when he proposed their venturing against Huwawa to Enkidu, and Enkidu proved reluctant, he sternly upbraided his friend in just such terms:

> Who, my friend, was ever so high (that he could)
>   rise up to heaven and lastingly dwell with Shamash?
> Mere man, his days are numbered,
>   whatever he may do, he is but wind.
> You are—already now—afraid of death.
> What about the fine strength of your courage?
> Let me lead,
>   and you (hanging back) can call out to me: "Close in,
>   fear not!"
> And if I fall I shall have founded fame
> "Gilgamesh fell (they will say) in combat with terrible
>   Huwawa." [= II, 191–200]

He goes on imagining how in later years his children will climb on Enkidu's knee, and how Enkidu will then tell them how bravely their father fought and what a glorious death he died.

But all of this was when death was known to Gilgamesh only in the abstract. Now, with the death of Enkidu, it touches him in all its stark reality, and Gilgamesh refuses to believe it:

> My friend, the swift mule, the wild ass of the mountain,
>   the panther of the plain.
> Enkidu, my friend, the swift mule, the wild ass of
>   the mountain, the panther of the plain,
> who with me could do all, who climbed the crags,
> seized, killed the bull of heaven,
> undid Huwawa dwelling in the cedar forest,
> now—what sleep is this that seized you?
> You have grown dark and cannot hear me!
> But he was not raising his eyes.
> (Gilgamesh) touched his heart, it was not beating.
> Then he covered the face of his friend, as if he were a bride . . .
> Like an eagle he was circling around him;
> as does a lioness when (returning and) meeting its whelps,

he kept circling in front and back of his friend;
tearing the while his hair and scattering the tufts,
stripping and flinging down the finery off his body.
                                        [= VIII, 50–64]

The loss he has suffered is unbearable. He refuses with all his soul
to accept it as real:

> He who ever went through all hazards with me,
> Enkidu whom I love dearly,
> who ever went through all hazards with me,
> the fate of man has overtaken him.
> All day and night have I wept over him,
> and would not have him buried—
> as if my friend might yet rise up at my (loud) cries—
> for seven days and nights,
> until a maggot dropped from his nose.
> Since he is gone I can no comfort find,
> keep roaming like a hunter in the plains. [= X, 55–64]

Death, fear of death, has become an obsession with Gilgamesh.
He can think of nothing else; the thought that he himself must die
haunts him day and night and leaves him no peace. He has heard
about an ancestor of his, Utanapishtim, who gained eternal life and
now lives far away at the ends of the world. He decides to go to him
to learn the secret of immortality.

So Gilgamesh sets out on his quest. It takes him through the known
world to the mountains where the sun sets in the West. The gate the
sun enters is guarded by a huge scorpion man and his wife, but when
Gilgamesh tells them of Enkidu's death and his quest for life, they
take pity on him and let him enter the tunnel into the mountains
through which the sun travels by night. For twelve double miles,
then, Gilgamesh makes his way through the dark tunnel: only as he
nears the gate of sunrise at the other end does he feel the wind on his
face then at last sees the daylight ahead. At the gate of sunrise is a
wondrous garden in which the trees bear jewels and precious stones
as fruits, but its riches hold no temptation for Gilgamesh whose
heart is set on one thing only, not to die. Beyond the gate lie vast des-
erts over which Gilgamesh roams, supporting himself by killing wild
bulls, eating their flesh, and dressing in their skin. To get water he
digs wells where wells never were before. Without any goal he follows
the prevailing winds. Shamash, the sun god—always the soul of
moderation—becomes vexed at seeing him thus, and he reasons with
Gilgamesh from the sky. But Gilgamesh will not listen to reason, he
just wants to live:

> Is it (so) much—after wandering and roaming around
>   in the desert—

to lie down to rest in the bowels of the earth?
I have lain down to sleep full many a time all the(se) years!
(No!) Let my eyes see the sun and let me sate
  myself with daylight!
Is darkness far off? How much daylight is there?
When may a dead man ever see the sun's splendor? [= IX, 28–33]

Roaming thus, Gilgamesh eventually comes to the shore of the sea that encircles the earth and here he finds an inn kept by an alewife. His unkempt looks and hide clothing frighten the alewife and she hastens to lock her door, thinking him a bandit. As Gilgamesh comes close, however, he tells her who he is and speaks of Enkidu who died and of his own quest for eternal life, the secret of which he hopes to learn from Utanapishtim. The alewife—as had Shamash—sees the hopelessness of his quest and tries to dissuade him:

Gilgamesh, whither are you roaming?
Life, which you look for, you shall never find.
(For) when the gods created man, they set
death as share for man, and life
snatched away in their own hands.
You, Gilgamesh, fill your belly,
day and night make merry,
daily hold a festival,
dance and make music day and night.
And wear fresh clothes,
and wash your head and bathe.
Look at the child that is holding your hand,
and let your wife delight in your embrace.
These things alone are the concern of man. [= X, 77–91]

But Gilgamesh cannot be reached:

Why, my (good) alewife, do you talk thus?
My heart is sick for my friend.
Why, my (good) alewife, do you talk thus?
My heart is sick for Enkidu! [= X, 94–97]

and he asks her to tell him the way to Utanapishtim. She does so. The boatman of Utanapishtim, Urshanabi, happens to be on the mainland to cut timber, perhaps he will let Gilgamesh cross over with him. Gilgamesh finds him, but there are difficulties at first. Gilgamesh, it seems, has broken in anger the stone punting poles that Urshanabi uses to propel his boat across the waters of death, probably because Urshanabi did not immediately grant his request for passage.[4] So now he has to cut a considerable number of wooden (and so perishable) punting

4. Jacobsen thinks that the words translated in this Norton Critical Edition as "Stone Charms" refer to "stone punting poles." This is contradicted by the Hittite version so has not been accepted here (see p. 79).

poles needed to make up for the durable stone ones. But in the end he is taken across to the island on which Utanapishtim lives.

And so at long last, after incredible hardships, Gilgamesh has reached his goal. There on the shore of the island is his forbear Utanapishtim, and he can ask him how one obtains eternal life.

Yet, the moment Gilgamesh lays eyes on him, he senses that things are not quite what he had thought, something is subtly wrong:

> I look at you Utanapishtim,
> your proportions are not different, you are just like me!
> Nor are you different, you are just like me!
> My heart was all set on doing battle with you,
> but you in idleness lie on your back.
> Tell me, how came you to stand in the assembly of
>   gods and seek life? [= XI, 2–7]

Utanapishtim then tells him the story of the flood, how he alone was warned by his lord Ea, built an ark and saved his family and pairs of all animals in it and eventually, after the flood, was granted eternal life by the gods as a reward for having saved human and animal life. It is the story of a unique event which will never recur, not a secret recipe or set of instructions for others to follow. It has no relevance for Gilgamesh and his situation, and so destroys utterly all basis for the hope that drove him on his quest:

> But for you, now, who will assemble the gods for you,
> that you might find life, which you seek? [= XI, 231–32]

Utanapishtim leaves Gilgamesh no time to answer. Perhaps this is because he wishes to bring his point home through an object lesson, the contest with sleep that is to follow, perhaps it is merely an indication that the flood story was a not too skillful insertion in a shorter tale that originally had only the object lesson. At any rate, Utanapishtim immediately suggests to Gilgamesh that he try not to sleep for six days and seven nights. Gilgamesh accepts the challenge—a contest, it would seem, with Death's younger brother Sleep—but as he sits down Sleep sends a blast down over him and Utanapishtim sardonically says to his wife:

> Look at the strong man who craved life!
> Sleep is sending a blast down over him like a rainstorm.
>   [= XI, 237–38]

Utanapishtim's wife, however, takes pity on Gilgamesh, knowing that from this sleep he will never waken by himself, that fighting it is in fact fighting death; and she begs her husband to wake him, that he may go back in peace. Utanapishtim is not too keen. He knows only too well that man is by nature deceitful, and he expects that

Gilgamesh will prove no exception. He therefore tells his wife to prepare food for Gilgamesh each day and to mark the days on the wall behind him. She does so, and on the seventh day Utanapishtim touches him and he wakes. His first words—as Utanapishtim had foreseen—are:

> As soon as sleep poured down over me you quickly touched
>   me so that you awakened me. [= XI, 255–6]

but the marks on the wall and the food portions in various states of staleness bear witness to a different truth. There is no hope, then, and terror holds Gilgamesh in its grip more desperately than ever.

> Gilgamesh said to him, to the faraway Utanapishtim:
> "What can I do, Utanapishtim, where will I go?
> The one who followed behind me, the rapacious one,
> sits in my bedroom, Death!
> And wherever I may turn my face, there he is, Death!"
>   [= XI, 266–70]

Utanapishtim has no solace to offer, only tells the boatman Urshanabi to take Gilgamesh to a place where he can wash, and to give him clean clothes for the return journey. These clothes will stay fresh until he gets home. Then Gilgamesh and Urshanabi launch the boat once more, but as they move off, the wife of Utanapishtim again intercedes for Gilgamesh, asking her husband what he will give Gilgamesh now that, after so many hardships, he is on his way home. Gilgamesh brings the boat back to shore and Utanapishtim tells him of a thorny plant growing in the Apsû, the sweet waters deep under the earth, which has power to rejuvenate. Its name is "As Oldster Man Becomes Child." Gilgamesh, overjoyed, makes haste to open the valve down to the Apsû, ties stones to his feet, as do the pearl divers in Bahrein, to drag him down, finds the plant and plucks it, though it stings his hand, cuts loose the stones, and lets the flood carry him up and cast him ashore. Delighted, he shows the plant to Urshanabi—both, apparently, are now on the shore of the Persian Gulf rather than at Utanapishtim's island—and tells him of its qualities and how he is taking it back to Uruk where he will eat it when he grows old and thus return to childhood.

But the weather is warm and as he travels back Gilgamesh sees an inviting, cool pond, doffs his clothes, and goes in to bathe. A serpent smells the odor of the plant which he has left with his clothes, comes out of its hole, snatches, and eats it. As it disappears again into its hole it sloughs off its old skin and emerges new and shiny and young.

This spells the end of Gilgamesh's quest. It has come to nothing. The serpent, not he, has obtained the power of rejuvenation. And so at last he has to admit defeat, final and utter defeat:

> On that day Gilgamesh sat down and wept,
> tears streaming down his cheeks:
> "For whose sake, Urshanabi, did my arms tire?
> For whose sake has my heart's blood been spent?
> I brought no blessing on myself,
> I did the serpent underground good service!" [= XI, 332–38]

The mood in which he meets this final defeat, however, is new and other than what he has been capable of before; it is one of composure, one of resignation, even humorous, self-ironical resignation, not of terror and despair. It is a mood not unlike Dryden's:

> Since ev'ry man who lives is born to die,
> And none can boast sincere felicity,
> With equal mind, what happens, let us bear,
> Nor joy nor grieve too much for things beyond our care.
> Like pilgrims to th' appointed place we tend;
> The world's an inn, and death the journey's end.

This late and dearly won resignation, this acceptance of reality, finds symbolic expression in the epic in a return to where we began, to the walls of Uruk which stand for all time as Gilgamesh's lasting achievement. Man may have to die, but what he does lives after him. There is a measure of immortality in achievement, the only immortality man can seek.

And so, when Gilgamesh finally arrives home, his first act is to show the walls to Urshanabi.

> Gilgamesh said to the boatman, Urshanabi:
> "Go up, Urshanabi, on the wall of Uruk, walk around!
> Examine the terrace, look closely at the brickwork!
> Is not the base of its brickwork of baked brick?
> Have not seven masters laid its foundations?
> An acre town and an acre orchards,
> an acre riverbed, also precinct of the Ishtar temple.
> Three acres and the precinct comprises Uruk." [= XI, 346–53]

This ends the story.

Sources

To clarify to ourselves what this ancient story is about and what its author was driving at, we may profitably ask two fundamental questions, one about sources and another about the theme. The question about sources asks what the author had to work with or—if the Old Babylonian fragments do not yet represent an epic, merely a cycle of tales—within what frame of reference, within what world of traditional Gilgamesh lore, the telling of these tales moved. The question about theme probes further. It asks what the author (or authors) did with those materials: how they were aimed, what meanings were seen in them or given to them. What made them the stuff of poetry?

The sources—what is known about them or can be surmised—we have tried to present succinctly in a diagram headed "Gilgamesh Tradition." It begins with the "historical Gilgamesh," a ruler of Uruk at circa 2600 B.C., in the period known as Early Dynastic II. The reason we assume that the Gilgamesh traditions cluster around an actual historical figure is that the tradition seems to be remarkably informed about the period with which it deals. Personages encountered in the episodes, such as Enmebaragesi, the father of Agga of Kish, mentioned in the tale "Gilgamesh and Agga,"[5] have been proved to be historical by contemporary inscriptions. The name Gilgamesh itself is composed of elements that were current in proper names at that time, but fell out of use later; the custom of burying a ruler's court with him when he died, implied in the tale of "The Death of Gilgamesh," is actually known to us from the only slightly younger Royal Tombs at Ur, after which time it was abandoned.

As ruler of Uruk in the Early Dynastic period the historical Gilgamesh would have had the title ofen and would have united in his person the two distinct aspects of that office, magical and martial, which we have called on the chart respectively, the Heros and the Hero aspects.

The magical, or Heros, aspect of the office of en we have touched upon earlier, in our discussion of the yearly rite of the sacred marriage, in which a human en priest or priestess married a deity.[6] In Uruk, the en was male and was the ruler of the city. In the rite he took on the identity of Dumuzi-Amaushumgalanna and married the goddess Inanna, or Ishtar. Their union magically ensured fertility and plenty for all. As shown by the famous Uruk Vase on which the rite is pictured, it was celebrated in that city as early as Protoliterate times.[7]

The magic powers of the en were not limited to his ritual role in the sacred marriage. They belonged to him in his own right and continued to be effective after his death when he dwelt in the underworld, in the earth from which emanated the powers that made trees and plants, orchards, fields, and pasturage all grow and thrive. Notably successful en priests, in whose time there had been years of plenty,

5. Included in this Norton Critical Edition as "Gilgamesh and Akka," above, pp. 104–09. "The Death of Gilgamesh," which Jacobsen references below, is also included here, above, pp. 146–58.
6. It is the custom of some Sumerologists to set Sumerian words with spaces between the letters. The passage alluded to has not been reprinted here. Jacobsen uses "Heros" to refer to religious functions of a ruler.
7. The Uruk Vase is a stone vessel from Uruk, about 3000 B.C.E., that shows a goddess receiving offerings from a man in a distinctive fringed garment. Jacobsen thinks that the goddess is Inanna and the man is an "en," a Sumerian term sometimes understood to be a ruler with priestly, military, and political responsibilities. "Protoliterate times" refers to the period of Mesopotamian civilization between 3500 and 3000 B.C.E.

continued, therefore, to be worshiped with funerary offerings after their death to insure that they would continue their blessings. The historical Gilgamesh, we may assume, was such a figure, credited with the power to produce plentiful years and continuing to be worshiped after his death. Our first tangible indication that this was so comes from account texts from Girsu of around 2400 B.C.[8] They show that funerary offerings for successful dead en priests and other figures credited with fertility powers were made at a sacred locality called "The (River-) Bank of Gilgamesh." Further evidence of Gilgamesh's prominence as a power in the netherworld comes in a composition of about 2100 B.C. dealing with the death of the first king of the Third Dynasty of Ur, Urnammu. Here Gilgamesh appears as a judge in the realm of the dead. He occurs again in that role much later, in magical texts of the first millennium, where he is appealed to for judgment against wayward ghosts and other evils. Lastly, copies of laments, which may have been composed in the first half of the second millennium, mention Gilgamesh as a form of the dying god Dumuzi side by side with the god Ningishzida.

It is clear, thus, that there was a vigorous and continuous nonliterary religious tradition arising from the magical aspect of the historical Gilgamesh's office as en.

The martial aspect of the office of en implies that the historical Gilgamesh must have headed the army of Uruk; and here again the fact that traditions cluster around his name suggests that he was a military leader of extraordinary stature. Whether the later literary tradition celebrating him as leader in a war of liberation against Kish actually contains a historical kernel is not easy to say, though it is not implausible. At any rate, the role of liberator ascribed to him would seem to be the reason why the god Dumuzi-Amaushumgalanna chose to model himself on Gilgamesh when he served as divine deputy with the army of Uruk in a later war of independence, the one against the hated Gutian mountaineers in about 2100 B.C. Utuhegal, who led that army to victory, tells us in his inscription how he reported this decision of Dumuzi-Amaushumgalanna to his troops in a speech to them when they set out.

The tradition about Gilgamesh's war with Kish is referred to also in a royal hymn written for Shulgi of Ur only a generation or so after Utuhegal, and another military achievement, the building of the city walls of Uruk, is ascribed to him in a tradition attested to around 1800 B.C. in an inscription of the ruler Anam who made repairs on them.

Against the background of these two nonliterary lines of tradition, one about a power for fertility in the netherworld (the Heros

8. Girsu was a Sumerian city important during the last half of the third millennium B.C.E.

Gilgamesh Tradition

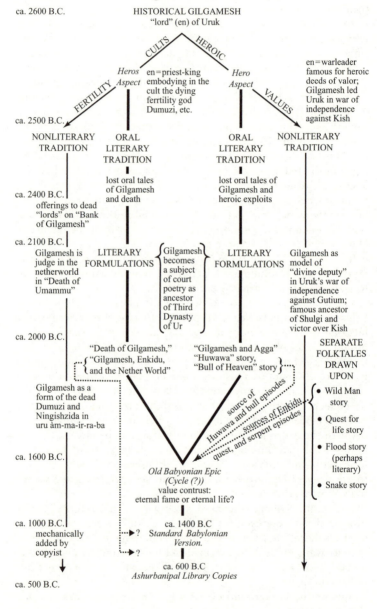

ca. 2600 B.C.
HISTORICAL GILGAMESH
"lord" (en) of Uruk

CULTS   HEROIC

Heros Aspect   en=priest-king embodying in the cult the dying ferrtility god Dumuzi, etc.   *Hero Aspect*

en=warleader famous for heroic deeds of valor; Gilgamesh led Uruk in war of independence against Kish

FERTILITY   VALUES

ca. 2500 B.C.
NONLITERARY TRADITION   ORAL LITERARY TRADITION   ORAL LITERARY TRADITION   NONLITERARY TRADITION

lost oral tales of Gilgamesh and death   lost oral tales of Gilgamesh and heroic exploits

ca. 2400 B.C.
offerings to dead "lords" on "Bank of Gilgamesh"

ca. 2100 B.C.
Gilgamesh is judge in the netherworld in "Death of Umammu"

LITERARY FORMULATIONS   { Gilgamesh becomes a subject of court poetry as ancestor of Third Dynasty of Ur }   LITERARY FORMULATIONS

Gilgamesh as model of "divine deputy" in Uruk's war of independence against Gutium; famous ancestor of Shulgi and victor over Kish

ca. 2000 B.C.
"Death of Gilgamesh," { "Gilgamesh, Enkidu, and the Nether World" }   "Gilgamesh and Agga" "Huwawa" story, "Bull of Heaven" story }

SEPARATE FOLKTALES DRAWN UPON

Gilgamesh as a form of the dead Dumuzi and Ningishzida in uru àm-ma-ir-ra-ba

source of Huwawa and bull episodes
sources of Enkidu, quest, and serpent episodes

• Wild Man story
• Quest for life story
• Flood story (perhaps literary)
• Snake story

ca. 1600 B.C.

Old Babylonian Epic (Cycle (?)) value contrast: eternal fame or eternal life?

ca. 1000 B.C.
mechanically added by copyist

--▶?   ca. 1400 B.C *Standard Babylonian Version.*

--▶?   ca. 600 B.C *Ashurbanipal Library Copies*

ca. 500 B.C.

line), one about a famed warrior and wall builder of old (the Hero line), we may then set what we might call the literary development. Of its beginnings we know nothing at all, but we may surmise a body of oral tales and songs handed down and lost to us, except as they furnished material for later written compositions.

It seems such written compositions appear first with the accession of the Third Dynasty of Ur around 2100 B.C. The kings of that dynasty not only took great interest in literature and the preservation of old works generally, but considered themselves descendants of Gilgamesh, so that traditions and works about him would have special claim to their attention. What we have preserved (almost all in later copies) are separate short epic compositions in Sumerian, and they divide quite neatly into the Heros and Hero lines of tradition, with works where Gilgamesh confronts the problem of death and works celebrating his martial prowess. Among the former is the tale called "The Death of Gilgamesh," which tells how death came to him in due time, how he violently protested, and how Enlil himself personally argued with him that there was no way for man to avoid it. The story is known to us only in fragments and its full meaning may only become clear through future lucky finds. Another Gilgamesh story concerned with death is called "Gilgamesh, Enkidu, and the Netherworld."[9] It tells how in the beginning of time the goddess Inanna, wandering along the banks of the Euphrates, found a tree floating on it, pulled it ashore, and planted it with the hope that when it grew to maturity she could have a table and a bed made from its wood. The tree grew apace, and when it had reached the proper size Inanna wished to fell it but found that the thunderbird Imdugud[1] had built its nest in the crown, the demoness Kiskillilla had made her abode in its trunk, and a huge serpent nestled at its root. Poor Inanna, therefore, could not get to her tree and appealed to her brother Utu, the sun god, for help, but he refused. She then turned to Gilgamesh, who gallantly took up arms and drove the intruders away, felled the tree, gave her its wood for a table and a bed, and made for himself a puck and stick—for a game which seems to have resembled modern hockey—out of its roots. Uruk played and feasted, celebrating the victory, and all were happy except a poor waif, a little girl who had neither father, mother, or brother, and felt left out and lost. In her anguish she cried out to the sun god, the god of justice and fairness, with the dread "i - U t u," and he heard her. The earth opened and the playthings Gilgamesh had made for himself fell down into the netherworld as a reproof to the thoughtless revelers. Gilgamesh was disconsolate and Enkidu rashly offered to bring them back up. Accordingly, Gilgamesh gave him elaborate instructions about how to conduct himself in the

9. Included in this Norton Critical Edition, above, pp. 146–58 and pp. 109–25.
1. Imdugud is another way of reading the name of Anzu, a monstrous bird.

netherworld, to be very quiet, not to call attention to himself by wearing fine clothes and anointing himself, not to show emotion by kissing the dead child and wife he had loved or striking the dead child or wife he had hated. As it turned out, Enkidu did all these things and the netherworld held him fast. Gilgamesh appealed to the gods but all they could do for him was to open a vent to allow Enkidu's ghost to come up to speak with him. The friends embraced, and at Gilgamesh's questioning Enkidu told in detail what the netherworld was like. Conditions were dismal, although there were gradations of misery. Those with large families, those who fell in battle, those who had lived a good life, were better treated than the rest. But no clear general principles of a moral or ethical nature seem to have governed the infernal regions.

Among the compositions belonging to the Hero line of the tradition are, first of all, "Gilgamesh and Agga of Kish,"[2] a short Sumerian composition which tells how Gilgamesh led Uruk in a war of freedom against Kish. After Uruk had refused to do the usual corvée work, Agga's shipborne troops appeared before its walls and began a siege. A first sortie by the warrior Birhurturra proved unsuccessful. A second by Enkidu and Gilgamesh cut its way to Agga's boat and took him captive. The story raises intricate problems of heroic honor and loyalty. Gilgamesh had at one time, it appears, been a fugitive whom Agga received kindly. In fact, it would seem likely that it was Agga who made Gilgamesh his vassal ruler in Uruk, the position from which Gilgamesh now foments a rebellion against him. As a true hero, Gilgamesh cannot bear to owe anything to the largess of another, but must win what he has through his own prowess in battle, must prove himself by defeating Agga. Only after he has taken Agga captive can he acknowledge his debt to him: he sets him free and of his own free will promises to recognize him as overlord. The largess is now his: he is repaying the good turn Agga originally did him and is no more in his debt.

Gilgamesh's Hero aspect also dominates the Sumerian tale about his expedition against Huwawa which we have in two different versions, one elaborate, the other brief. The adventure is undertaken so that Gilgamesh may establish a name for himself, but the tale differs from the one about Agga in its more romantic, almost fairy tale setting. Unlike Agga, who is an entirely human opponent, Huwawa seems more ogre than warrior. Altogether mythical in character, finally, is the Sumerian tale about "Gilgamesh, Inanna, and the Bull of Heaven."[3] Here, as in the corresponding episode in the epic, Gilgamesh's valor is pitted against a deity and a mythical monster.

2. Included in this Norton Critical Edition as "Gilgamesh and Akka," above, pp. 104–09.
3. Included in this Norton Critical Edition as "Gilgamesh and the Bull of Heaven," above, pp. 138–46.

As will be seen, then, the two lines of the Gilgamesh tradition find literary expression in compositions showing diametrically opposed attitudes toward death. In the Hero tales death is almost recklessly courted by the hero: to repay Agga and no longer feel in his debt, to establish a name by killing Huwawa, to stand up to Inanna. In the Heros tales death is the great unavoidable evil: "the darkness that cannot be resisted has arrived for you," Gilgamesh is told in the "Death of Gilgamesh." "If I instructed you about the netherworld, you sitting down weeping. I would want to sit down and weep," Enkidu tells him in "Gilgamesh, Enkidu, and the Netherworld." These contradictory attitudes united in the person of Gilgamesh prefigure, as it were, what was to become the theme of the later epic: the change from an earlier disdain for death to the obsessive fear of it which drives Gilgamesh on his quest after Enkidu's death.

If we ask more specifically which parts of the Sumerian literary Gilgamesh tradition were used in the epic we would point to the Huwawa story and the "Gilgamesh, Inanna, and the Bull of Heaven" story as obvious prototypes of the corresponding episodes in the epic. Both of these episodes are represented in the Old Babylonian materials. No Sumerian prototypes, on the other hand, have been found for the "Coming of Enkidu" and the "Quest for Life" episodes, which also are part of the Old Babylonian materials; and it may in fact be doubted whether these tales ever did form part of the Sumerian Gilgamesh tradition. The likelihood is that they came from elsewhere.

In the case of the "Coming of Enkidu" tale, the motif of the hairy wild man who lives with the animals and is lured into human society by a woman is found in many forms in the folklore of Asia, and has been studied in detail by Charles Allyn Williams in his dissertation, *Oriental Affinities of the Legend of the Hairy Anchorite* (Urbana, 1925–26). His data show that the basis of the story is wonder at the orangutan, which was seen as a "wild man" deliberately shunning the company of other men. Its origin must therefore be looked for in the Far East.[4]

The motif of the "Quest for Life" is also well known outside Mesopotamia. We find it in the story of "The Water of Life" in Grimm's *Hausmärchen*,[5] which tells about a dying king whose three sons set out to find the water of life to revive him. Only the youngest son, helped by animals to whom he has been kind, succeeds in reaching the island where the water of life is and bringing it back. He also, of course, wins a princess and, after further trials, lives happily ever after.

---

4. Jacobsen refers here to the story of Enkidu, Tablet I, lines 110–20, and to the story in Tablets IX and X.
5. Fairy tales.

Lastly, there is the motif of the serpent stealing the plant of rejuvenation. This motif has been convincingly traced to Melanesian and Annam folklore by Julian Morgenstern in a study called "On Gilgamesh—Epic XI" in *Zeitschrift für Assyriologie* 29, pp. 284–300.

At what time these Far Eastern folktale motifs spread to Mesopotamia is not easy to determine. The first two must have been there in Old Babylonian times, as shown by the Gilgamesh materials, and there is no reason to assume that they had come in earlier. Why they were drawn into the Gilgamesh tradition is a further puzzle. The simplest answer—which can of course be no more than a surmise—is clearly to assume that the Old Babylonian materials do indeed belong to an epic, the author of which obtained his theme from the contrastive attitudes to death in the Gilgamesh tradition but supplemented his materials with other tales he knew that would serve to develop it. If one would see, rather, the Old Babylonian materials as representing merely a loose cycle of independent tales, it becomes more difficult to imagine what, if anything, about these tales could have made anybody think they referred to Gilgamesh.

If we are right in surmising the existence of an Old Babylonian Epic of Gilgamesh, that epic would almost certainly have been shorter than the version credited to Sîn-liqi-unninnī from perhaps the end of the second millennium, and that shorter again than the version in twelve tablets we have from the library of Ashurbanipal.[6] To begin with the latter, the twelfth tablet is a mechanical addition of an Akkadian translation of the last half of "Gilgamesh, Enkidu, and the Netherworld," a tale which has no organic connection with the rest of the epic. The adding on has indeed been done so mechanically that the first lines make no sense and can only be understood in the light of those parts of the original story which were dropped when it was attached to the Gilgamesh Epic. Without this addition—which seems more the work of a copyist than an editor—the epic shows a frame: it begins and ends with the same hymn in praise of the walls of Uruk. Probably this was the form Sîn-liqi-unninnī gave it, and to his version belongs probably also the long account of the flood which is put in the mouth of Utanapishtim and which takes up almost half of the eleventh tablet. That it belongs with the frame is suggested by the stress which the introduction to the epic places upon it, for in a passage omitted in our retelling of the story the introduction lists as one of Gilgamesh's achievements that he brought back information from before the flood. On the other hand the unwieldy length of the flood story, which badly upsets the flow and balance of the quest narrative, and the fact that it duplicates—in

6. Jacobsen refers to a large collection of tablets assembled and copied at the capital city Nineveh by the Assyrian king Ashurbanipal (see p. 177, note 1). Most of the manuscripts of the standard version are from this collection.

fact renders meaningless—the following contest of Gilgamesh with Sleep, strongly suggests that it is an addition and not part of the original story. Its source is obviously the tradition about the flood represented both by the Sumerian flood story and the elaborate account in the Atrahasis Myth.[7] In neither of these settings, of course, does the flood have any relation to the traditional Gilgamesh materials. Probably, therefore, we should imagine the Old Babylonian epic (or story of the quest) as not yet having it—at least not at such length—and assume that it was included because of its intrinsic interest by Sîn-liqi-unninni in his version.

Structural Analysis: Themes

The question about the sources of the Gilgamesh Epic, which led us back to a historical Gilgamesh, en of Uruk and point of origin for two lines of tradition with contrasting attitudes toward death, suggests that precisely in this contrast lay, *in nuce*,[8] the central theme of the later epic. The further question about how that theme was developed, what the author did with his materials and how he focused them, is perhaps best asked in terms of Sîn-liqi-unninni's version. It may be phrased either in positive terms as a quest for achieving immortality or in negative terms, as a flight, an attempt to avoid death. In the accompanying diagram we have indicated progress toward the story goals by upward movement of the story curve, and shown hindrance by a downward turn.

As the story begins Gilgamesh shares the heroic values of his times, and his aspirations to immortality take the form of a quest for immortal fame. Death is not yet truly the enemy; it is unavoidable of course but somehow part of the game: a glorious death against a worthy opponent will cause one's name to live forever. In his pursuit of this goal Gilgamesh is extraordinarily successful and scores one gain after another. He fights Enkidu and gains a friend and helper. Together they are strong enough to overcome the famed Huwawa and to treat with disdain the city goddess of Uruk, Ishtar. At that point they have undoubtedly reached the pinnacle of human fame. And at that point their luck changes. In ruthlessly asserting themselves and seeking ever new ways to prove their prowess they have grievously offended the gods, paying no heed to them whatever. Huwawa was the servant of Enlil, appointed by him to guard the cedar forest; their treatment of Ishtar was the height of arrogance. Now the gods' displeasure catches up with them, and Enkidu dies.

When he loses his friend, Gilgamesh for the first time comprehends death in all its stark reality. And with that new comprehension comes

7. See note 1 on p. 87.
8. In essence (Latin).

the realization that eventually he himself will die. With that all his previous values collapse: an enduring name and immortal fame suddenly mean nothing to him any more. Dread, inconquerable fear of death holds him in its grip; he is obsessed with its terror and the desirability, nay, the necessity of living forever. Real immortality—an impossible goal—is the only thing Gilgamesh can now see.

Here, then, begins a new quest: not for immortality in fame, but for immortality, literally, in the flesh. As with his former quest for fame Gilgamesh's heroic stature and indomitable purpose take him from one success to another. Setting out to find his ancestor, Utanapishtim, in order to learn how to achieve, like him, eternal life, he gains the help of the scorpion man and his wife, Sidûri, the alewife, and Urshanabi. When after great travail he stands before Utanapishtim it is only to have the whole basis for his hopes collapse. The story of the flood shows that the case of Utanapishtim was unique and can never happen again and—to make his point—Utanapishtim's challenging him to resist sleep, proves how utterly impossible is his hope for vigor strong enough to overcome death.

However, at the point of the seemingly total and irreversible failure of his quest, new hope is unexpectedly held out to Gilgamesh. Moved by pity, Utanapishtim's wife asks her husband to give Gilgamesh a parting gift for his journey home, and Utanapishtim reveals a secret. Down in the fresh watery deep grows a plant that will make an oldster into a child again. Gilgamesh dives down and plucks the plant. He has his wish. He holds life in his hand. Any time he grows old he can again return to childhood and begin life anew. Then on the way back there is the inviting pool and the serpent who snatches the plant when he carelessly leaves it on the bank.

Gilgamesh's first quest for immortality in fame defied the gods and brought their retribution on him; this quest for actual immortality is even more deeply defiant; it defies human nature itself, the very condition of being human, finite, mortal. And in the end it is Gilgamesh's own human nature that reasserts itself; it is a basic human weakness, a moment of carelessness, that defeats him. He has nobody to blame but himself; he has ingloriously blundered. And it is perhaps this very lack of heroic stature in his failure that brings him to his senses. The panic leaves him, he sees himself as pitiful and weeps; then as the irony of the situation strikes him, he can smile at himself. His superhuman efforts have produced an almost comical result. This smile, this saving sense of humor, is the sign that he has, at last, come through. He is finally able to accept reality and with it a new possible scale of value: the immortality he now seeks, in which he now takes pride, is the relative immortality of lasting achievement, as symbolized by the walls of Uruk.

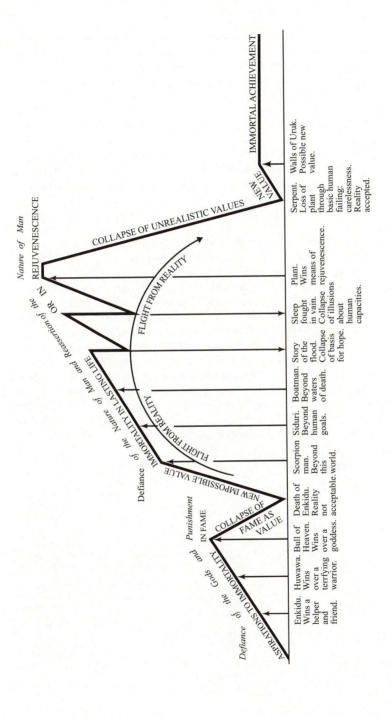

The movement from heroic idealism to the everyday courage of realism illustrated by the Gilgamesh story gains further in depth if one analyzes it not only positively as a quest, but also negatively as a flight, an avoidance. A flight from death rather than a quest for life—but a flight in what terms?

Throughout the epic Gilgamesh appears as young, a mere boy, and he holds on to that status, refusing to exchange it for adulthood as represented by marriage and parenthood. Like Barrie's Peter Pan he will not grow up.[9] His first meeting with Enkidu is a rejection of marriage for a boyhood friendship, and in the episode of the bull of heaven he refuses—almost unnecessarily violently—Ishtar's proposal of marriage. She spells disaster and death to him. So when Enkidu dies, he does not move forward seeking a new companionship in marriage, but backward in an imaginary flight toward the security of childhood. At the gate of the scorpion man he leaves reality; he passes literally "out of this world." In the encounter with the alewife he again firmly rejects marriage and children as an acceptable goal, and eventually, safely navigating the waters of death, he reaches the ancestors, the father and mother figures of Utanapishtim and his wife, on their island where, as in childhood, age and death do not exist. True to his images, Utanapishtim sternly attempts to make Gilgamesh grow up to responsibility; he proposes an object lesson, the contest with sleep, and is ready to let Gilgamesh face the consequences. The wife of Utanapishtim, as mother, is more indulgent, willing for Gilgamesh to remain a child, and she eventually makes it possible for him to reach his goal with the plant "As Oldster Man Becomes Child." Gilgamesh is fleeing death by fleeing old age, even maturity; he is reaching back to security in childhood. The loss of the plant stands thus for the

9. Note Harry Stark Sullivan, *The Interpersonal Theory of Psychiatry* (New York, 1953), p. 245: "The beginning of preadolescence is equally spectacularly marked, in my scheme of development, by the appearance of a new type of interest in another person . . . . This new interest in the preadolescent era is . . . a specific new type of interest in a *particular* member of the same sex who becomes a chum or a close friend. This change represents the beginning of something very like full-blown, psychiatrically defined *love*. In other words, the other fellow takes on a perfectly novel relationship with the person concerned: he becomes of practically equal importance in all fields of value." And ibid., p. 264: " . . . the change from preadolescence to adolescence appears as a growing interest in the possibilities of achieving some measure of intimacy with a member of the other sex, rather after the pattern of the intimacy that one has in preadolescence enjoyed with a member of one's own sex."

The appearance of Enkidu provides Gilgamesh with a "chum" and allows him to remain in preadolescence rather than moving on to a heterosexual relationship such as is characteristic of adolescence and adulthood. Note that in explaining Gilgamesh's dream about Enkidu's arrival his mother says [see Tablet I, lines 300–02 (*Editor*)]: "The axe you saw is a man, you will love him as (you would) a wife, so that I will make him your compeer" and that at his arrival Enkidu prevents Gilgamesh's marriage to Ishhara [see Tablet II, lines 92–5 (*Editor*)]. Also when he rejects the adult goal of marriage and children urged by the alewife he does so in terms of his attachment to Enkidu [see Tablet X, lines 94–97 (*Editor*)]: "Why my (good) alewife do you talk thus? / My heart is sick for my friend! / Why, my (good) alewife do you talk thus? / My heart is sick for Enkidu!" Throughout the epic the relationship with Enkidu competes with, and replaces, marriage. [*Jacobsen's note.*]

loss of the illusion that one can go back to being a child. It brings
home the necessity for growing up, for facing and accepting reality.
And in the loss Gilgamesh for the first time can take himself less seri-
ously, even smile ruefully at himself; he has at last become mature.

> For whose sake, Urshanabi, did my arms tire?
> For whose sake has my heart's blood been spent?
> I brought no blessing on myself,
> I did the serpent underground good service! [= XI, 335–38]

The Gilgamesh Epic is a story about growing up.

WILLIAM L. MORAN

The Epic of Gilgamesh: A Document of Ancient Humanism[†]

Philology has been described as the "art of slow reading," and nowhere
else is this art more appropriate, indeed at times even essential, than
in reading an epic. For distinctive of the epic and lending it its pecu-
liar power and dignity is the leisure with which the epic poet moves
through his tale. His pace is slow; he may even digress. He lingers
over scenes and events. And, as we read his work, we should linger
too, and not only linger, but, as Schiller once wrote to Goethe, linger
with love—*sich mit Liebe verweilen.*

It is as a philologist, a lover of words, a slow reader, with Schiller as
my guide, that I speak to you this evening. I can hardly hope, I know,
to introduce you to the Gilgamesh epic. Most of you are familiar with
it, I am sure, and some of you will recall Thorkild Jacobsen's lecture
on the epic before this Society not many years ago.[1] You may also be
acquainted with Bernarda Bryson's splendid adaptation of the epic
for your children and grandchildren,[2] and as these children have
grown to high school and college age and have been introduced to
the genre of the epic in various languages and cultures, you may have
heard them discussing Gilgamesh and comparing it with, say, the
Odyssey or *Beowulf.*

In fact, in the last decade it has become almost impossible to
ignore our epic. Two more scholarly translations have appeared, one

---

[†] *Canadian Society for Mesopotamian Studies Journal* 22 (1995): 15–22. Reprinted by per-
mission of the publisher. Originally delivered as a lecture to the society on Nov. 14, 1990.
Notes are by the editor of this Norton Critical Edition. The translations from the epic are
Moran's, but line numbers in square brackets refer to this Norton Critical Edition.
1. Thorkild Jacobsen's 1976 essay on the epic is reprinted in this Norton Critical Edition,
pp. 176–201.
2. Bernarda Bryson, *Gilgamesh: Man's First Story.* New York: Holt, Rinehart & Winston,
1961.

by Stephanie Dalley,[3] another by Maureen Kovacs.[4] Robert Silver-
berg, the distinguished science-fiction writer, turned the epic into a
first-rate novel, *Gilgamesh the King*.[5] Another novelist, the late John
Gardner, shortly before his tragic death completed his re-englishing
of the text, and it was published in 1984.[6] In this decade, too, our
epic returned to the world of music. On October 18, 1988, at the
Theatre der freien Volksbühne in Berlin, a seven-act opera, *The For-
est*, by Robert Wilson and David Byrne, was performed for the first
time, and not long after that at the Brooklyn Academy of Music. It
was conceived, we are told, as a modern response to the ancient mes-
sage of the Gilgamesh epic.

In a word, the Gilgamesh epic is becoming part of world literature.
Its appeal is universal. Its images and tale arrest the fancy of a child.
The profundity of these images, their immense, almost endless, sig-
nificance, and the understanding of man in a tale told with a simple
but compelling art, command the esteem and admiration of even the
most sensitive and the most critical. One of the most renowned poets
of the 20th century, Rainer Maria Rilke, could declare the Gil-
gamesh epic the greatest thing one could experience.[7]

If therefore I cannot introduce you to the Gilgamesh epic, I
must ask you to allow me to linger over the text, here and there, in
various ways, but always with love, and to introduce you to *my* Gil-
gamesh epic.

This request is not as egotistical as it may sound. It has been said
that everyone should write his own *Faust*.[8] In a very real sense, every-
one *must* write his own Gilgamesh. We have two versions of the epic,
one from the Old Babylonian period, written in the early second mil-
lennium, which is extremely fragmentary.[9] This version a poet-editor,
in the late second millennium, in still undetermined proportions of
revision, expansion, deletion, and oral variation, reworked into the
standard version that will be our concern. But this version too is frag-
mentary, in places extremely so. This situation, together with our still
very imperfect knowledge of the Mesopotamian literary tradition in
general, renders any interpretation tentative and subjective. The best
I can do, then, is present to you *my* Gilgamesh.

3. Stephanie Dalley. *Myths from Mesopotamia*. Oxford: Oxford UP, 1989, pp. 39–153.
4. Maureen Kovacs. *The Epic of Gilgamesh*. Stanford: Stanford UP, 1985.
5. Robert Silverberg. *Gilgamesh the King*. Westminster, MD: Arbor House, 1984.
6. John Gardner and John Maier, with the assistance of Richard Henshaw. *Gilgamesh:
   Translated from the Sîn-leqi-unninī Version*. New York: Alfred A. Knopf, 1984.
7. William L. Moran, "Rilke and the Gilgamesh Epic," *Journal of Cuneiform Studies* 32
   (1980): 208–10.
8. *Faust* refers to a German legend of a doctor who sold his soul to the devil in exchange
   for youth, knowledge, and magic powers, best known from the retelling by Johann
   Wolfgang von Goethe (1808).
9. In this Norton Critical Edition, what Moran calls the "Old Babylonian version" is
   referred to as "old versions" or "an old version."

I begin at the beginning. Among relatively recent discoveries bearing on the reconstruction of the epic, the most important concern the prologue. One fragment has restored a few precious signs at the end of the opening lines; another has filled in a 25-line break that had so tormented interpreters of the past. We now have almost intact the entire introduction. Moreover, we now know that the first 26 lines are the creation of the later poet-editor of whom I just spoke. Obviously, these lines merit the closest attention, for here, if anywhere, we may expect to hear the authorial-editorial voice speaking most clearly. Here, if anywhere, we may hope to determine his point of view, how he read, and would have us read, the ancient tale that follows.

He immediately presents Gilgamesh, introducing him as "one who saw everything,"

> Possessed of wisdom, knowing all.
> He saw what was secret, revealed what was hidden,
> Brought back knowledge of days before the Flood,
> From a long journey returned, weary but at peace.
> On stone he chiselled each wearying toil. [= I, 6–10]

There is a paradox here that my translation obscures. When the two words for "weary" and "at peace", or their congeners, are elsewhere used together as here, they are antonyms: one means "weary, exhausted", and it is related to the word for "wearying toil" in the next line: the other word means just the opposite, "rested, refreshed". Gilgamesh is both. The paradox is brief but important. It focusses our attention on the contrast of the externally exhausted body and what can only be, internally, a spirit refreshed and at peace, a peace which the context implies came to Gilgamesh with wisdom and knowledge. What this wisdom and knowledge were the epic will reveal.

The poet-editor continues. He refers briefly to two other achievements of Gilgamesh, the building of the famous walls of his native city Uruk and of its famous sanctuary, the temple of the goddess Ishtar. Then suddenly he addresses us, you and me, individually, a fact that is almost always lost in translation. As Leo Oppenheim so rightly stressed, the poet is no bard, real or fictive, Homer-like, singing his tale in some banquet hall. He speaks to a "thou," "look thou at its wall . . . gaze thou on its bastions, go thou up on the wall of Uruk and walk about; examine thou the terrace, study thou the brickwork, if its brickwork not be all of baked bricks, its foundations not laid by the Seven Sages. One sar is city, one sar orchards, one sar pasture and pond—and the fallow fields of Ishtar's house—three sar and fallow fields . . . "[1] [=I, 13–22] The poet addresses us as

---

1. A. Leo Oppenehim, *Ancient Mesopotamia: Portrait of a Dead Civilization*, Revised Edition completed by Erica Reiner. Chicago: U of Chicago P, 1977, pp. 255–64 (p. 259).

readers, and we are alone, with tablet in hand. No other epic begins this way, and we are becoming increasingly aware, first from the theme of wisdom, now from this unparalleled form, that if what we are reading is epic it is perhaps epic of a special kind.

On reading the next five lines, which conclude the poet-editor's expansion of his earlier source, the impression of novelty yields to conviction, and the author's purpose, I believe, becomes clear. I shall read them but continue on into the hymn to Gilgamesh of the earlier source, and this will bring us to the end of the old 25-line gap and to the beginning of the narrative. (The tablet is slightly broken on the left edge and therefore some readings, none of which seriously affects the sense, are dubious.)

> Find the copper chest,
> Remove the locks of bronze,
> Open the cover to the treasure there,
> Take up and read diligently the tablet of lapis lazuli.
> How he, Gilgamesh, every hardship bore. [= I, 25–9]

(Now begins the old hymn, and note the change of style.)

> He was a giant among kings, in stature most renowned,
> Brave, in Uruk born, a butting ox,
> Marching in the vanguard, the leader.
> In the rearguard marching too, the one his brothers trust.
> A mighty net, protector of his band.
> A raging flood, destroying even walls of stone,
> Son of Lugabanda, Gilgamesh, perfect in strength.
> Child of the noble cow, Lady Wild-Cow Ninsun,
> Gilgamesh, proud, perfect, awesome,
> Opening passes in the hills,
> Digging wells on mountain slopes,
> Crossing Sea, Wide-Deep, to the rising sun,
> The universe surveying, life ever seeking,
> In his power reaching Utnapishtim, the Faraway One.
> Restoring shrines by the Flood destroyed.
>
> Who among the multitudes of men
> Can rival him in kingship,
> Like Gilgamesh can say, "I am king".
> Like Gilgamesh was chosen the day that he was born,
> Two parts being god, one part man? [=I, 30–50]

Before turning to the lines about the chest and the lapis lazuli tablet, let us consider briefly the prologue is a whole, this long (46 lines), unparalleled combination of quasi hymn, address to a reader, and concluding hymn. You will perhaps have noted that it is only in the very last line of the expansion, as the poet-editor is about to join his older source, that he mentions his hero's name. For 25 lines, directly or indirectly, we have been reading about him without being told just who he is, so that when we finally do come to the name Gilgamesh, it emerges from the previous silence with a certain emphasis or foregrounding. And this leads to the lines that follow, in which the name reappears in line 33, again in line 35, and in a kind of crescendo, at the very end:

> Who among the multitudes of men
> Can rival him in kingship
> Like Gilgamesh can say, "I am king".
> Like Gilgamesh was chosen the day he was born? [= I, 47–9]

A more literal translation in the last line, instead of "was chosen", would be "his name was called". Another reading that has been proposed is "his name was famous" In any reading, the nameless hero of lines 1–25 is nameless no more. The prologue looks like a baroque elaboration of the old simple poetic device of speaking of an action and identifying the subject in only a general way, and then in a parallel line saying the very same thing, only this time identifying the subject by name.

Since we know the hymn only here and from a reference elsewhere to the opening line. "He was a giant among kings. In stature most renowned," we cannot be sure in what follows of what belongs to the older source, and what, if anything to our poet-editor. It is true that no king is called a "wild ox" or a "net" after the Old Babylonian period, and in the references to physical strength, birthplace, royalty, and legitimation, we recognize themes of the ancient royal hymnology. But that does not take us very far. We can say only that, if anything was added, it was nothing discordant. The hymn is of a piece to the unique dignity, kingship, and power of Gilgamesh.

This Gilgamesh, I hardly need point out, is not the Gilgamesh of the opening lines. This Gilgamesh is a powerful giant, the strongest of men, performing one feat of strength after another, moving across the world and the cosmic sea, reaching Utnapishtim, and finally stopping there, we feel, only because there is no more distant place to go. Of course when we get to these lines now, we have read what has gone before and we are conditioned by it. We know that there is another Gilgamesh. But think how different it would be if we didn't.

Far different is the figure of the Gilgamesh to whom we are first introduced. This Gilgamesh is a man who has suffered and is spent. Every one of the feats that the hymn celebrates is here simply "wearying toll." And lest we forget this, just as we are about to begin the hymn, we are reminded that "Gilgamesh every hardship bore." Opening passes in the hills, digging wells on mountain slopes, and so on— all hardships, pain, exhaustion. There is something almost unheroic in the tenor of all this, in insistence on pain and exhaustion, usually dominant considerations only for non-heroes. Here Gilgamesh seems as much the sage who has suffered as the hero who has triumphed.

To the difference of the two figures there is, as we noted in passing, a corresponding difference of styles: for the traditional hero, the traditional hymn and the conventional celebratory tone; for the exhausted man of suffering, language that is flatter, more matter of fact, a style that, fittingly, reports more than celebrates.

And now to the copper chest and the lapis lazuli tablet lying within. Certainly we must identify the inscription mentioned earlier, "on stone he chiselled each wearying toil", with the lapis lazuli tablet we are now instructed to read so diligently. Not only does it seem, in context, unlikely that the two are distinct, but, as we shall see, good and proper kings were supposed to leave inscriptions in chests. Note, too, how strongly "each wearying toil", *kalū mānaḫti*, is echoed in sound and paralleled in sense by what we are now told to read about on the tablet, how Gilgamesh bore *kalū marṣāti*, "every hardship."

Open to discussion is the proper rendering of the term *narū*, the object on which Gilgamesh chiselled the account of his labors, usually a "stele" and hitherto so translated here. But if the lapis lazuli tablet and the *narū* are the same thing, we should no longer think of a stele like the Code of Hammurabi, a large inscribed standing stone on public display. Our *narū* lies in a chest.

And where is the chest? A text that I shall cite shortly suggests that we should think of it as lying in a room of some temple, perhaps the temple of Ishtar, the only temple that has been mentioned. That the chest was part of a foundation deposit, as has been proposed, to me does not seem likely. Perhaps, however, since we are dealing with literary fiction, the question should not be pressed.

These are minor issues. The main one is the implications of these lines for interpretation. It has been argued that by implying that his source for the narrative that follows—and certainly this is implied— was the *narū* inscribed by Gilgamesh himself, and by inviting the reader to a comparison with the original, our poet-editor wishes to authenticate his tale. And this is true, I believe, but I also believe that such an analysis does not go far enough, for it ignores the implications within the literary tradition of the particular type of authentification.

The best parallel for this particular type is found in the composition known as the *Legend of Narām-Sîn*.[2] Now this composition is the clearest example of what Professor Grayson calls "pseudo-autobiography".[3] The formal characteristics of the genre, due to the

---

2. *Muses*, pp. 344–56.
3. A. K. Grayson, *Babylonian Historical–Literary Texts*. Toronto: U. of Toronto P, 1975, p. 5.

accidents of preservation, are still not firmly established, but the genre certainly imitates, with modifications, the old *narū*-stele form. It has a famous king of the past speak in the first person and tell of some events in his life, often fabulous and legendary. Then, where the old *narū*-stele form concluded with blessings and curses depending on how the stele was treated, "pseudo-autobiography" has the king address the reader and instruct him on the conduct of his life, basing the instruction on his own experiences as just recounted. On the evidence at hand, this didacticism is an essential feature of the genre.

In the *Legend of Narām-Sīn*, which in its later rather than its Old Babylonian form is instructive for our purposes, we find Narām-Sīn, the famous king of Akkad, in the broken first line already addressing the reader: "Read diligently the *narū* . . . " It is, moreover, now virtually certain that we should restore the beginning of the line to read "Open the chest." The text that follows is at first badly broken. Narām-Sīn tells of an earlier king's failure to leave a *narū*, as he should have done, thereby depriving Narām-Sīn of his guidance. A fabulous tale about bird-men follows, and the narrative section concludes with Narām-Sīn's reporting an oracle he says he received from the goddess Ishtar. The king then addresses the reader:

> Whosoever thou art, whether governor or prince
> or anyone else,
> Whom the gods shall call to rule over a kingdom,
> I have made for thee a chest and inscribed a *narū* for thee,
> And in the city of Cuthah, in the temple Emeslam,
> In the chamber of the god Nergal, deposited it for thee.
> Find this *narū* and listen to what this *narū* says,
> and then . . .

And there follows a long exhortation reflecting the oracle of Ishtar as just reported.

I need not belabor the obvious parallels to our Gilgamesh passage: the address to the reader, the chest, the *narū* within, the command to read it dillgently. Were these parallels from a form of didactic literature isolated, and were there no other indications of didacticism, latent or expressed, in the rest of the epic, then naturally one would hesitate to draw from these parallels any firm conclusions. But, of course, as we have just seen, this is not true. Gilgamesh is presented as a wise man from the very opening lines, and this has not been overlooked by modern interpreters. Jean Nougayrol, Erica Reiner, Thorkild Jacobsen, Giorgio Buccellati—to name only some of the more recent ones—have in various ways analyzed the epic as a kind of *Bildungsroman*, the story of Gilgamesh's education and progress to maturity, and the implications we would see in these lines only confirm how essentially correct they have been.[4] I propose, therefore, that in this imitation of "pseudo-autobiography" our poet-editor gives us final and formal guidance on how we are to read what follows: as *narū*-epic, epic but epic in a new key, epic in "the key of wisdom" (Buccellati).[5]

The hymn is over, the narrative begins. At this point I feel like Aeneas when asked by Dido to tell of the fall of Troy and all that had befallen him. Not, of course, that for me to tell my tale would be an "unspeakable sorrow" (*infandum dolorem*).[6] On the contrary. But I share with Aeneas the obvious problem of time.

> The dewy night is falling from the sky,
> And sinking stars summon us to sleep.

I cannot tell the whole tale, let alone linger over it, but let me remind you of all that follows: Gilgamesh oppressing Uruk: Enkidu, given by the gods to be a match for Gilgamesh, born in the steppe, seduced by the harlot, drawn from his animal state into the civilized life of Uruk; the struggle and then friendship of Gilgamesh and Enkidu; their expedition against the monster Huwawa: their triumphant return to Uruk; the confrontation with the goddess Ishtar and the vision of *eros* as also *thanatos*[7]; the death of Enkidu; the unassuageable grief of Gilgamesh and his new, obsessive fear of death; his journey across the world to the one immortal, the survivor of the Flood, Utnapishtim, only to learn the terrible truth of the inevitability of death, even for him, even for the greatest of kings and the strongest of men, a man indeed even partly divine.

Let us now step back, if only briefly, look at the narrative as whole, and linger long enough to see at least the structure of this truly epic tale.

The principal structure, I submit, is articulated by repetition, repetition of periods of time associated with a repeated symbolism. The periods of time are three periods of "six days and seven nights" ("seven days and seven nights" in the Old Babylonian version); the symbolism, that of bathing and clothing, "rites of passage", symbols of an inner transformation.

The first period is the "six days and seven nights" during which Enkidu and the harlot make uninterrupted love. As you will recall,

4. Jean Nougayrol, "L'Épopée babylonienne," *Atti del Convegno Internazionale sul Tema: La Poesia Epica e la sua Formazione (Roma, 28 marzio-3 aprile 1969)*. Rome: Accademia Nazionale dei Lincei, 1970, pp. 839–58; Erica Reiner, "Die akkadische Literatur." In Wolfgang Röllig, ed., *Neues Handbuch der Literaturwissenschaft, Altorientalische Literaturen*. Wiesbaden: Athenaion, 1978, pp. 151–210 (pp. 169–71). For Buccellati, see note 5, this page. *Bildungsroman* is a literary term that refers to a novel that shows how a character develops and matures.
5. Giorgio Buccellati, "Tre Saggi sulla Sapienza Mesopotamica I." *Oriens Antiquus* 11 (1972): 1–30 (p. 2: "Gilgamesh in chiave sapienzale").
6. Moran refers here to Virgil's epic poem, *The Aeneid,* the end of Book I and the beginning of Book II.
7. "*Love* as also *death*."

this epic performance over, Enkidu tries to run again with his animal companions, and he falls. He is no longer an animal; he has been transformed within. As the poet says, "He now has wisdom, broad understanding." He has begun his transformation into a human being.

Then on the way to Uruk with the harlot, he meets shepherds who place before him bread and beer, the food and drink of men. Here the text breaks off and for the sequel we must go to the Old Babylonian version. There we find Enkidu adjusting very quickly and in truly heroic fashion; of the beer he drinks seven kegs. Then, relaxed and singing away, his face aglow,

> With water he washed
> His hairy body,
> Anointed himself with oil,
> Became a man,
> Put on a garment,
> Was human. [= I, 40–2]

The humanization of Enkidu, it is generally and perhaps correctly held, is complete at this point, but I would like to propose one last step, and it is the moment—described so far, I admit, only in the Old Babylonian, but certainly present in the later version—when Enkidu bows down and acknowledges the kingship of Gilgamesh:

> It is as one unique your mother bore you,
> Wild-Cow of the pen, Ninsuna.
> Placed high, high over man, are you.
> The kingship of the people Ellil has decreed for you.
>   [= II, 107–10]

This event must be seen, I believe, against the background of the Mesopotamian view of kingship. In this view, kingship is the final and perfect ordering principle of human existence, and in its absence humanity is incomplete, even savage. This is implied, for example, by the Sumerian King List, where we and kingship bringing order to human affairs.[8] It is in the myth of Etana[9]; without kingship man lacks counsel. And it has a new and striking illustration in a recently published myth where we find the Birth-goddess told, "It was you who created primal-man (*lullū-amēlu*), so Fashion too a king, counsellor-man."[1]

Enkidu was born primal-man (*lullū-amēlu*), and I propose that until he comes into the city and begins life under a king he is still

---

8. Jean-Jacques Glassner, *Mesopotamian Chronicles*, ed. Benjamin R. Foster. Writings from the Ancient World 19. Atlanta: Society of Biblical Literature, 2004, pp. 117–26.
9. *Muses*, pp. 533–54.
1. *Muses*, pp. 495–97.

not entirely removed from his original condition. Only in Gilgamesh does he find counsel, and in counsel his full humanity.

The narrative then moves on until another period of six days and seven nights intervenes, a period associated this time, however, with the negative symbolism of a refusal to bathe and to dress in the clothes of men. I refer to the mourning of Gilgamesh over the death of his friend Enkidu.

The fragmentary state of the seventh and eighth tablets leaves the actual course of events at Enkidu's death somewhat obscure. According to the Old Babylonian version, however, paralleled by a fragment of the standard version, Gilgamesh later on tells the alewife that when Enkidu died,

> All day and night I wept over him
> And would not have him buried,
> As if my friend might rise at my cries,
> For seven days and seven nights,
> Until a maggot dropped from his nose. [= X, 58–60]

And I think we may safely assume that somewhere in the breaks of the seventh or eighth tablet the description of the grief of Gilgamesh included this information.

In the course of his protracted and unremitting grief, as Gilgamesh rocks back and forth over his friend's corpse, he pulls out his hair, tears off his finery as though something taboo and untouchable, and in his last words to his beloved friend he says:

> I will leave my body covered with grime,
> Wrap it in a lion-skin and roam in the steppe.
> [= VIII, 79–80]

The transformation of Gilgamesh in this week of mourning is profound. We witness not only the physical death of Enkidu, but the ethical death of Gilgamesh as well. The hero who had once voiced so eloquently the heroic ideal, declaring his contempt for death, chiding Enkidu for fearing it even for a moment as long as there be prospect of fame, is about to reject that ideal utterly and all the values associated with it. Consumed with a fear of death, Gilgamesh the hero dies and Gilgamesh the anti-hero is born.

And the transformation goes even deeper. In setting out, as he is about to do, to find immortality, Gilgamesh rejects not only conventional heroism but his very humanity.

Therefore, the grime, the unbathed body, the animal skin, the absence of human garb, speak of more than an identification with the dead Enkidu and a return to the world of the steppe from which his friend had once come. They are also emblematic of the anti-hero and the would-be god, the anti-man.

There remains a last week and a last transformation. Utnapish-tim tells Gilgamesh the story of the Flood. Then to convince him that he does not have the stuff of immortality, Utnapishtim chal-lenges Gilgamesh:

> Lie not down to sleep
> For six days and seven nights. [= XI, 233]

And immediately sleep, an image of death as an old man, death's twin for the Greeks, pours over Gilgamesh and he sleeps and sleeps until Utnapishtim touches and wakes him. It is the seventh day.

And now, finally, Gilgamesh yields. Now, finally, he accepts his mortality and therefore his humanity. Now, finally, the would-be god, the anti-man, is no more. In evidence of this he allows himself to be bathed, his skins cast off and carried away by the sea, and a new cloak to cover him. Thus he is ready for the journey back, back from the rim of the world, where the immortals dwell, back from the steppe, the haunt of animals and death, back to Uruk, where he as a man belongs.

The consistency and comprehensiveness of this overall analysis convinces me of its essential correctness. It was first proposed, though only partially and tentatively, by Hope Wolff, a student of comparative literature, who buried it in a footnote.[2] She recognized the repetitions of the time periods and their association with changes of character, though the changes she proposed were some-what different from mine. She did not see the repeated association with bathing and clothing, which recognized, her position becomes, I believe, immeasurably stronger, for the symbolism not only bears on changes of character but cuts to the very heart of the epic and its central concern, on being human.

Of the many merits of Emily Vermeule's 1975 Sather Lectures, *Aspects of Death in Early Greek Art and Poetry*,[3] not the least was the inclusion among her illustrations of the old Charlie Brown strip showing Snoopy lying at the entrance to his doghouse, under a huge icicle, and fearing imminent death, saying to himself with ever increasing emphasis, "I don't want to die. I'm too young to die. I'm too nice to die. I'm too ME to die."

Of what Snoopy speaks we all surely know, and how often have we not said to ourselves essentially the same thing. And for the same reason we sympathize with the terrified Gilgamesh who felt very much "too me to die", and in him we recognize the very prototype of the ego's massive resistance to the prospect of death and extinc-tion. And in his subduing that resistance, in his finally accepting, if

2. Hope N. Wolff, "Gilgamesh, Enkidu, and the Heroic Life," *Journal of the American Oriental Society* 89 (1969): 392–98 (p. 392, n. 2).
3. Emily Vermeule, *Aspects of Death in Early Greek Art and Poetry*. Berkeley: U of Califor-nia P, 1979.

reluctantly and fearfully, his destiny, we also recognize the essential and enviable wisdom that brought him peace.

But is this all there is to the wisdom of Gilgamesh, much though it be? I think not, but here I must warn you that my Gilgamesh epic now becomes indeed very much my own.

It is generally conceded that the Flood story was not part of the original epic. There are several arguments. The long account of 188 lines seems to be told for itself. It seriously interrupts the flow of dialogue between Utnapishtim and Gilgamesh, and if one removes the Flood story one makes the very smooth and natural transition from Utnapishtim's telling Gilgamesh about the assembly of the gods after the Flood to Utnapishtim's rhetorical question, "Now who is going to assemble the gods for you?" Finally, the story us told here is not an independent account; it draws on an identifiable source.

It is also generally conceded, though perhaps a little less commonly, that the one who added the story was the poet-editor of the prologue. He has a manifest interest in, and esteem for, "the knowledge of days before the Flood" that Gilgamesh brought back. He speaks too, in the prologue, of the secret things revealed by Gilgamesh, and of secret things the epic makes only two formal identifications, one of them the Flood story. If our poet-editor was not the one who added the story, he certainly directs us to it and implies its importance.

And what is that? Undoubtedly, Gilgamesh is presented in the prologue as a kind of culture-hero through whose sufferings we share to some extent in his experience and knowledge, knowledge especially of such arcane matters as what exactly happened at the Flood. After all, it might well be asked: If there was only one survivor of the Flood and he lives at the end of the world, how do we know the story at all? Who contacted this survivor? The epic supplies the answer.

But I think that in an epic to be read as a wisdom tale there is more to the importance of the Flood story than that. It is important, I submit, because it makes no sense.

There were two versions of the Flood story, a long and a short. In the long one, the Flood comes as the culmination of a long series of events reaching back into mythic time when man did not exist at all. It is a story that begins with some gods forced to labor for the others until they go on strike and refuse to work any longer. The solution to the crisis, proposed by the crafty god Ea, is the creation of man to form a new labor force. But this only leads to another crisis: man's ever increasing numbers eventually produce such a din that the god in charge of the earth, Ellil, can get no sleep. And so he sends the plague god to diminish man's numbers, but the crafty Ea, who is also the personal god of Utnapishtim, tells his client to have the people give the plague god all the food and presents they ordinarily give their personal gods and goddesses, thereby embarrassing the plague god at afflicting those so generous to him and thus forcing him to desist. And, of course, the plan works.

Then again, the same crisis with essentially the same solution. And then again, the same cycle once more. At which point the frustrated and furious Ellil decides to annihilate man by a flood, and he puts all the gods under oath not to tell any man lest there be somehow a survivor. And once more the crafty Ea finds a way out: he keeps his oath and still informs Utnapishtim of the impending disaster and how to escape, speaking not to Utnapishtim but to a reed wall behind which Utnapishtim lies.

In this amusing, naive tale the frustrated Ellil may be a somewhat pathetic figure, bringing very much to mind that neurotic noise-hater. Ben Jonson's character Morose in *The Silent Woman*.[4] His anger may be excessive and his decision to destroy mankind reprehensible and even short-sighted. After all, the gods need man. But his decision is also understandable, and it does make some sense.

The short version is quite different. We have two examples of it, one the account in the Gilgamesh epic, the other on a tablet from the 13th century discovered at Ras Shamra in Syria, ancient Ugarit.[5] The latter is extremely fragmentary, but enough is preserved—the very beginning and the very end—to show its basic similarity to the Gilgamesh version. It begins:

> When the gods took counsel about the lands
> They sent a flood upon the world.

Then Utnapishtim introduces himself and begins to tell of Ea's speech to the reed wall. At the very end, Utnapishtim and his wife are being given immortality.

In the Gilgamesh version, the story of the Flood begins like this:

> Shurippak—a city you yourself know,
> lying on the Euphrates' bank—
> This city was old, the gods too within it,
> And their heart moved the gods to send a flood.
>   [= XI, 11–14]

It continues, as does the Ugarit tablet, with Ea's speech to the reed wall, and ends with Ellil's touching the foreheads of Utnapishtim and his wife, as they kneel at his feet, and declaring that they would no longer be like men, but like gods, immortal.

What distinguishes the short version, as you will certainly have noted, is the absence of any clear motivation for sending the Flood. In this version, the decision to destroy mankind has no prior history, no background; it simply happens. If it is not an act of sheer

4. Ben Jonson, *Epicoene, or The Silent Woman* (1609).
5. *Muses*, p. 255.

caprice, the motives remain a mystery. In this version, the waters wash over man for reasons we shall never know.

Unfortunately, the part of the long version in which Utnapishtim may have been given immortality is lost, and so we cannot extend the comparison of the two versions. It should be noted, however, that in the short version, or, more cautiously, the short version as preserved in the epic, the gift of immortality must strike one as no less capricious or mysterious than the sending of the Flood. The god Ellil, who had been mainly responsible for the destruction of man, and who only moments before, on arriving and finding a few survivors, had become quite enraged, now not only spares these survivors but makes them immortal. Why this extraordinary largesse? The conclusion of the story makes no more sense than its beginning. We start with an apparently arbitrary destruction of life, we end with an apparently equally arbitrary extension of life into eternity.

Recognition of the inscrutability of the gods was ancient and common in Mesopotamian religious literature, and it became an essential part of the wisdom of the sage. Indeed, in approximately the same period as the composition of the standard version of the Gilgamesh epic, we find the reflective concluding from their experience of life that not only were the gods inscrutable, but they held man to norms of behavior which they would not reveal and he could not discover. It even seemed that good was evil and evil good. It is within this tragic view of man that I would place the short version of the Flood, the primeval paradigm of the human situation.

Equally paradigmatic is the episode of the Plant of Life. The latter is the second secret identified as such and the story about it we also owe, I believe, to our poet-editor. Through the kindness of Utnapishtim and his wife, who wish to give him a farewell present and some reward for his labors, Gilgamesh secures the Plant of Life, which will give him youth if not immortality. On the way back to Uruk, however, he lays it down and plunges into the cool waters of a pool, only to watch helplessly as a serpent (or some other creature) makes off with it, sloughing its skin as it goes.

What betrays Gilgamesh here is simply his humanity, its frailty and its limitations, and he draws a conclusion that echoes the words of the alewife he had heard earlier. To his proposal to cross the sea to Utnapishtim she had said, "If it may/can be done [the word in question is ambiguous], cross over; if not, turn back." Weeping, Gilgamesh now says, "I should have turned back." With this experience of human frailty and the recognition of the radical impropriety of the whole enterprise—one should attempt neither to escape death nor even to cheat it—Gilgamesh has achieved the final wisdom.

The tale, however, does not end there. We must still hear the very end and, in my opinion, very important words of the epic. As

they reach Uruk Gilgamesh says to Urshanabi, Utnapishtim's boat-
man who had accompanied him:

> Go up on the walls and walk about,
> Examine the terrace and study the brickwork,
> If its brickwork be not all of baked bricks,
> Its foundation not laid by the Seven Sages,
> One sar city, one sar orchards, one sar pasture and pond—
>   and fallow fields of Ishtar's house—
> Three sar and fallow fields . . . [= XI, 347–53]

We have come full circle. Hearing the prologue, the very words
earlier addressed to us as readers, we have a sense of finality and
completeness. We begin in Uruk, we end there, but now, in the new
context, after all that has gone before, the verifiable materiality of
it all—walls and measurements and topography—tells us, and tells
us forcibly, that Gilgamesh is back from a world of jewelled trees
and monsters and regions not meant for man, into a definable,
measurable, human world, a world indeed made by man.

And in this man-made world of Uruk, this human achievement,
one senses, too, a real, if muted, pride. There seems to be an intuitive
if inarticulate perception that this is the work proper to man and his
destiny: to build, to create a world of his own, as well as to die. It is
this consciousness of the dignity as well as of the tragedy of man that
we may, with the great art historian Erwin Panofsky, describe as
humanism: insistence on human values, acceptance of human limi-
tations.[6] For me, then, the Gilgamesh epic, *my* Gilgamesh epic, is a
document of ancient humanism.

SUSAN ACKERMAN

Liminal Women: Shamhat, Siduri, Ishtar, and Utnapishtim's Wife[†]

I hope to demonstrate that the women in the *Epic of Gilgamesh* who
are particularly able to do the work of moving Gilgamesh and Enkidu
in and out of the Epic's liminal phases are able to do so not only
because they, like almost all Mesopotamian women, are liminal from

---

6. For Erwin Panofsky (1892–1968), see Sylvia Ferretti, *Cassirer, Panofsky, Warburg: Sym-
bol, Art and History.* New Haven, CT: Yale UP, 1989.
† From *When Heroes Love: The Ambiguity of Eros in the Stories of Gilgamesh and David.*
New York: Columbia UP, 2005, pp. 138–50. Copyright © 2005 Columbia University
Press. Reprinted with permission of the publisher. Abridged by the editor with the
author's permission. Bibliographic information has been supplied in full and in some
cases updated. Some of the author's notes have been omitted. Unless otherwise indi-
cated, notes are by the author.

the point of view of the Epic's male authors but also because they are *especially* liminal women, women who live, for example, not just a woman's typically marginal existence, but a life on the extreme margins of society (the prostitute Shamhat), or women who manifest an extremely exaggerated form of a liminal being's betwixt-and-between identity (the human yet immortal wife of Utnapishtim). In all, I will examine the liminal nature of four of the Epic's women characters: the prostitute Shamhat as she is described in Tablets I and II, the ale-wife Siduri as presented in Tablet X, the goddess Ishtar as depicted in Tablet VI, and the portrayal found in Tablet XI of Utnapishtim's wife.

The Prostitute Shamhat

Almost all commentators have suggested that the role Shamhat plays in the acculturation of Enkidu in the opening tablets of the *Epic of Gilgamesh* is pivotal, since it is immediately after Shamhat's and Enkidu's six days and seven nights of uninterrupted lovemaking that Enkidu's animal nature leaves him ("Enkidu was diminished, he could not run as before"; Tablet I, line 209) and the transformation that makes him human begins ("he had grown in broad understanding"; Tablet I, line 210.)[1] This is an interpretation with which I by no means disagree, and I also by no means disagree with the analysis of Moran, who associates the profound transformation effected by Shamhat with rites-of-passage imagery that especially includes rituals of cleansing and clothing (Enkidu being anointed and donning his first human attire).[2] What I would like to suggest here, however, is that combining these two sets of observations allows us to assign a heightened significance to Shamhat's role as a pivotal character. In my estimation she is particularly able to propel the admittedly already liminal Enkidu into what I have described as the fully liminal world of tests and trials, of divine revelation, and of egalitarian communitas that he experiences together with Gilgamesh because she, as a prostitute, is herself a highly liminal being and so especially able to bring about Enkidu's entry into the liminal phase of the Epic in which his interactions with Gilgamesh take place.[3]

1. Tablet and line numbers have been converted to correspond to those of this Norton Critical Edition, but the translation given in the original publication has been retained [*Editor*].
2. William Moran, "The Gilgamesh Epic: A Masterpiece from Ancient Mesopotamia." In Jack M. Sasson, with John Baines, Gary Beckman, and Karen S. Rubinson, eds., *Civilizations of the Ancient Near East*. New York: Scribner, 1995, pp. 2327–36.
3. Rivkah Harris, *Gender and Aging in Mesopotamia: The Gilgamesh Epic and Other Ancient Literature*. Norman, U of Oklahoma P, 2000, p. 122, somewhat similarly comments that Shamhat performs a "mediating role" in the acculturation of Enkidu because she herself, as a prostitute, stands at an intermediate position within Mesopotamian society . . . On Shamhat as mediator, see also Neal Walls, *Desire, Discord, and Death: Approaches to Ancient Near Eastern Myth*. Boston: American Schools of Oriental Research, 2001, pp. 29–32.

That prostitutes are liminal characters has been noted by several scholars of the ancient Near Eastern world. Susan Niditch, for example, has written that as liminal entities generally are those who fall "betwixt and between neatly defined categories," so does a prostitute according to ancient Near Eastern tradition fall "between the two allowable categories for women. She is neither an unmarried virgin, nor a non-virgin wife." Yet, while for most women the prostitute's participation in sexual intercourse outside the bounds of marriage would mean condemnation, Niditch argues that because the prostitute is in a certain sense officially recognized as liminal within her society, and thus acknowledged as an individual not constrained by the customs and conventions of the social order, she is tolerated. As Niditch writes, "In effect, one could fall between the proper categories and survive, once that outside betwixt-and-between status was itself institutionalized and categorized."[4] Phyllis A. Bird similarly describes prostitution in Mesopotamia as a "tolerated liminal activity"[5] and has elsewhere tried to capture the ambiguous qualities that characterize the prostitute's liminal nature by describing her using the paradoxical phrase "legal outlaw."[6] As Bird suggests, the activity of the prostitute is something the society (at least as represented by its male members) feels is needed and even desired, and therefore the role of the prostitute is accommodated. But because the prostitute threatens the conventions of her society by "standing outside the normal social order and its approved roles for women," she is nevertheless "ostracized and marginalized" with "a stigma . . . always attached to her role and her person."[7]

Bird further suggests that there is a stigma attached to the fact that the prostitute controls the financial transactions in which she engages with her clients, something that again stands outside the normal social order in the ancient Near Eastern world, where financial transactions are typically controlled by men.[8] According to Bird, moreover, the prostitute even lives on the outskirts of a city, her very place within urban geography demarcating, to use Bird's terminology, her "marginal" character.[9] This aspect of a

---

4. Susan Niditch, "The Wronged Woman Righted: An Analysis of Genesis 38," *Harvard Theological Review* 72 (1979): 143–49, p. 147 and note 13 on that page, cited by Phyllis Bird, "The Harlot as Heroine: Narrative Art and Social Presupposition in Three Old Testament Texts," in Miri Amihai, George W. Coats, and Anne M. Solomon, eds., *Narrative Research on the Hebrew Bible, Semea* 46 (1989): 119–39 (p. 135, n. 17).
5. Phyllis Bird, "The Bible in Christian Ethical Deliberation Concerning Homosexuality: Old Testament Contributions," in David L. Balch, ed., *Homosexuality, Science, and the "Plain Sense" of Scripture.* Grand Rapids: Eerdmans, 2000, pp. 142–76 (p. 160).
6. Bird, "Harlot as Heroine," p. 125.
7. Bird, "Harlot as Heroine." See similarly Walls's descriptions of the "prostitute's ambiguous social status" and of prostitutes as "socially marginal women" in *Desire, Discord, and Death,* p. 21.
8. Bird, "Harlot as Heroine," p. 125.
9. Bird, "Bible in Christian Ethical Deliberation," p. 160, note 46.

prostitute's existence may be indicated in the Gilgamesh Epic in Tablet VII, in which Enkidu, among the curses he heaps upon Shamhat, says, "May the shadow of the city walls be where you stand!" (line 82).

The curses of Shamhat that Enkidu utters are interesting to us for another reason, which is that they are similar to the curses that the goddess Ereshkigal, the queen of the netherworld, utters against a male impersonator of women who has been sent to petition her in the myth of Ishtar's Descent to the Netherworld.[1] Ereshkigal, for example, begins her tirade against the impersonator by claiming she will curse him with a great curse, just as Enkidu opens his invective against Shamhat by saying, "Let me curse you with a great curse" (Tablet VII, line 68). Also, both Ereshkigal and Enkidu denounce the objects of their disdain by saying, "May the drunkard and the thirsty strike your cheek" (Tablet VII, line 84). Finally, as Enkidu says of Shamhat, Ereshkigal expresses hope that the impersonator will find a place to stand only on the outskirts of the city, under the shadow of its walls. These parallels are significant for our purposes because of the similarities they posit between Shamhat and the female impersonator, a cult functionary of Ishtar who is well characterized as liminal. This confirms what I have already suggested, that Shamhat as a prostitute is well understood as liminal too.

Shamhat is further understood to be a liminal figure who propels Enkidu into a world of liminal engagement with Gilgamesh. Indeed, her very first words to Enkidu, which are spoken after their weeklong bout of lovemaking is completed, urge Enkidu to go to Uruk to meet Gilgamesh (Tablet I, lines 217–20). Crucial to notice here is that the idea Enkidu might go to Uruk and engage with Gilgamesh after being "tamed" by Shamhat is *never* part of the original plan that brought the prostitute into the wilderness. Rather, the huntsman's father, who is the one who originally proposed that the huntsman ask Gilgamesh for a prostitute to seduce Enkidu, suggests she entice Enkidu only because he knows the seduction will break Enkidu's bond with the wild beasts and so end Enkidu's abetting of his animal companions through his disabling of the huntsman's snares. Gilgamesh, too, when he responds to the huntsman's appeal by sending Shamhat into the countryside, does so only with the intent of distracting Enkidu from his attacks

---

1. For translations of this text, Stephanie Dalley, *Myths from Mesopotamia: Creation, the Flood, Gilgamesh, and Others.* Oxford: Oxford UP, 1991, pp. 154–62, and *Muses,* pp. 498–505. For comments on the parallels between Ereshkigal's curses of the *assinnu* (female impersonator) sent to her and Enkidu's curses of Shamhat, Dalley, *Myths from Mesopotamia,* p. 161, nn. 15 and 16; also the comments of Bird, "The Bible in Christian Ethical Deliberation," p. 160, note 46; Gwendolyn Leick, *Sex and Eroticism in Mesopotamian Literature.* London: Routledge, 1994, pp. 166–67; Martti Nissinen, *Homoeroticism in the Biblical World: A Historical Perspective.* Minneapolis: Fortress, 1998, p. 32.

against the huntsman's livelihood; there is never any mention that the huntsman might send the subdued Enkidu back to Uruk for Gilgamesh to encounter. This idea instead is unique to Shamhat, and the fact that she expresses it in the first words she speaks to Enkidu suggests it has a special significance. Once again, I propose its significance is that Shamhat as an exceptionally liminal character is particularly well positioned, from the narrative's perspective, to effect Enkidu's movement into the world of liminal time and space in which his interactions with Gilgamesh will take place. In fact, we might say that *only* a liminal character like Shamhat can effect Enkidu's movement into liminal time and space, as opposed to, say, the huntsman's father, who seems oblivious to this possibility.

The Alewife Siduri

Several scholars have commented on how similar Shamhat is structurally to the alewife Siduri. Rivkah Harris points out, for example, that both Shamhat and Siduri are working women who support themselves, that both function within the extradomestic domain of Mesopotamian society, and that both are engaged in professions that were important in the leisure activities of Mesopotamian men. Taverns such as Siduri is depicted as managing, moreover, were places where men went to meet prostitutes like Shamhat, and thus taverns were accommodated yet stigmatized in some of the same ways in Mesopotamian society that prostitution was accommodated yet stigmatized.[2] Tzvi Abusch adds that as Shamhat sought to humanize the animalistic Enkidu in the early scenes of the Epic, so too toward the Epic's end, at least in the Old Babylonian version, does Siduri seek to rehumanize the animal-like and corpselike Gilgamesh, by urging him to put his overwrought mourning behaviors aside. Indeed, Abusch notes that many of the specific features of human existence to which Shamhat originally introduced Enkidu are those later urged upon Gilgamesh by Siduri in an old version [Tablet X, lines 82–92]: a clean body, human clothing, and sex. Abusch follows up as well on an interpretation first put forward by Moran, who argues that the episode describing Enkidu's acculturation in the Gilgamesh Epic derives from an older story "of the humanization of a primitive by a prostitute that would have been told in the *aštammu*, 'tavern/inn,'" to which Abusch adds: "Siduri's advice would also seem to . . . have its setting in the *aštammu* . . . " Through these and other connections, Abusch concludes, "the author links the Siduri–Gilgamesh encounter with the earlier Shamhat-Enkidu encounter and suggests that

2. Harris, "Gender and Aging," p. 122 and note 16.

they parallel each other."[3] This observation allows us in turn to conclude that, as the prostitute Shamhat is represented in the Epic as an exceptionally liminal figure, so too should the alewife Siduri be identified as highly liminal in nature.

Other evidence supports this interpretation. Dalley notes, for example, that alewives in Mesopotamia "lived outside the normal protection of male members of a family," which is the sort of position we now readily recognize as liminal.[4] Abusch in addition points out that Mesopotamian taverns served ritually "as a transition-point back to normal life for the patient who has undergone magical rites,"[5] which implies that those who kept taverns were themselves transitional figures. Abusch, moreover, follows Lambert in identifying Siduri as a goddess, "perhaps of the Ishtar type."[6] If this is so, however, then we must quickly note that, unlike Ishtar and the other gods, Siduri does not live in the heavens. Yet the otherworldly location in which Gilgamesh encounters her, on the shores of a cosmic sea, is surely not the earthly domain of humans. Siduri, that is, lives in a locale betwixt and between the realms of gods and mortals, which suggests that, if she is a goddess, she is one who, like her more famous neighbors Utnapishtim and his wife, represents a betwixt-and-between or liminal sort of divinity.[7]

Abusch further suggests that some version of the Gilgamesh Epic that predates the old versions ended shortly after Gilgamesh's encounter with Siduri and did not include any of the Utnapishtim episode. As Abusch sees it, Gilgamesh, in this account, while wandering aimlessly, would have come across Siduri, who, after delivering her famous speech about the need for Gilgamesh to abandon his futile quest, would have concluded by advising "his immediate return home to Uruk and the resumption there of a normal life." The text then "may well have ended with Siduri sending Gilgamesh back to Uruk in the care of a boatman, perhaps Urshanabi."[8] Were

3. Tzvi Abusch, "Gilgamesh's Request and Siduri's Denial, Part 1: The Meaning of the Dialogue and Its Implications for the History of the Epic," in Mark E. Cohen, Daniel C. Snell, and David B. Weisberg, eds., The Tablet and the Scroll: Near Eastern Studies in Honor of William W. Hallo. Bethesda: CDL, 1993, pp. 1–14 (pp. 7–8). Compare also Abusch's comments in "The Development and Meaning of the Gilgamesh Epic: An Interpretive Essay," Journal of the American Oriental Society 121 (2001): 614–22, p. 617: "Just as a prostitute, a woman, humanized and acculturated Enkidu at the beginning of this [an old] version, so a tavern-keeper, another woman, humanized and acculturated Gilgamesh at the end"; similarly Gregory Mobley, "The Wild Man in the Bible and the Ancient Near East." Journal of Biblical Literature 116 (1997): 217–33 (p. 222): "Women—first Siduri, then tavern-keeper, and later Utnapishtim's wife—figure in the wild man Gilgamesh's return to culture, just as Shamhat was the principal agent of Enkidu's domestication."
4. Dalley, Myths from Mesopotamia, p. 132, n. 106.
5. Abusch, "Gilgamesh's Request and Siduri's Denial, Part 1," p. 7, n. 29, and the references cited there.
6. Ibid, p. 5.
7. Harris, Gender and Aging, p. 123.
8. Abusch, "Gilgamesh's Request and Siduri's Denial, Part 1," pp. 11, 12.

this hypothesis to hold, it would suggest still more of the structural parallels between Shamhat and Siduri that were so significant for our analysis above, for as Shamhat effected Enkidu's movement out of the wilderness where he was born and toward the city of Uruk, so too would Siduri have effected the end of Gilgamesh's wilderness wanderings and his journey back toward Uruk. As Shamhat, moreover, in effecting Enkidu's movement toward Uruk, propelled him into the liminal time and space that are represented in the stories of his interactions with Gilgamesh, so analogously would Siduri, in effecting Gilgamesh's return to Uruk, be propelling him out of the liminal time and space that have defined his existence since shortly after he and Enkidu met. We could then further propose that the reason Siduri, like Shamhat, is particularly able to effect a hero's transformation with respect to liminal time and space is that Siduri, like Shamhat, is a highly liminal figure.

Yet even if Abusch's reconstruction cannot be sustained (and he himself notes it is speculative),[9] the basic fact of Siduri's liminal nature remains, and I believe that this is a significant feature of the Epic, even in the Standard version, in which Siduri's role is greatly downplayed. Siduri as a liminal figure serves, as do the theriomorphic scorpion-men and Utnapishtim and his wife, as an ideal representative of all the aspects of liminality Gilgamesh has experienced and is experiencing at the point in the Epic at which she appears: the liminal lands in which Gilgamesh has wandered; the liminal tests and trials Gilgamesh has endured; and the liminal identity Gilgamesh manifests. As Gilgamesh lives betwixt and between worlds, that is, he appropriately interacts with other betwixt-and-between characters, and even in her downplayed role in the Standard version Siduri functions as one of those beings. In the old versions [Tablet X, lines 82–92], she is more, a liminal being who, I would argue, uses her liminal position to try and move Gilgamesh out of his liminal existence and into a reaggregated life.

The Goddess Ishtar

In an essay entitled "Images of Women in the Gilgamesh Epic," Rivkah Harris quotes a hymnic passage in which the goddess Ishtar sings of herself, "When I sit at the entrance of the tavern, I am a loving prostitute,"[1] and then correctly notes that this passage suggests some association between the prostitute Shamhat, the tavern keeper Siduri, and the goddess Ishtar, who plays such a large role in Tablet VI of the Gilgamesh Epic. This is indicated by other evidence as well. Ishtar, for example, is the patron of prostitutes within Mesopotamian

9. Ibid., p. 9.
1. Harris, *Gender and Aging*, p. 122.

tradition, including the subcategory of prostitutes known as the *šamḫātu*, or "shamhat-prostitutes," who in the *Epic of Gilgamesh* give Shamhat her name (Tablet VI, line 157). Also, in several god lists, the name Siduri occurs as a name of Ishtar.[2] These data linking Shamhat, Siduri, and Ishtar intimate, in terms of our analysis, that Ishtar, like Shamhat and Siduri, is to be understood in certain respects as liminal. Indeed, in a second article, "Inanna-Ishtar as Paradox and a Coincidence of Opposites," Harris makes precisely this point. In Harris's words, Ishtar, "represented both order and disorder, structure and anti-structure. In her psychological traits and behavior she confounded and confused normative categories and boundaries." Later, in the same essay, Harris, quoting Turner, specifically identifies the goddess as "liminal," one who, as a goddess of love and sexuality but of war as well, is represented in ways both benign and horrific. To illustrate more fully, Harris cites two texts in particular. The first lists several aspects of existence that are said to fall in the domain of Ishtar: to destroy and to tear up, yet to build up and to settle; business savvy and great winnings, yet financial loss and deficit; slander and hostile words, yet joking and smiling. The second text speaks of Ishtar as the one who has "thrown into confusion threads which have been ordered," yet simultaneously as the one who has "organize[d] those threads which bring confusion." As Harris says, these are "vivid expressions of the goddess's innate contradictions."[3]

As I have suggested above regarding Shamhat and Siduri, I would propose that because of Ishtar's generally liminal nature, the Epic associates her with its heroes' movement in and out of liminal time and space. Crucial to recall here is that, as I have interpreted at least the Standard version (the Tablet VI materials are not represented in the old versions and may not even have been a part of that corpus),[4] there seems to be a brief movement toward Gilgamesh's and Enkidu's reaggregation or reintegration into Uruk's community at the beginning of Tablet VI, when the two heroes return successful from their expedition against Huwawa/Humbaba and Gilgamesh bathes and reclothes himself in his royal robes and so apparently resumes his position as king. But almost immediately, there is, to use Turner's language, another "breach of regular, norm-governed social

2. W. G. Lambert, "The Hymn to the Queen of Nippur," in G. Van Driel, T. Krispijn, M. Stol, and K. R. Veenhof, eds., *Zikir šumim: Assyriological Studies Presented to F. R. Kraus on the Occasion of His Seventieth Birthday*. Leiden: Brill, 1982, pp. 173–82 (p. 208).
3. Harris, *Gender and Aging*, p. 159; see further, on Ishtar's contradictory nature, Tzvi Abusch, "Ishtar's Proposal and Gilgamesh's Refusal: An Interpretation of *The Gilgamesh Epic*, Tablet 6, Lines 1–79," *History of Religions* 26 (1986): 143–87, p. 159, who speaks of Ishtar both as a goddess of fertility and life but also of death; H. L. J. Vanstiphout, "Inanna/Ishtar as a Figure of Controversy," in H. G. Kippenberg, ed., *Struggles of the Gods: Papers of the Groningen Work Group for the Study of the History of Religions*. Amsterdam: Mouton, 1984, pp. 225–38.
4. Abusch, "Ishtar's Proposal and Gilgamesh's Refusal," pp. 180–87; and Abusch, "Development and Meaning," p. 615, note 3 and p. 618.

relations"—Gilgamesh's rejecting of Ishtar's proposal of marriage, and in the most insulting of terms—which provokes the sending of the Bull of Heaven and throws the narrative back into a liminal phase.[5] The scene of Ishtar's proposition is thus pivotal in terms of the narrative's movement in and out of liminal time and space,[6] as was the scene of Enkidu's humanization by the prostitute Shamhat and, perhaps, the scene in the old versions and its potential precursors in which the alewife Siduri counsels Gilgamesh to abandon his futile wanderings. The liminally characterized Ishtar, in short, helps propel movement with respect to liminal time and space in much the same way that the liminally characterized Shamhat and, possibly, Siduri are able to do. The imagery that surrounds this Ishtar-related transition, moreover, is identical to the imagery that surrounds the transition effected by Shamhat and, at a minimum, proposed by Siduri: cleansing, clothing, and sex.

Ishtar is very like the prostitute Shamhat (of whom, she is, after all, the patron goddess), as her proposal to engage, as did Shamhat with Enkidu, in a non-normative yet marriagelike relationship with Gilgamesh propels him into a liminal existence.[7]

Utnapishtim's Wife

The pivotal roles played by the women Shamhat, Siduri, and Ishtar in the *Epic of Gilgamesh* lead me to suspect that we need to pay more attention, in the Standard version, to another woman, Utnapishtim's wife, and especially to the role she may play in bringing about Gilgamesh's ultimate return to Uruk. As I have already indicated, this woman, like all the other women I have described, is surely liminal, defined in terms of a betwixt-and-between identity (a mortal who became immortal) and living in the betwixt-and-between space (neither the heavenly abode of the gods nor the earthly domain of humans). She also, it might be argued, provides some of the crucial impetus of getting Gilgamesh back to Uruk.[8] Particularly significant here is the scene in the Standard version's Tablet XI, in which Gil-

5. Victor W. Turner, *The Dreams of Affliction*. Ithaca, NY: Cornell UP, 1968, p. 38.
6. H. L. J. Vanstiphout, "The Craftsmanship of Sîn-leqi-unninnī," *Orientalia Lovaniensia Periodica* 21 (1990): 45–79, *passim*, also reads the Tablet VI material as pivotal in terms of the Epic's structure, although his overall understanding of its significance differs from mine.
7. Further aspects of the relationship between the Shamhat and Ishtar episodes in the *Epic of Gilgamesh* are provocatively explored by Walls, *Desire, Discord, and Death*, pp. 36–40; see also the comments of Benjamin R. Foster, "Gilgamesh: Sex, Love, and the Ascent of Knowledge." In John H. Marks and Robert M. Good, eds., *Love and Death in the Ancient Near East: Essays in Honor of Marvin H. Pope*. Guilford, CT: Four Quarters, 1987, pp. 21–42 (p. 36).
8. Note the somewhat similar comments of Harris, *Gender and Aging*, p. 125; see also Benjamin R. Foster, "Humor and Wit in the Ancient Near East." In Sasson, ed., *Civilizations of the Ancient Near East*, pp. 2459–69 (p. 2468), cited by Walls, *Desire, Discord, and Death*, p. 82, note 15.

gamesh tries to stay awake for six days and seven nights yet immedi-
ately falls into a "sleep like a fog" (Tablet XI, lines 235 and 238). Upon
witnessing this, Utnapishtim speaks scornfully to his wife about Gil-
gamesh's failure. But he says nothing about what he plans to do with
the somnolent Gilgamesh, so that, for all the Epic tells us, Utnapish-
tim could be planning to let Gilgamesh lie comatose forever. It is only
Utnapishtim's *wife* who urges that he be awoken, and that he be awo-
ken, significantly, so that he might "go back on the way that he came
in well-being" (Tablet XI, lines 241–42).

In addition, Utnapishtim's wife urges Utnapishtim to tell Gilgamesh,
after he is awakened, about the Plant of Rejuvenation; otherwise,
Utnapishtim might again, for all the Epic tells us, have done nothing.
To be sure, the knowledge of the Plant of Rejuvenation becomes a bit-
tersweet gift, as Gilgamesh claims the Plant only to lose it to the ser-
pent, but it is nevertheless, in the Standard version account, a gift
that finally forces Gilgamesh to acknowledge the basic truths of
human existence that have theretofore eluded him. Utnapishtim's
wife, that is, does much more in the Standard version than commen-
tators usually acknowledge to bring about the resolution of Gil-
gamesh's angst-ridden existence. Or, to speak in the terms of our
analysis here, it is *she,* by making sure that Gilgamesh does not sleep
forever and by prodding her husband to tell Gilgamesh of the Plant
that inspires his ultimate realization of life's truths, who puts Gil-
gamesh in a position to move out of the liminal phase of his life story
and be reaggregated or reincorporated into his community.

Moreover, although there is no sex involved (unless one finds an
allusion to it deeply veiled, in the phallic image of the serpent), there
are, in conjunction with this transition Utnapishtim's wife helps
bring about, the same rites of cleaning and clothing that accompa-
nied the transition of Enkidu effected by Shamhat and the transition
in Tablet VI associated with Ishtar. Thus, immediately after Gil-
gamesh awakens from his week-long sleep, and just before he is told
the secret of the Plant of Rejuvenation, he bathes and redons his
royal robes. Bathing and the donning of clean clothing are rites also
urged upon Gilgamesh by the alewife Siduri within an old version as
she seeks to effect his reintegration into Mesopotamian society.
Indeed, it may be that as Siduri becomes downplayed in the Stan-
dard version, Utnapishtim's wife in some sense replaces her in her
role as a liminal woman whose function in the narrative is to help
move an epic hero out of his liminal existence. It may further be
that the sexual motifs that are present in the old-version Siduri epi-
sode and present in conjunction with liminal women's roles else-
where in the epic tradition are absent in relation to Utnapishtim's
wife because of the observations I advanced earlier regarding the
Standard version's concluding proposition, that marriage and family

are insufficient paths to fulfillment in life for the reaggregated or reintegrated Gilgamesh.

Yet whatever the merits of these last points of speculation, it seems clear that we must view many of the Epic's women characters—Shamhat, Siduri, Ishtar, and Utnapishtim's wife—generally through the lens of liminality and see more specifically that these women's exceptionally liminal nature places them in an especially good position to move the Epic's two heroes in and out of liminal time and space. As such, these women function simultaneously as mirrors of the liminal imagery that predominates in the Epic's text and as crucial linchpins that facilitate the narrative's movement through the phases of the rites-of-passage model.

ANDREW R. GEORGE

The Mayfly on the River: Individual and Collective Destiny in the *Epic of Gilgamesh*[†]

The Babylonian narrative poem that today we call the *Epic of Gilgamesh* underwent a long evolution. The earliest-known manuscripts are Old Babylonian[1] and date to about the eighteenth century BC. Subsequent centuries witnessed the proliferation of variant versions of the poem, its growing use as an academic tool in scribal schools, and its diffusion outside Babylonia to Syria, Anatolia and Palestine. Towards the end of the second millennium, an attempt was made to standardize the text. The poem was known in this late period as "He who Saw the Deep", after its incipit.[2]

In the first millennium, Babylonian scholarship attributed the poem "He Who Saw the Deep" to a man called Sîn-leqi-unninni, otherwise known only as the supposed ancestor of a family of late scribes. How big a part he played in fixing the text of "He Who Saw the Deep" is uncertain, but his name is a convenient identifier for whatever intellect it was that produced the standardized text that was the vehicle for the Gilgamesh narrative in the first millennium. His was an intellect that had more than an editorial impact on the poem. Modern readers of *Gilgamesh* are often more receptive to the poetry of the earlier,

† From KASKAL, *Rivista di storia, ambienti e culture del Vicino Oriente Antico* 9 (2012): 227–42. Reprinted with permission of the publisher. Abridged by the editor of this Norton Critical Edition with the author's permission. The line numbers used by the author refer to his own translations (George 1999, 2003). These have been keyed to the line numbers in this Norton Critical Edition in square brackets, such as [= I, 1–29].
1. "Old Babylonian" refers to the manuscripts called "old versions" in this translation [*Editor*].
2. "Incipit" means here the first half of the opening line of the poem [*Editor*].

Old Babylonian fragments. Sîn-leqi-unninni does not have a great reputation as a poet. But close reading of his poem reveals a profound thinker, who gave the poem a structure and tone that were certainly the result of a deliberate and consistent policy to focus less on heroic grandeur and glory and more on human frailty and failure. The confident exuberance of the Old Babylonian poem is clearly audible in its prologue, which began with the words "Surpassing All Other Kings". By contrast "He Who Saw the Deep" begins at once as a melancholy reflection on the trials and tribulations of human existence, for which wisdom is the only compensation.

Since its rediscovery by modern western scholarship, the poem "He Who Saw the Deep" has usually been read as the story of an individual, the hero-king Gilgamesh, and his struggle against his mortal doom as a human being. The gods send to Gilgamesh, a tyrant in Uruk, a friend called Enkidu. The pair go on adventures but offend the gods, so that Enkidu must die. Gilgamesh travels to the ends of the earth in a vain quest to avoid death. His tale can be read symbolically as the story of any human life. Modern readers easily identify with Gilgamesh as individual to individual, and recognize his existential struggle as their own, but magnified to an heroic scale. The preoccupation with the individual reflects a salient feature of modern western society, in which the rights and place of the individual are dominant in social contexts and the community is expected to serve the interests of the individual. But there is another social entity in the Babylonian life: the community as a whole.

The poem's disapproval of Gilgamesh's tyrannous treatment of his townspeople (Tablet I 67 [= I, 69]) can be seen in this light, not as a political rejection of the institution of kingship itself, but as a condemnation of a perversion of that institution whereby the community suffered by the antisocial action of a single individual instead of benefiting from him playing his proper role.

Concentration on the individual figure of the hero magnifies the risk of ignoring what the poem has to say about human society as a collective. In the following I shall explore one aspect of the poem's contrast of the individual human being and the collective mankind. In particular I shall further the case for a view already expressed in my critical edition (2003), that Sîn-leqi-unninni's poem differentiates the mortality of the individual from the collective immortality of the human race. This will be done with a grateful nod to great minds of Heian-period Japan, nineteenth-century Russia and twentieth-century France.

The poem begins like this:

> He who saw the Deep, the country's foundation,
>   who knew the proper ways, was wise in everything!

Gilgamesh, who saw the Deep, the country's
    foundation,
  who knew the proper ways, was wise in everything!

5   He everywhere explored the seats of power,   [5]
      knew of everything the sum of wisdom.
    He saw what was secret, discovered what was hidden,
      brought back a tale of before the Deluge.

    He came a far road, was weary but at peace;
10 all his labours were set on a tablet of stone.   [10]
    He had the rampart built of Uruk-the-Sheepfold,
      of holy Eanna, the sacred storehouse.

    See its wall like a strand of wool,
      view its parapet that none could copy!
15 Take the stairway of a bygone era,   [15]
      draw near to Eanna, seat of Ishtar the goddess,
    that no later king could ever copy!

    Climb Uruk's wall and walk back and forth!
      Survey its foundations, examine the brickwork!
20 Were its bricks not fired in an oven?   [20]
      Did the Seven Sages not lay its foundations?

    [A square mile is] city, [a square mile] date-grove, a
      square mile is clay-pit, half a square mile the
      temple of Ishtar: [three square miles] and a half is
      Uruk's expanse.

    Open the tablet-box of cedar,   [25]
25   release its clasp of bronze!
    [*Lift*] the lid of its secret,
      pick up the tablet of lapis lazuli and read out—
    the travails of Gilgamesh, all that he went through.
                          Gilgamesh I 1–28 [= I, 1–29]

The poem continues with the Old Babylonian incipit, "Surpass-
ing All Other Kings", so it is very probable that we should read ll.
1–28 [= 1–29] as a self-contained prologue. As such, it sets out the
main concerns of the poem in its standardized, first-millennium
form. I would make three comments at this point.

  First, the prologue clearly asserts the experience of the poem's
protagonist as a life of pain and hardship, a life which when taken
to the heroic extreme brought the compensation of unsurpassed

wisdom—not, as the Old Babylonian incipit avers, the reward of unsurpassed glory.

Second, when the poet enjoins the reader to climb Uruk's wall and admire its structure and antiquity, the final focus is not the wall, but the city, in lines which announce their presence, their topic and their seriousness with a stark dissonance, by abandoning verse for prose. This is no lapse, for this very same passage of prose is repeated at the end of the poem as its very last stanza. There can be no doubt that, as the framing device for the entire poem, this passage bears the full intent of the poet, and the choice of prose as its form can only be a strategy to draw attention to that burden. I shall return to this burden later.

The third comment arises from a consideration of the prologue's formal structure and a point of philology. The first ten lines tell in the shortest possible style the adventure that Gilgamesh was best known for: he made a long journey to the ends of the earth in search of immortality and returned exhausted, not with the object of his quest but with words of wisdom from a primeval time. The next ten lines have become eleven, for l. 17 rehashes l. 14 and looks like an awkward interpolation. They move on to the topic of the great wall, ancient and enduring, that provides such a contrast with the ephemeral lives of its antediluvian creators, the Seven Sages, and especially its renewer, the hero Gilgamesh.

The hinge of this transition, from Gilgamesh's frantic adventure to the solid immobility of the wall, is a succession of four clauses relating his homecoming (ll. 9–10). Placed deliberately at the mid-point of five four-line stanzas, these clauses contain the following four verbs: "he came", "he was exhausted", "he was put at ease", and "it was set". Gilgamesh returns home, collapses exhausted, and can do no more. It is not he who places his story on the tablet of lapis lazuli. That is done for him. After so long in motion, now he has arrived at a condition of stasis. The uneven distribution of the four clauses across the two lines of poetry—three crammed into l. 9; one alone in l. 10—serves to emphasize further the transition from journey to homecoming, from restless activity to calm inaction. The journey has come to a halt.

I shall quote the end of the poem in full, because much of it forms a doublet with the prologue. Prologue and epilogue are the matching book-ends of the poem, vital parts of a carefully structured frame that gives all the more reason to seek in them the poem's most urgent and essential message.

> At twenty leagues they broke bread,
> 320   at thirty leagues they stopped for the night.
> When they arrived in Uruk the Sheepfold,   [345]

Gilgamesh spoke to him, to Ur-shanabi the
    boatman:

"O Ur-shanabi, climb Uruk's wall and walk back and
    forth,
    "survey its foundations, examine the brickwork!
325 "Were its bricks not fired in an oven?
    "Did the Seven Sages not lay its foundations?   [350]

"A square mile is city, a square mile date-grove, a
square mile is clay-pit, half a square mile the temple of
Ishtar: three square miles and a half is Uruk's
expanse."
                    Gilgamesh XI 319–28 [= XI, 343–53]

Here the transition from motion to stasis is implicit. Gilgamesh
and his companion come to Uruk, in motion. But upon that arrival,
Gilgamesh moves no more. All he can do is enjoin his companion to
go up on to the wall and view the city, in words that repeat the
poem's prologue. He has no energy for that himself. And he has no
need, for his words reveal that he has already gained the insight
that he urges on Ur-shanabi. The important point is that, having
reached the end of his adventure, Gilgamesh comes to a stop. And
so, therefore, must the poem.

The view that Gilgamesh makes a transition from motion to stasis
is reinforced by comparative reading. Assyriology is traditionally a
historicist discipline, founded on the evidence of known facts. His-
torically, it has not paid much attention to the less empirical, more
subjective field of comparative literature. But in the study of ancient
literature there is much to learn from reading eclectically, for it is
axiomatic that all reading is enriched and conditioned by the reader's
knowledge of and response to other texts. Literary studies have
already deployed Gilgamesh alongside the masterpieces of such
authors as Plato, Ovid, and Dante (George 2003, 54 n. 137). In this
essay other great writers and thinkers are introduced to their com-
pany. They come from medieval Japan, imperial Russia and twentieth-
century France. The Russian comes first.

Tolstoy's novel *War and Peace* owes nothing to *Gilgamesh*, for it
was finished in 1868, eight years before George Smith published the
first attempt at translating the major Babylonian poetic narratives
into a modern language. Nevertheless, there is common ground. *War
and Peace* is in part the story of a man, Count Pierre Bezuhov, who
searches vainly for meaning in life. In that respect it is a literary ana-
logue of the *Epic of Gilgamesh*. The respective protagonists share
prominence in social station and spiritual malaise. Both lack nothing

in material comforts but are deeply unhappy with their lives. Like Gilgamesh in his quest for immortality, Pierre Bezuhov seeks fulfillment everywhere but in vain. He tries carousing, gambling, marriage, politics, Freemasonry, religion, intellectual pursuits: nothing gives him the answer he is looking for. Gilgamesh embarks on more heroic tasks, but equally in vain.

The two searchers after meaning become wise through contact with a teacher. Gilgamesh, in revolt against death, travels across the Waters of Death to the Babylonian counterpart of the Isles of the Blessed, intending to win immortality from the flood hero, the immortal Uta-napishti. There he learns from the instruction of this ancient sage, and then, his eyes opened, from his own conspicuous failures. A series of exclamations punctuates what can be understood as his passage from revolt to submission. When Uta-napishti demonstrates to Gilgamesh his powerlessness before sleep, Gilgamesh faces up at last to the inevitability of death and cries out in anguish (XI 244–45 [= XI, 269–70]), "There in my bed-chamber Death does abide, / and wherever I turn, there too will be Death!" When later a snake robs him of the Plant of Youth and even the compensation of rejuvenation slips beyond his grasp, he realizes the full vanity of his quest, and despairs that it would have been better if he had never made the voyage (XI 317–18 [= XI, 342]): "Had I only turned back, and left the boat on the shore!"

The mental journey that led Gilgamesh first to anguish and despair and thence to wisdom is completed by the first-millennium prologue's description of him at his return (I 9): "He came a far road, was weary but at peace". That second verb of stasis, "at ease, peace", signifies Gilgamesh's final reconciliation with his mortal destiny. Because the prologue gives foreknowledge of this, the end of the poem does not repeat it, but consists only of a third, more elaborate exclamation, beginning "Climb Uruk's wall!" The three exclamations witness a refocusing of Gilgamesh's attention, from the stark encounter of Death and himself, to his failure to escape that encounter, to the city of Uruk and its wall. Thus his preoccupation with his personal existential crisis gives way to an impersonal topic, in which suddenly self-reference is completely lacking. At the end, the poem reveals that Gilgamesh has learned to reflect not on the struggle inside himself, but on that which is external to him.

In *War and Peace* Pierre Bezuhov learns from an old soldier called Platon Karatayev. Pierre and Platon meet in prison in 1812, as Moscow burns, and march together as captives in Napoleon's retreat from Russia. In his uncultured simplicity Platon is a little reminiscent of Enkidu, the friend whose death aroused in Gilgamesh his terror of dying. Platon's only possession, apart from his dog, is an unthinking happiness. His combination of unfailing cheerfulness and uncomplaining surrender to life's vicissitudes has a profoundly liberating effect on Pierre. Eventually Platon falls sick and lacks the strength to go on, and a French guard shoots him where he sits. Platon offers no resistance to death, but accepts it as he has accepted life. Pierre is rescued by Cossacks a little further down the road, and convalesces in Orel, attended by servants from home. Here, in enforced idleness, his gloom lifts at last. He finds himself surrendering to life as Platon had. He does not wish to do anything more than just observe what is going on around him:

> "Well, what next? What am I going to do now?" And immediately he would answer himself: "Nothing. I am going to live".[3]

In this passive frame of mind Pierre achieves happiness and peace with himself. The development derives from a sudden revelation, and this was clearly personal to Tolstoy, for he spends many words of the novel in explaining this revelation—too many, in fact, to be quoted here in full, but the following excerpts will serve well enough to make a comparison between Pierre's new state of mind and Gilgamesh at the wall of Uruk:

> The very thing that had haunted him in the old days [before 1812] and that he constantly sought in vain—an object in life— did not exist for him now. That search for an object in life was over not merely temporarily, for the time being—he felt that it no longer existed for him and could not present itself again. And it was precisely this absence of an aim which gave him the complete and joyful sense of freedom that constituted his present happiness . . .
>
> All his life he had been seeking over the heads of those around him, while he had only to look straight in front without straining his eyes . . . now . . . he . . . joyfully feasted his eyes on the ever-changing, eternally great, unfathomable and infinite life around him. And the closer he looked, the more tranquil and happier he was. The awful question that had shattered all his mental edifices in the past—the question *Why?*—no longer existed for him.

Pierre achieves happiness when forced by great events to exchange a life of unceasing activity for passive captivity, and gradually then to learn to enjoy submissive inaction. When he emerges from his voyage of change, he does nothing; he does not want to do anything; everything is done around him. He has reached a point of stasis similar to Gilgamesh at his return from the ends of the earth. Both heroes have shed the self-absorption that made them unhappy. The

3. This and the following quotations from Tolstoy are taken from Rosemary Edmonds' translation of *War and Peace* Book 3, Part 4, Chapter 12 (Tolstoy 1957, 1308–1309).

reader understands of both that now they are, like Platon Kara-
tayev, indifferent to the prospect of death.

In the passages just quoted Tolstoy makes very clear his view that
meaning in life does not derive from what one does, but from what
goes on around one, the human society of which one is a part. The
secret is passive enjoyment of human life observed in all its mystery:
"ever-changing, eternally great, unfathomable and infinite", as he
puts it. And these words, especially, lead me to visit again the strange
passage of prose that concludes the Babylonian poem of Gilgamesh.

In writing a commentary on *Gilgamesh* for my critical edition, I was
forced to confront the implications of the poem's final lines. The con-
ventional view was that Gilgamesh found personal consolation in the
wall of Uruk as his enduring monument. If he must die, then he could
leave behind no more impressive memorial to his individual existence
than this most lasting structure (it still stands today). But then why
does the poem not end with XI 326 [= XI, 350]? The wall is indeed a
mighty symbol of the permanence of some human achievement, in
contrast to the transience of human life. But it is not the last word.
That lies in XI 327–28 [= XI, 351–53].

My insight was that the wall is a stage from which Gilgamesh's
companion will gain a view of the city, for it is with the life of the
city that the poem concludes: "The epilogue of the epic tells its
audience a self-evident truth: gaze on the generations that surround
you and learn that human life, in all its activities, is collective and
not individual. The symbol of that life is the great city that we con-
template from the wall" (George 2003, 527; also 2007: 58). The Uruk
that Gilgamesh urges Ur-shanabi to look upon is divided into four:
city, date-grove, clay-pit and temple. These terms do not describe the
city topographically; they organize its contents thematically. For
me they symbolized four fundamental activities of human existence:
raising of family, production of food, manufacturing, and intellec-
tual and spiritual life.

This insight gains new strength from Roland Barthes' essay on
"La tour Eiffel", first published in 1964. Barthes saw that contem-
plating a panorama from a height provokes the intellectual observer
to a structural decipherment of what is viewed. The panorama
"requires to be divided up, identified, reattached to memory" (1997,
11), so that what is seen from an unfamiliar angle is deciphered, made
recognizable and organized in the mind. Barthes' structuralist gaze
gave the Eiffel Tower the same function as the wall of Uruk, a plat-
form with an urban view. His decipherment of the Paris he observed
from that platform led him to make the same intellectual leap as
the poet of *Gilgamesh*: to compartmentalize and rearrange the
panorama of a great city in terms of four basic "functions of human
life" (as he puts it):

The visitor to the Tower has the illusion of raising the lid which covers the private lives of millions of human beings; the city becomes an intimacy whose functions, *i.e.*, whose connections he deciphers; on the great polar axis, perpendicular to the horizontal curve of the river, three zones stacked one after the other, as though along a prone body, the functions of human life: at the top, at the foot of Montmartre, pleasure; at the center, around the Opéra, materiality, business, commerce; toward the bottom, at the foot of the Pantheon, knowledge, study; then, to the right and left, enveloping this vital axis like two protective muffs, two large zones of habitation. (Barthes 1997, 12–13)

Barthes' human functions are "pleasure" (in the brothels of Pigalle below Montmartre), commerce, intellectual life and dwelling. The Babylonian poet's four categories are city (dwelling), date-grove (agriculture), clay-pit (industry) and temple (learning). If one allows a match between modern commerce and ancient industry, the two symbolic lists differ in one category only: Gilgamesh includes food production where Barthes saw sexual gratification. Perhaps it is unsurprising that a resident of a modern European city should consider the pursuit of individual sensual pleasure more essentially human than the social necessity of agriculture.

The fourfold division of the city of Uruk also encourages interpretation in terms of psychological theory. In the context of a contrast between individual and community, however, it is more important that at the end of *Gilgamesh*, as at the beginning, the individual reader is prompted to look down from the wall of Uruk, like Barthes from the Eiffel Tower, and reflect on all human endeavour. In ancient Mesopotamia the ideal city was believed ancient and eternal, built by the gods and enduring forever. The exact same history and destiny were attributed to mankind, whose life the cityscape explicitly represents. In a world where no final apocalypse was contemplated, where indeed the gods had been chastened by the flood and thereafter vouchsafed the future of mankind for all time (George 2003, 527), the human race stretched forth in the imagination into an unending and infinite future.

The ending of the poem, then, abrupt and anticlimactic though it is, makes a grand statement about man and mankind. Essentially it subordinates the concerns of man the individual to those of man the collective. A recent analysis of the poem from the perspective of narrative analysis makes the same point, observing that the "quest for personal gratification must gradually give way for what is good for the community" (Altes 2007, 192). It is not an accident that this carefully structured poem begins with a poetic stanza on the hero Gilgamesh and ends with a prose stanza on the city Uruk. The change in topic, from individual to collective, is reinforced by the change in form.

The prologue of "He Who Saw the Deep" insists that Gilgamesh returns from his quest wise, as wise as no man before or since. The words that he speaks at the very end of the poem are certainly intended as a distillation of that wisdom. For me they achieve a greater meaning if one considers the city wall in "He Who Saw the Deep" to play a supporting role to the city, rather than the other way around. Of course, the wall is a powerful icon full of hermeneutic potential (e.g. Dickson 2009) and in an older version of the poem it may not have been subordinate to the city. As it is, the wall gives way to the city. And is it not so, that the poem, through Gilgamesh's speech to Ur-shanabi, directs our gaze on to what Tolstoy later called the "ever-changing, eternally great, unfathomable and infinite life around him"? Had not Gilgamesh, like Pierre Bezuhov, used all his life a figurative telescope to search the horizons restlessly for meaning and truth? "All his life he had been seeking over the heads of those around him".

The prologue and epilogue combine subtly to show Gilgamesh, like Pierre, come at last to the conclusion that in the end what he had been looking for was to be found at home, in the passive observation of the life that surrounds him and of which he is part. "And the closer he looked, the more tranquil and happier he was". Or, as the poet of *Gilgamesh* puts it with those verbs of stasis, "he was weary but at peace".

On his journey home from the sage Uta-napishti, Gilgamesh recognizes with sudden insight that his quest to the ends of the earth can bring only despair. As remarked above, he laments that it would have been better not to have gone. His quest was a personal disaster. But, as we have seen, in its hero's homecoming the poem turns from the individual to the collective population, from the mortal to the immortal. For Gilgamesh, at a standstill, life is over and ends in failure, even before he is overtaken by death, the greatest human failing. But the collective life—symbolized by the city—goes on forever.

What I have described above as the "grand theme of man and mankind", the theme of individual fate contrasted with collective, is not limited to the prologue and epilogue of "He Who Saw the Deep". It is also central to what the sage flood hero, Uta-napishti, tells Gilgamesh at their meeting. His sermon is the first stage of the instruction that Gilgamesh undergoes in Uta-napishti's presence. It contains an elegy of lyrical beauty.

> "Man is snapped off like a reed in a canebrake!   [295]
> "The comely young man, the pretty young woman—
> "all [too soon in] their [prime] Death abducts them.

"No one at all sees death,
305   "no one sees the face [of Death,]
"no one [hears] the voice of Death,   [300]
         "Death so savage who hacks man down!

"At some time do we build a household,
         "at some time do we start a family,
310   "at some time do brothers divide their inheritance,
         "at some time do feuds arise in the land.   [305]

"Ever has the river risen and brought us flood,
         "the mayfly floating on the water.
"On the face of the sun its countenance gazes,
315   "then all of a sudden nothing is there!"
                    Gilgamesh X 301–22 [=X, 295–309]

The first three stanzas set out with great clarity the contrast
between the individual's fate and the collective destiny of men.
The individual is scythed down suddenly like a harvested reed, an
image found elsewhere in ancient Near Eastern poetry. A Hebrew
poet combined it with a lament for the pain of life that echoes
another theme of Gilgamesh (Job 14: 1–2): "Man that is born of
woman is of few days and full of trouble. He cometh forth like a
flower and is cut down". The third stanza makes a rarer observa-
tion, that men endure forever through the cycle of generations.
The fourth stanza restates the same contrast between man and
men as a metaphor, in which the brief-lived insect symbolizes the
individual and the eternal river stands, as elsewhere, for the cur-
rent of time. Like the insect, men too have only a brief share of time
alive on earth.

There is a very prominent and instructive mayfly metaphor in the
Japanese *Genji-monogatari*. This sprawling work of the Heian
period, in English usually entitled "The Tale of Shining Genji", is
attributed to the gentlewoman Murasaki Shikibu (fl. AD 1000). It
tells mainly of the life and loves of a great nobleman, but the narra-
tive does not end with Genji's death, for it is impelled forward by its
own momentous force. The hero being dead, and his loves long
gone, the tale turns to the amorous exploits of his son, the Com-
mander (Kaoru). One story dwells on his wooing of a lady who sud-
denly disappears. Having lost her, and thinking she must be
drowned, Kaoru sits in twilight as mayflies flit back and forth, and
the sight of them causes him to reflect on her too brief presence in
his life with a short poem:

There it is, just there, yet ever beyond my reach, till I look
  once more,
and it is gone, the mayfly (*kagerou*), never to be seen again.[4]

The chapter is entitled *Kagerou*, "The Mayfly", in honour of this
verse. Murasaki glosses the poem by having Kaoru add a prose
afterthought: "'It might not be there at all,' they say he murmured
to himself." Here, as in *Gilgamesh*, the mayfly symbolizes the brev-
ity of human existence and also, because of its evident characteris-
tic of being there one moment, and gone the next, it symbolizes the
finality of death, which acts to wipe individual men out as if they
had never been, drowned in the river of time. "All of a sudden,
nothing is there!"

The prologue of the poem of Gilgamesh implies that his visit to
the flood hero, the sage Uta-napishti, made Gilgamesh wise, and
that he brought this wisdom back with him to Uruk. Other Babylo-
nian traditions acknowledge his reputation as one whose return
from his quest brought knowledge of the ideal order of the antedilu-
vian age, when human life was as the gods had originally planned it.
Uta-napishti's sermon, which ends with the elegy quoted above,
makes clear the distinction between the fragile brevity of a man's life
(the mayfly) and the infinite repetition of mankind's generations
through past and future time (the flooding river). For the poet of
Gilgamesh, perhaps Sîn-leqi-unninni, perhaps another, the wisdom
attained by his hero, the archetypal searcher after immortality, per-
mits the hero to see that mankind's destiny—eternal life—is the
essential compensation for the pain of individual oblivion. Accep-
tance of this as the truth of the human predicament thus brings
final peace and reconciliation even to those, like Gilgamesh, who go
most in fear of death.

It is no accident that Gilgamesh, like Pierre Bezuhov, achieves a
calm state of mind only after vain struggle. For both, the change
from activity to passive participation, from motion to stasis, is a
mark of wisdom. It brings the end of the self-centred aspirations of
ambitious youth and signals the onset of contemplative and recon-
ciled age. "He Who Saw the Deep" tells a story about finding a new
balance between individual and collective, a story that asserts a
belief that a human life gains meaning as part of a greater whole.
Steinbeck's reaction to intensive study of marine ecology was a pro-
found reflection on the human species, leading him to write on one
occasion in *The Log from the Sea of Cortez* that "it is through strug-
gle and sorrow that people are able to participate in one another"

4. Taken from Royall Tyler's translation of *Genji-monogatari*, Chapter 52 (Murasaki
   2001, p. 1073).

(1960, 176–77). The path from ego to Self is not an easy journey.[5] The poem of Gilgamesh agrees: this realization is attained, this wisdom won, only by hard experience of life and death.

This essay has sought to demonstrate that a contrast between individual fate and collective destiny, and the resolution of that distinction, lie at the heart of the most profound parts of the poem of Gilgamesh. It would be a surprise if such a universal theme did not find literary expression by other great imaginations in history. Tolstoy, as one would expect, summed up the eternal truth succinctly. Simple but innately wise, Platon Karatayev tells Pierre Bezuhov in jail, "Suffering lasts an hour but life goes on for ever!" They are words that once again oppose individual fate and collective destiny, the mayfly and the river. It is my contention that in the shade of Uruk's wall the hero Gilgamesh, come at last to a standstill after a life of suffering (*mānaḫtu*) and seeing before him the teeming metropolis, might very well have said the same.

Bibliography

Altes, L. K. 2007. "Gilgamesh and the Power of Narration." *Journal of the American Oriental Society* 127: 183–93.

Barthes, R. 1997. *The Eiffel Tower and Other Mythologies*. Trans. R. Howard. Berkeley: U of California P.

Dickson, K. 2009. "The Wall of Uruk: Iconicities in Gilgamesh." *Journal of Ancient Near Eastern Religions* 9: 25–50.

George, A. R. 1999. *The Epic of Gilgamesh: The Babylonian Poem and Other Texts in Sumerian and Akkadian*. London: Penguin.

———. 2003. *The Babylonian Gilgamesh Epic: Introduction, Critical Edition and Cuneiform Texts*. Oxford: Oxford UP.

———. 2007. "The Epic of Gilgameš: Thoughts on Genre and Meaning." In J. Azize and N. Weeks, eds., *Gilgameš and the World of Assyria: Proceedings of the Conference Held at Mandelbaum House, the University of Sydney, 21–23 July 2004*. Leeuven: Peters. Pp. 37–65.

Murasaki Shikubu. 2001. *The Tale of Genji*. Trans. R. Tyler. London: Penguin.

Steinbeck, J. 1960. *The Log from the Sea of Cortez*. London: Penguin.

Tolstoy, L. 1957. *War and Peace*. Trans. R. Edmonds. London: Penguin.

5. George here refers to a psychological reading of Gilgamesh using the theories of Carl Jung, discussed in the unabridged version of his essay, pp. 239–41; see further Rivkah S. Kluger, *The Archetypal Significance of Gilgamesh, a Modern Ancient Hero*. Einsiedeln, Switzerland: Daimon Verlag, 1991 [*Editor*].

HILLARY MAJOR

Gilgamesh Remembers a Dream[†]

I have not been able to loose
that image,
the rosy root coils
of that nether plant
shining for the first time
in my palm, looping
to my elbows,
damp as I was,
soft in a sodden slimy way
like fish skin,
entrails pumping with blood.
Your lips had no tenderness
like its leaves, clinging on fingertips,
your voice no depth
like the dark places where I found it.
I have sifted through
piles of carnelians
in search of that hue
that holds my eyes like sunspots.
All brightness caught
in water drops,
reflected leaf to root,
beads of sweat on desert skin,
sea to sky, all
one burning opal
out of time.
The sands we crossed together
have slid with our footsteps
into story,
and I cannot recall
the lines of your face,
sitting again behind brick walls;
but every morning I am stunned
by the seconds I held eternity
in helpless arms.

† From Hollins University's *Album* (spring 2000). Reprinted by permission of the author.

Glossary of Proper Names

Ab Sumerian name for the tenth month of the Mesopotamian calendar. In the first millennium B.C.E., it was described as the "the month of Gilgamesh. For nine days [or: on the ninth day] young men compete in boxing and wrestling matches by their city gates."

Adad God of thunderstorms.

Adapa Ancient sage of the city Eridu in Sumer who was a favorite of the god of wisdom, Enki, but who lost a chance for immortality; see *Muses*, pp. 525–32.

Agga Alternative spelling for Akka.

Akka King of the city Kish and a contemporary of Gilgamesh. His unsuccessful siege of Uruk is described in the Sumerian poem "Gilgamesh and Akka."

Akkadian One of the two major languages spoken in ancient Mesopotamia; the other was Sumerian.

Amorites A Semitic-speaking people, originally at home in north Syria and the upper Euphrates region, who migrated in large numbers to Mesopotamia at the beginning of the second millennium B.C.E. In Sumerian literature they were disdained as uncivilized nomads and marauders.

An Sumerian name for the sky god, Akkadian Anu.

Antum Wife of Anu, the sky god.

Anu Akkadian name for the sky god, supreme in the pantheon but remote from human affairs.

Anunna gods Literally, "Noble Seed"; a class of important gods in heaven and the netherworld, sometimes said to number fifty.

Anzu Monstrous bird with the head of a lion, subject of a mythological story wherein he steals power from the god Enlil but is defeated in battle by Enlil's son Ninurta; see *Muses*, pp. 555–78. This creature was a byword for something hideous and terrifying.

Apsu The fresh water under the earth, abode of the god Enki/Ea.

Aratta A city fabled by the Sumerians for its wealth, especially in the precious blue stone lapis lazuli. They believed that it lay far to the east of Sumer in present-day Iran; see *Harps*, pp. 275–319, and *Epics*, pp. 49–96.

Aruru A goddess of birth, credited with the creation of human beings.

Ashimbabbar "Who comes out brightly," a Sumerian epithet for Nanna, the moon god.

239

Atrahasis   Literally, "Super-wise," the Akkadian name of the immortal Flood hero Utanapishtim/Ziusudra in the Babylonian story of the Flood; see *Muses,* pp. 227–80.

Aya   Goddess of dawn and wife of Shamash, the sun god, often called upon in prayers to intercede with her husband.

Babylonia   The southern half of Mesopotamia, roughly the region from present-day Baghdad to the Gulf. The Babylonian language was a dialect of Akkadian. The old versions of *The Epic of Gilgamesh* were written in Old Babylonian, the form of the language in use during the first half of the second millennium B.C.E., the middle and later versions in Standard Babylonian, the literary form of the language preferred after that.

Belet-ili   A goddess of birth, said in the Atrahasis version of the Flood story to have created the human race along with the god Enki.

Belet-seri   Literally, "Lady of the Steppe"; scribe and bookkeeper in the netherworld.

Bibbu   In the epic, a deity serving as butcher or meat carver in the netherworld.

Birhurturre   Hero of the city Uruk, who served as negotiator during the siege of Uruk in the Sumerian poem "Gilgamesh and Akka."

Bitti   Another spelling of Pitti, a netherworld deity.

Bull of Heaven   Monster bull belonging to Anu, the sky god, killed by Gilgamesh and Enkidu.

Dilmun   Sometimes said to be the remote home of the immortal hero of the Flood story, Utanapishtim/Ziusudra. Dilmun was the ancient name of the island of Bahrein and was celebrated in Sumerian poetry as a place where nothing unpleasant ever happened.

Dimpiku   A netherworld deity.

Dumuzi   (1) Early king of Uruk, before Gilgamesh. (2) Akkadian Tammuz, shepherd god, youthful lover of Inanna/Ishtar, who forces him to go to the netherworld; see *Harps,* pp. 1–84, and *Muses,* pp. 488–96.

Ea   Akkadian name for Sumerian Enki, god of wisdom, magic, and fresh water, known for his ingenious solutions to dilemmas and for his beneficence to the human race.

Eanna   Name of the temple of the goddess Inanna/Ishtar at Uruk, originally the temple of Anu, as in Tablet II, lines 9 and 11, to which later versions add "and Ishtar."

Ekur   Name of the temple of the god Enlil at Nippur, later a generic term for "temple."

Endashurima   Husband of the goddess Nindashurima and paternal ancestor of the god Enlil.

Endukuga   Literally, "Lord of the Holy Mound"; husband of Nindukuga and paternal ancestor of the god Enlil.

Enki   (1) Sumerian name for the god of wisdom, magic, and fresh water, Akkadian Ea. (2) Literally, "Lord Earth"; husband of Ninki and paternal ancestor of the god Enlil.

Enkidu   Shaggy man from the steppe, Gilgamesh's match and closest friend.

Enkimdu   Sumerian god of irrigation and agriculture.

Enlil   Chief god on earth, residing at Nippur, often harsh and inimical to the human race.

Enmebaragesi   King of Kish and father of Akka in "Gilgamesh and Akka." In "Gilgamesh and Huwawa," Gilgamesh names Enmebaragesi as his older sister, presumably a humorous touch.

Enmerkar   Gilgamesh's ancestor, hero of two Sumerian epic poems; see *Harps*, pp. 275–319, and *Epics*, pp. 23–96.

Enmesharra   Literally, "Lord of All Cosmic Powers"; paternal ancestor of the god Enlil.

Enmul   Literally, "Lord Star"; husband of Ninmul and paternal ancestor of the god Enlil.

Ennugi   A minor deity in charge of water courses.

Enutila   Literally, "Lord of the Finished Days"; paternal ancestor of the god Enlil.

Ereshkigal   Queen of the dead and the netherworld, sister of the goddess Ishtar; see *Muses*, pp. 506–24.

Eridu   City in Sumer with a sanctuary to the god Enki, regarded by the Sumerians as the oldest in their land.

Erish   Probably Eresh, a city in Sumer with a sanctuary to the goddess Nisaba.

Errakal   A name for Nergal, god of the netherworld.

Etana   Ancient Mesopotamian king who was said to have flown up to heaven on an eagle; see *Muses*, pp. 533–54.

Euphrates   One of the two major rivers of ancient Mesopotamia, the other being the Tigris. In ancient times, the city Uruk lay on the banks of the Euphrates River.

Fate   A netherworld deity (Sumerian name: Namtar), courier of death.

Gilgamesh   King of Uruk, hero of this epic.

Great City   A euphemism for the netherworld.

Great Mountain   Epithet of the god Enlil.

Hamran   Otherwise unknown, in the epic an upland or mountain in northern Syria.

Hanish   A god of destructive storms.

Hattusha   Capital city of the Hittites in central Anatolia.

Hittite   The language of the Indo-European–speaking people who settled in central Anatolia during the first half of the second millennium B.C.E. and created a powerful nation-state in that region.

Holy Mound   Name of a shrine in the temple of Enlil at Nippur; also the name of the ceremonial throne for the chief god presiding at the cosmic assembly of the gods.

Humbaba   Monster appointed by the god Enlil to guard the forest of cedars, famous in Mesopotamian tradition for his frightening face.

Hushbishag   Housekeeper for Ereshkigal, queen of the netherworld.

Huwawa   Earlier form of the name Humbaba.

Igigi gods   A class of gods of heaven, sometimes thought to number seven. The Sumerians called them the "Great Princes," but in Babylonian tradition they were often considered inferior in status to the Anunna gods.

Inanna   Sumerian goddess of fertility and reproduction, equated with the Akkadian goddess Ishtar. One of her main temples was Eanna at Uruk.

Irnina   Another name or a local form of the goddess Ishtar.

Ishtar   Goddess of sex, love, and warfare; the planet Venus; and the principal female deity in the Mesopotamian pantheon.

Ishullanu   According to a Sumerian myth, Inanna, while on a journey, seduced a gardener, whom she then sought to kill. In the epic, the gardener is called Ishullanu and is said to have resisted her advances.

Itiha   A city mentioned only in "The Hittite Gilgamesh," location unknown.

Kish   City in Babylonia that competed with Uruk for control over Mesopotamia in the time of Gilgamesh.

Kullab   A city quarter of the greater city Uruk, with a temple of An.

Land of No Return   A name for the netherworld.

Larsa   City in Babylonia with a temple to the god Shamash.

Lugalbanda   Early king of Uruk, father of Gilgamesh, and hero of several Sumerian epic poems; see *Harps*, pp. 320–44, and *Epics*, pp. 97–165.

Lugalgabagal   Gilgamesh's minstrel.

Lugalgirra   A god of war and death.

Mala   Hittite name for the upper Euphrates River or one of its tributaries.

Mami   A name for the birth goddess, Belet-ili.

Mammetum   A name for the birth and mother goddess.

Marduk   God of Babylon.

Mashum   Mythological mountains where the sun rose and set.

Meslamtaea   A name for the netherworld deity Nergal.

Mount Lebanon   Mountain ranges along the Mediterranean coast of present-day Lebanon, famous in antiquity for their cedar trees.

Mount Nimush   High peak sometimes identified with Pir Omar Gudrun in Kurdistan, landing place of the ark in the Gilgamesh epic.

Nahmizulen   Another name for Siduri in Hittite Gilgamesh.

Namrasit   Akkadian equivalent of Ashimbabbar, an epithet of the moon god.

Namtar   God of destiny or fate, courier of death and the netherworld.

Nanna   Sumerian name of the moon god, Akkadian Sin. His main temple was at the city Ur.

Nergal   Sumerian name for the chief god of the netherworld, husband of Ereshkigal.

Ninazu   Literally, "Lord Physician"; a healing deity, son of Ereshkigal.

Nindashurima   Wife of Endashurima and paternal ancestor of Enlil.

Nindukuga   Literally, "Lady of the Holy Mound"; wife of Endukuga and paternal ancestor of Enlil.

Ninegal   Literally, "Lady of the Palace"; a goddess at Nippur sometimes identified with Inanna.

Ningal   Literally, "Great Lady"; wife of Sin, the moon god.

Ningishzida   Literally, "Lord of the Upright Tree"; a netherworld deity, son of Ninazu, sometimes depicted as a horned snake.

Ninhursag Literally, "Lady of the Mountain"; Sumerian birth and mother goddess.

Ninki Literally, "Lady Earth"; wife of Enki and paternal ancestor of Enlil.

Ninlil Wife of the god Enlil.

Ninmul Literally, "Lady Star"; wife of Enmul and paternal ancestor of Enlil.

Ninshuluhhatumma A netherworld deity in charge of ritual washing and cleaning.

Ninsun Sumerian goddess, called the "wild cow," wife of Lugalbanda and mother of Gilgamesh.

Nintu Literally, "Lady Who Gives Birth"; a name for the Sumerian birth goddess.

Ninurta Son of Enlil, agricultural and warrior god, who defeated the monstrous bird Anzu in combat; see *Harps,* pp. 233–72.

Nippur City in Babylonia with the principal temple to the god Enlil.

Nisaba Sumerian goddess of grain and scribal learning.

Nudimmud Epithet of Enki evidently referring to his role in creation and inspiration and as patron deity of artisans and craftsmen.

Nungal Sumerian goddess in charge of jails and the household of the temple of Enlil at Nippur.

Palil A protective deity.

Peshtur Literally, "Little Fig"; younger sister of Gilgamesh.

Pitti A netherworld deity.

Puzur-Enlil Boat builder put in charge of the ark by Utanapishtim.

Qassa-tabat A minor netherworld deity who swept the floors of sacred spaces.

Sebettu Literally, "The Seven"; violent and destructive warrior brothers, incarnation of the Pleiades, beneficent guides in "Gilgamesh and Huwawa."

Shamagan A form of Sumuqan, the Sumerian god of wild beasts and cattle.

Shamash Akkadian name of the sun god, concerned with justice, honesty, and oracles, Sumerian Utu.

Shamhat/Shamhatu Literally, "Joy Girl"; the harlot who seduces Enkidu.

Shangashu Literally, "Murderer"; in "The Hittite Gilgamesh" the name of the hunter who encounters Enkidu in the steppe outside Uruk.

Shanhatu Name of Shamhat the harlot in "The Hittite Gilgamesh."

Shulgi King of the city Ur (ca. 2094–2047 B.C.E.), patron of Sumerian literature, who claimed kinship with Gilgamesh.

Shullat God of destructive storms.

Shulpa'e Literally, "Hero Who Comes Forth Magnificently"; god sometimes identified with the planet Jupiter, mentioned in "The Death of Gilgamesh" as a god of the netherworld.

Shuruppak City in Babylonia reputed to antedate the Flood, long abandoned at the time the epic was written, sometimes considered the birthplace of the Flood hero.

Siduri Tavern-keeper whose establishment lay at the edge of the world. Her name has variously been interpreted as Akkadian or Hurrian.

Silili Mother of the horse in *The Epic of Gilgamesh*, otherwise unknown.

Sin Akkadian name for the moon god, Sumerian Nanna, ruler of the sky during the night.

Sisig Sumerian god of dreams, evidently visualized as a puff of air, mentioned in "The Death of Gilgamesh" as the sole illuminating spirit in the dark netherworld.

Sumer The southern half of Babylonia, especially during the third millennium B.C.E.

Sumerian The major language spoken in Sumer, or the southern half of Babylonia, during the time of Gilgamesh, maintained as a cultural language throughout Mesopotamian history.

Sumuqan Sumerian name of the god of wild beasts and cattle.

Sur-Sunabu Earlier form of the name Ur-shanabi, Utanapishtim's ferryman.

Tammuz Akkadian name for Sumerian Dumuzi; in "The Death of Gilgamesh," a netherworld deity.

[Tammuz]-absu A netherworld deity who ritually assumed the blame for the faults of others.

Tigris One of the two major rivers of ancient Mesopotamia, the other being the Euphrates.

Ubar-Tutu Father of Utanapishtim, the Flood hero.

Ulaya Modern Karun River in southwestern Iran, an important cultural boundary in the time of Gilgamesh.

Ullu The name for Utanapishtim in "The Hittite Gilgamesh."

Ur City in Babylonia with the principal temple of Nanna/Sin, the moon god.

Ur-lugal Son of Gilgamesh and builder of his tomb.

Ur-Shanabi Servant of Utanapishtim, ferryman who crosses the ocean and waters of death.

Uruk Largest city in Mesopotamia in the time of Gilgamesh, with principal temples of An and Inanna.

Utanapishtim Literally, "He Found Life"; Akkadian name for the immortal Flood hero, called Ziusudra in Sumerian, Atrahasis in the Babylonian Flood story, and Ullu in Hittite. Some scholars spell it "Utnapishtim."

Utu Sumerian name for the sun god, Akkadian Shamash.

Zababa God of warfare and the city Kish.

Zabala City in Babylonia with an important temple to Inanna.

Ziusudra Literally, "Long-Lived"; Sumerian name for the Flood hero, Akkadian Utanapishtim.

Selected Bibliography

• indicates works included or excerpted in this Norton Critical Edition.

• Ackerman, Susan. *When Heroes Love: The Ambiguity of Eros in the Stories of Gilgamesh and David.* New York: Columbia UP, 2005.

Black, J., G. Cunningham, E. Robson, and G. Zólyomi, eds. *The Literature of Ancient Sumer.* Oxford: Oxford UP, 2004. Important anthology.

Bryce, Trevor. *The Kingdom of the Hittites.* Oxford: Clarendon Press, 1998.

Cavigneaux, Antoine, and Farouk N. H. Al-Rawi. *Gilgameš et la mort: Textes de Tell Haddad VI, avec un appendice sur les textes funéraires sumériens.* Cuneiform Monographs 19. Groningen: Styx, 2000.

Edzard, Dietz O. "Gilgameš und Huwawa A. I. Teil." *Zeitschrift für Assyriologie* 80 (1990): 165–203.

———. "Gilgameš und Huwawa A. II. Teil." *Zeitschrift für Assyriologie* 81 (1991): 165–233.

———. *"Gilgameš und Huwawa": Zwei Versionen der sumerischen Zedernwaldepisode nebst einer Edition von Version "B."* Sitzungsberichte der Bayerischen Akademie der Wissenschaften, Philosophisch-historisch Klasse 1993/4. Munich: Beck, 1993.

Ehrich, Carl, ed. *From an Antique Land: An Introduction to Ancient Near Eastern Literature.* Lanham, MD: Rowman and Littlefield, 2009. Chapters on Sumerian, Akkadian, and Hittite literature.

Foster, Benjamin R. *Before the Muses: An Anthology of Akkadian Literature,* 3rd ed. Bethesda, MD: CDL Press, 2005.

Gadotti, Alhena. *'Gilgamesh, Enkidu, and the Netherworld' and the Sumerian Gilgamesh Cycle.* Untersuchungen zur Assyriologie und vorderasiatischen Archäologie 10. Berlin: De Gruyter, 2014.

George, Andrew. *The Epic of Gilgamesh: A New Translation.* London: Allen Lane, Penguin, 1999. Authoritative translation with the versions treated separately, together with the Sumerian Gilgamesh poems.

———. *The Babylonian Gilgamesh Epic: Introduction, Critical Edition and Cuneiform Texts.* Oxford: Oxford UP, 2003. Essential for study of the epic.

• ———. "The Mayfly on the River: Individual and Collective Destiny in the Epic of Gilgamesh." KASKAL, *Rivista di storia, ambienti e culture del Vicino Oriente Antico* 9 (2012): 227–42.

• Jacobsen, Thorkild. *The Treasures of Darkness: A History of Mesopotamian Religion.* New Haven, CT: Yale UP, 1976.

———. *The Harps That Once . . . : Sumerian Poetry in Translation.* New Haven, CT: Yale UP, 1987. Important anthology.

Maier, John, ed. *Gilgamesh: A Reader.* Wauconda, IL: Bolchazy-Carducci, 1997. Essays on the epic from various viewpoints.

Maul, Stefan. *Das Gilgamesch-Epos, Neu Übersetzt und Kommentiert.* Munich: Beck, 2005.

• Moran, William L. "*The Epic of Gilgamesh*: A Document of Ancient Humanism." *Canadian Society for Mesopotamian Studies Journal* 22 (1995): 15–22.

———. "The Gilgamesh Epic: A Masterpiece from Ancient Mesopotamia." In Jack M. Sasson, with John Baines, Gary Beckman, and Karen S. Rubinson, eds. *Civilizations of the Ancient Near East.* New York: Scribner, 1995. Pp. 2327–36.

Radner, Karen, and Eleanor Robson, eds. *The Oxford Handbook of Cuneiform Culture.* Oxford: Oxford UP, 2011. Essays on ancient Mesopotamian written culture.

Römer, W. H. P. *Das sumerische Kurzepos 'Gilgameš und Akka.'* Alter Orient und Altes Testament 209/1. Neukirchen-Vluyn: Neukirchener Verlag, 1980.

Sasson, Jack M., with John Baines, Gary Beckman, and Karen S. Rubinson, eds., *Civilizations of the Ancient Near East.* New York: Scribner, 1995. Essays on ancient Near Eastern history, culture, and literatures.

Shaffer, Aaron. "Sumerian Sources of Tablet XII of the Epic of Gilgamesh." Ph.D. diss., U of Pennsylvania, 1963.

Vanstiphout, Herman. *Epics of Sumerian Kings: The Matter of Aratta.* Writings from the Ancient World 20. Atlanta: Society of Biblical Literature, 2003.